BREADS

BREADS

Sharon Tyler Herbst

Illustrated by
Michelle Burchard

HPBooks

HPBooks
are published by
The Berkley Publishing Group
200 Madison Avenue
New York, NY 10016

LIBRARY OF CONGRESS CATALOGING-IN-PUBLICATION DATA
Herbst, Sharon Tyler.
Breads/by Sharon Tyler Herbst.—1st HPBooks ed.
    p. cm
"HPBooks"
Includes index.
ISBN 1-55788-192-8 (paper: acid-free paper)
1. Bread I. Title
TX769.H445 1994
641.8' 15—dc20   94-14296
                        CIP

Printed in the United States of America
2 3 4 5 6 7 8 9 10

NOTICE: The information printed in this book is true and complete
to the best of our knowledge. All recommendations
are made without any guarantees on the part of the author
or the publisher. The author and publisher disclaim
all liability in connection with the use of this information.

This book is printed on acid-free paper.

*To my dear friend, the late Bert Greene — a culinary Renaissance man
and an incredibly generous human being — who always said:
"Bread cast upon the waters comes back eclairs." And it does!*

ACKNOWLEDGMENTS

Heartfelt thanks to all my friends and family for their interest, love, support, and eagerness to be tasters for my recipe testing throughout the years. And a special thanks to:

Helen Fisher, one of the original owners of HPBooks, who had enough faith to give me a chance when I came to her 13 years ago with my first cookbook proposal; Jeanette Egan, my wonderful, talented editor, who gave me the freedom to virtually rewrite this book just the way I wanted; Kay and Wayne Tyler (Mom and Dad) and Tia Tyler Leslie (darling sister), for being the lifeline of my support system all these years; and, above all, Ron Herbst, my husband and best friend, for his love, support, and always perfectly timed words of inspiration, consolation, and motivation.

CONTENTS

Introduction

There are few things in the food world that can warm the heart and bring on a smile more quickly than a loaf of freshly baked homemade bread. Unless, perhaps, it's the spirit-warming satisfaction and sense of accomplishment you get from baking it . . . and sharing it with someone you love.

There's no doubt about it—home breadmaking is once again on the "rise." Probably because there's something special about baking bread that appeals to all our senses and positive emotions. First there's the delicious, earthy aroma of the yeast as it begins to ferment. Next comes the warm and responsive feel of the dough as you pummel and knead it—a perfect way to work out pent-up aggressions. As the dough begins to rise, there's a sense of wonder and excitement. Soon, the dough is puffy and rounded and ready for the oven. Before long, the comforting fragrance of baking bread begins to waft its delicious promise throughout the house, making mouths water in anticipation. Finally, you're cutting through the crisp, golden-brown crust to reveal a bread so tender and delicious it doesn't even need butter!

For some unknown reason, the difficulty and "mystery" of bread baking has long been exaggerated. Nonsense! Making bread is a fun, exciting, creative process—there's absolutely no mystery about it. The simple fact is that anyone can make bread—even a beginner. And using bread-kneading aids such as food processors, heavy-duty mixers, and bread machines means breadmaking is faster and easier than ever. If you know the basics, can read a recipe, and have an oven, a wholesome loaf of homemade bread is well within your reach. Later, after you begin to get the "feel" of breadmaking (and you will), you'll be able to relax and follow your instincts.

One of my aims with this book is to dissolve the "yeast mystique" that's intimidated would-be bakers for decades. The truth is, once you learn a few facts about yeast, you'll find it's really easy to work with. And once you're hooked by the wonders of yeast, you'll be a breadmaker for life. Just remember this easy breadmaking formula: Use the very best ingredients you can afford; learn a few basic breadmaking techniques; have the necessary equipment and ingredients on hand; start with a good recipe (which doesn't mean you can't improvise once you're experienced); and, most important, relax and have fun!

Whether you prefer moist quick breads, biscuits and muffins that take only an hour or so from start to finish, or tender yeast breads, rolls, or coffeecakes, which require a slightly longer time investment, you'll find a wide selection of each in the pages that follow. But remember, recipes aren't engraved in stone—they're simply blueprints from which your imagination should take wing. Part of the magic and excitement of breadmaking is adding your own personal touch to every loaf.

If you're already an experienced baker, you'll probably want to jump right in and start trying some of the many recipes in the following chapters. But if you're a beginner, or if you've never had any "luck" baking bread, take a few moments to read the following sections on ingredients and techniques. Come on—it won't take long to read a few pages. Breadmaking should be an adventure, not a trauma, and once you know the basics, you'll be baking bread with ease and flair.

Now that you see how simple and rewarding it can be to make your own bread, there's no longer any reason to tolerate tasteless, air-filled supermarket bread. Breadmaking is an incredibly rewarding experience—one of the most positive personal statements you can make. And there are few things more gratifying than baking a beautiful loaf of homemade bread and sharing it with someone you love.

Basic Bread Ingredients

There are basic ingredients that go into making most breads—flour, liquid (such as water, milk, or beer), leavening (like yeast, baking powder, and baking soda), sugar, and salt. Eggs, fat, herbs, spices, nuts, fruit, cheese, and other flavoring ingredients are also often used. The following information on basic breadmaking ingredients should help you become a more informed baker.

Common Flours

The most commonly used flour in breadmaking today is derived from wheat, which contains a protein called *gluten*. When dough is kneaded or a batter beaten, gluten forms the elastic network that holds in the carbon dioxide gas created by a leavener such as fermenting yeast. The gas bubbles cause the gluten to stretch and expand, making the dough rise. The less gluten (protein) in the flour, the weaker the dough's elasticity. And without a strong elastic network, the gas bubbles will escape into the air rather than leavening the bread.

The two types of wheat used to make flour for baking are high-gluten hard wheat and low-gluten soft wheat. Hard-wheat flour is particularly suitable for yeast breads, whereas soft-wheat flours are better for tender baked goods such as biscuits and muffins. To select a high-protein (good gluten-developing) flour, look at the "nutritional information" section on a flour-package label. Flours with 12 to 14 grams of protein per cup are best for yeast breads; those with 9 to 11 grams are better for quick breads.

Because the characteristics of flour vary greatly from one part of the country to another, it is almost impossible to give a precise amount of flour for each recipe. The way flour is milled can affect it, as can the temperature and humidity on your baking day. Flour absorbs less liquid during hot, humid months than in dry weather because it has already absorbed some moisture from the atmosphere. Your best guideline is to add only enough flour to keep the dough from being too sticky to work with. A dough that's slightly tacky to the touch but not sticky will yield a much nicer loaf than one that is too dry.

Storing flour Because flour readily absorbs and retains moisture, it should be stored in airtight containers. All-purpose and bread flours can be kept at room temperature for up to six months. However, temperatures above 75F (25C) invite bugs and mold. Flours containing part of the grain's germ (such as whole-wheat flour) turn rancid quickly because of the oil in the germ. Store these flours, tightly wrapped, in the refrigerator or freezer for up to six months. Always bring chilled flours to room temperature before using.

Stone-ground flour This variety of flour is processed between specially shaped granite stones at lower speeds than the steel hammer- or rollermills used to produce most commercial flours. This method splits the grain rather than crushes it, and the reduced speed protects the flour from overheating as it's ground. Stone-ground flour is coarser and heavier than steel-ground. If using all stone-ground flour in a recipe, and a medium-weight, even-textured loaf is desired, use about 1-1/2 times the yeast indicated.

All-purpose flour A combination of high-gluten hard wheat and low-gluten soft wheat, milled from the inner part of the wheat kernel, this fine-textured flour contains neither the germ (the sprouting section) or the bran (the outer shell). All-purpose flour comes in *bleached* and *unbleached* forms, which can be used interchangeably. Unbleached flour is lightened naturally through oxidation over a period of months. Bleached flour has been chemically treated. Because unbleached flour has a slightly higher protein content and has retained more of its nutrients than its bleached counterpart, it's a better choice for yeast breads. All-purpose flour is suitable for most kinds of baking, including quick and yeast breads, biscuits, muffins, cookies, and cakes.

Bread flour The baker's choice for yeast breads, bread flour is milled from hard wheat. This specially formulated flour is high in protein (usually about 14 grams per cup), which makes it perfect for yeast breads. Bread flour is 99.8 percent unbleached flour, with a minuscule amount of malted barley flour to improve yeast activity and either ascorbic acid (vitamin C) or potassium bromate to make gluten more extensible and thereby improve the dough's gas retention.

Rye flour Because of its extremely low gluten content, rye flour won't produce a satisfactory loaf of bread without the addition of a higher-protein flour. The same holds true of flours made of oats, corn, rice, barley, and buckwheat. Rye flour comes in light, medium, dark, and pumpernickel, the latter being the darkest and most coarsely ground. Medium rye flour is readily available in most supermarkets, whereas the others will more likely be found in natural food stores. Rye flour is heavier than bread, all-purpose, or whole-wheat flours and produces a sticky dough that requires patience and extra kneading.

Self-rising flour An all-purpose flour with the addition of salt and baking powder, it may be substituted for all-purpose flour with the following adjustments: Omit salt in yeast breads; omit baking powder and salt in quick breads.

Whole-wheat flour Milled from the entire wheat kernel, whole-wheat flour contains the germ. It has a higher fat content than all-purpose flour. It therefore will spoil more quickly and should be purchased in small quantities and stored in the refrigerator or freezer. Breads made with all whole-wheat flour produce a heavier, more compact loaf. The addition of some all-purpose or bread flour provides a better gluten structure, higher volume, and finer texture.

Whole-wheat pastry flour Made from finely milled soft wheat, this low-gluten flour is not suitable for yeast breads, with the exception of Whole-Wheat Croissants (page 145). However, it makes excellent biscuits, quick breads, and pastries. White pastry flour is generally sold as cake flour.

Special Flours, Meals & Grains

Though some of the following ingredients—like bran and cornmeal—are available in supermarkets, most will be found more readily in natural food stores. In general, these special flours, meals, and grains should be refrigerated or frozen in an airtight container for no more than six months. Always bring chilled ingredients to room temperature before adding to a bread dough.

Bran The outer layer of grains (such as wheat or oats), bran is a good source of carbohydrates, calcium, phosphorus, and fiber. It adds flavor, texture, and nutrients to bread.

Buckwheat flour Rich in vitamin E, calcium, and B-complex vitamins, buckwheat flour is low in protein and has a strong, musky flavor. It can be made at home by grinding buckwheat groats in a blender or food processor.

Cornmeal Depending on the type of corn used, cornmeal can be yellow, white, or blue. It can be steel-ground or stone-ground. Most cornmeal in supermarkets is steel-ground, which means the husk and germ have been almost completely removed. Such cornmeal can be stored in an airtight container in a cool, dark place for up to a year. Stone-ground cornmeal, found in natural food stores, is more nutritious because it retains some of the corn's hull and germ. It's also more perishable and should be stored in the refrigerator. Cornmeal comes in three grinds—fine (also known as corn flour), medium (the type found in supermarkets), and coarse, also known as *polenta*. All cornmeal gives bread a slightly sweet flavor; coarse cornmeal adds a crunchy, grainy texture.

Cracked wheat For cracked wheat, wheat kernels are cut into fragments rather than ground. It is the ingredient that gives bread a crunchy texture and a nutty, whole-grain flavor.

Gluten flour A high-protein, hard-wheat flour that's been treated to remove most of the starch, thereby preserving a high gluten content, gluten flour is used mainly in dietetic breads and as an additive to doughs made with flours (like rye) that have little or no gluten.

Oats There are two common forms of oats—rolled and steel-cut. Regular rolled oats—also called oat flakes—are made by rolling the whole grain into a flake. Quick-cooking oats are first cut into thirds, then steamed and rolled into flakes. Regular or quick-cooking rolled oats (not instant oatmeal) are used in the following recipes. Oat flour can be made by processing rolled oats in a blender or food processor. Oats are rich in minerals and protein, and add a nutty, slightly sweet flavor and chewy texture to bread.

Rice flour Milled from both white and brown varieties, rice flour has no gluten. It's added to breads mainly for its hearty flavor. Oriental sweet rice flour is a thickening agent and should not be used in baking.

Rye flakes Made by rolling the grain until flat, rice flakes add a coarse chewiness and pleasantly bitter flavor to bread.

Soy flour Made from soybeans, it is extremely high in vitamins, minerals, and protein. Soy flour creates a very brown crust, so the oven temperature should be reduced by 25F (5C). It has a strong, musty flavor and is generally used to enrich bread (see Cornell Enrichment Formula, page 57).

Triticale flour Made from a modern hybrid of wheat and rye, it has an even higher protein content than wheat flour. Because it's low in gluten, triticale flour should be combined with bread or all-purpose flour for the best results. Triticale flour can be substituted for whole-wheat flour in recipes. It contributes a nutty, ryelike flavor to bread.

Wheat berries These are the whole, unprocessed kernels, which must be softened before using either by soaking overnight in warm water or by sprouting (page 58). Wheat berries contribute a chewy texture and wholesome nutty flavor to bread.

Wheat flakes Rich in nutrients, wheat flakes are made from the whole kernel. They add a lightly sweet flavor and chewy texture to bread.

Wheat germ The flaky embryo of the wheat kernel, wheat germ is rich in vitamins, iron, protein, and fat. It's sold raw or toasted and has a nutty, slightly sweet flavor.

Leavening Agents

Simply stated, leavening agents are what make bread rise. The most commonly used leaveners are yeast, baking powder, and baking soda. Eggs can also contribute to leavening, but generally are not used specifically for that purpose.

Yeast

A living organism that thrives on the natural sugar in starch, yeast is commonly available in three forms— active dry yeast, quick-rising yeast, and compressed fresh yeast. Brewer's yeast is used for nutritional purposes, not leavening. When combined with sugar, moisture, and warmth, yeast begins to ferment, converting flour's starchy nutrients into alcohol and carbon dioxide gas. Gas bubbles trapped in a dough's elastic gluten mesh make it rise. During baking, oven heat kills the yeast, evaporates the alcohol, and causes the gas to expand and raise the bread in a final burst of energy called *oven-spring*.

Active dry yeast A yeast that's been dehydrated, it consists of cells that are alive but dormant. The cells become active again when mixed with a liquid. Active dry yeast comes in 1/4-ounce envelopes, 4-ounce jars, or in bulk. It should be stored in a cool, dry place, but can also be refrigerated or frozen. Properly stored, it's reliable when used by the expiration date stamped on the envelope or jar. Bulk dry yeast, available in natural food stores, is often risky because you don't know how old it is or under what conditions it has been stored. Such yeast could be dead and should always be proofed (page 11). Dry yeast should be dissolved in liquids at 105 to 115F (40 to 45C). One package of dry yeast is equal to about 2-1/4 teaspoons dry yeast or one cake compressed yeast.

Quick-rising yeast A different strain of dry yeast, it leavens bread in a third to half the time of regular active dry yeast. It comes in 1/4-ounce envelopes. There are two brands on the market—Fleischmann's RapidRise and Red Star's Quick-Rise. Though it was developed for the rapid-mix method (page 11) of combining the yeast with flour and adding 120F liquid, it can be dissolved conventionally, as with active dry yeast. Equal amounts of quick-rising yeast can be substituted for active dry yeast in most bread recipes, with an appropriate adjustment in rising times.

Compressed fresh yeast A moist, active yeast, it is extremely perishable. It's commonly sold in 0.6-ounce and 2-ounce cakes and can be found in a market's refrigerated section. Compressed fresh yeast must be refrigerated and used within one or two weeks, or by the date indicated on the package. It can be frozen for up to six months, but should be defrosted at room temperature and used immediately. Dissolve compressed fresh yeast in lukewarm liquids (95F, 35C). Always proof (see page 11) fresh yeast to be sure it's still alive. One 1/4-ounce envelope or 2-1/4 teaspoons dry yeast can be substituted for a 0.6-ounce cake of fresh yeast.

The temperature of the liquid in which any yeast is dissolved is very important. Too much heat will kill it; too little will slow its growth. Don't guess! Unless you're an experienced baker, use a thermometer for accurate temperature readings.

Generally, one envelope or a 0.6-ounce cake of yeast is used to raise 4 to 5 cups of flour. A little extra yeast may be used to speed the rising, but too much yeast will produce a bread with a porous texture and yeasty taste. Too little yeast creates a heavy, dense loaf. Doughs rich in butter, eggs, sweeteners, fruits, or nuts often need double the amount of yeast of plain doughs.

Baking powder This substance is a mixture of baking soda, an acid such as cream of tartar, and a moisture-absorber like cornstarch. When mixed with a liquid, baking powder releases carbon dioxide—just as fermenting yeast does, but with different results in flavor and texture. Single-acting baking powder immediately releases all its gas into a batter. The more commonly used double-acting baking powder releases some gas when it gets wet and the rest when the batter is exposed to oven heat. Double-acting baking powder is used in the recipes presented in this book. Store baking powder in a cool, dry place and use before the date on the bottom of the can. If you're unsure of a baking powder's freshness, combine 1 teaspoon of it with 1/3 cup hot water. If it bubbles enthusiastically, it's still active. The immediate rising speed of baking powder and baking soda makes it important to have the oven preheated and pans greased before mixing the batter. Too much baking powder or soda gives bread a crumbly, dry texture and bitter taste. It can also make the batter overrise, causing the bread to fall. Too little baking powder or soda produces a bread with a heavy, gummy texture.

Baking soda Also called bicarbonate of soda, it produces carbon dioxide gas when combined with an acidic liquid ingredient such as buttermilk, yogurt, or molasses. Because baking soda reacts immediately when moistened, it should always be mixed with the dry ingredients in the recipe before adding any liquid. Baking soda is very perishable and should be transferred from its box to an airtight container. Store in a cool, dry place for up to six months.

Sourdough starter (page 34) is a homemade leavening agent that is a mixture of flour and liquid into which yeast spores have been introduced. It's extremely temperamental but can produce a wonderfully tangy, slightly sour loaf.

Liquids

Liquids moisten dry ingredients and hold the bread together. Water and milk are the two most commonly used liquids, but many others, each bringing its own unique characteristic to bread, can be used.

Beer, cider, wine, and other alcoholic beverages These liquids give bread a smooth grain and distinctive flavor. The quality and flavor of the liquid you use will be reflected in the bread, so don't bake with anything you wouldn't drink. Though it has long been thought that alcohol evaporates when heated, a USDA study has discovered that from 5 to 85 percent of the alcohol may remain in cooked food, depending on the source of the alcohol and how it was heated. Even the smallest trace of alcohol may be ill-advised for alcoholics and those with alcohol-related illnesses.

Eggs Bread derives a rich, moist crumb, a creamy-yellow color, and a brown crust from eggs. They also contribute some leavening action.

Fruit and vegetable juices Available in an ever-growing variety, juices add flavor and body. Baking soda is added to quick breads made with fruit juices to neutralize the natural acid.

Meat and vegetable broths Homemade or canned, broths add flavor and create a lightly crisp crust. If a broth is salted, reduce the amount of salt called for in the recipe.

Milk products This category of liquids includes milk, buttermilk, sour cream, and yogurt. They produce a soft, brown crust and give the crumb a creamy color and fine texture. Breads made with milk stay fresher longer than those made with water. Modern pasteurization methods make scalding milk unnecessary. The only exception to this rule is raw, unpasteurized milk, which contains an organism that breaks down the gluten structure. Nonfat milk powder, buttermilk powder, and evaporated milk all contribute to producing a rich dough. Milk powders can be added to the dry ingredients without being dissolved. For each cup of buttermilk called for in a recipe, substitute 1/4 cup buttermilk powder plus 1 cup water. Baking soda is added to quick breads made with buttermilk, sour cream, or yogurt to neutralize their natural acidity.

Potato water The water in which peeled potatoes have been boiled contributes flavor, helps create a smooth crumb, and, because of the added starch, produces a slightly faster-rising dough.

Syrups Bread made with honey, maple syrup, and molasses has a moist crumb and a rich, dark crust.

Tea and coffee These popular beverages contribute flavor and create a richly colored crumb and a dark, crisp crust.

Water Last but not least, water creates a crisp crust and brings out a grain's natural flavor. If your water has a high mineral content, use bottled water to avoid transferring the flavor to the bread.

Sweeteners

Sweeteners—whether granulated sugar, brown sugar, honey, malt syrup, maple syrup, or molasses—add flavor and tenderness to bread, help brown the crust, and create a nicely textured loaf. They're also a quick-energy food for yeast, providing it with the power it needs to grow rapidly. Many classic yeast breads, such as French and Italian, do not use sugar; the yeast is nourished by the starch in the flour. Breads made without sugar take longer to rise. Too much sugar in a yeast bread overpowers the yeast's leavening action and inhibits rising. An excess of sugar in a quick bread produces a soggy loaf with a thick crust.

To substitute a liquid sweetener for granulated or brown sugar: For each 1/2 cup granular sugar, substitute 1/3 cup liquid sweetener and reduce the total liquid used in the recipe by 2 tablespoons. In quick breads, add 1/4 teaspoon baking soda to the dry ingredients. Liquid sweeteners like honey can cause overbrowning in baked goods. If you're using a recipe that wasn't specifically formulated for honey, reduce the oven temperature by 25F (5C).

Salt

Salt intensifies flavor; a salt-free bread tastes bland and flat. Cut salt down but not entirely out if you want a flavorful loaf. Salt also stabilizes the fermentation of yeast and strengthens gluten action. Too much salt will prevent yeast from fermenting; too little allows yeast to grow unchecked.

Fats

Fats—including butter, margarine, oil, lard, shortening, bacon fat, or other meat drippings—can generally be used interchangeably. Unsalted butter was used in the following recipes because it has a sweet creamery flavor and because it gives the cook more control over the final taste. Canola oil was used in the recipes calling for vegetable oil. Fat increases a bread's tenderness, keeps it soft and moist, and adds a rich flavor. In yeast breads, fat also lubricates the gluten strands, making the dough more elastic. Yeast breads made without fat, like French bread, begin to dry out within a few hours of baking. Too little fat in quick breads creates a dry, coarsely grained loaf. Too much fat produces an oily bread with a crumbly texture.

Eggs

Though eggs add to the liquid content of bread, they also contribute flavor, structure, fat (from the yolk), and leavening power. Store eggs in the refrigerator but bring to room temperature before adding to bread mixtures. To quickly take the chill off eggs, cover them with warm (not hot) water for 5 to 10 minutes. Recipes in this book use large, Grade AA eggs. One large egg equals a scant 1/4 cup liquid. For a richer dough, substitute 2 egg yolks for 1 whole egg. To cut cholesterol, substitute 1-1/2 egg whites for 1 whole egg. If cutting a recipe in half that calls for 3 eggs, use 1 whole egg and 1 egg yolk. If you only need 1/2 egg, lightly beat 1 whole egg, then measure out about 1-1/2 tablespoons.

Special Additions

Dried or fresh fruits, vegetables, nuts, cheese, seeds, spices, herbs, flavoring extracts, instant coffee powder, and unsweetened cocoa powder all add flavor and personality to bread. In yeast breads, cheese, dried fruits, and nuts are usually kneaded into the dough just before the final rise. Lightly flouring these ingredients helps to separate and incorporate them into the dough. Herbs, spices, and cocoa are added to the dry ingredients and flavoring extracts to liquid ingredients.

Techniques for Making Yeast Breads

The Yeast

There are three basic ways to begin a yeast bread: (1) proofing the yeast, (2) the sponge method, or (3) the rapid-mix method. Each method has its advocates and advantages, and most recipes can be adapted to make use of the technique you prefer.

Proofing yeast A simple procedure, proofing consists of testing the yeast to make sure it's alive. Because of the reliability of today's dry yeast, proofing isn't always necessary. However, bulk yeast should always be proofed, as should compressed fresh yeast (because it's so perishable) and dry yeast that's passed the expiration date on the package or jar. Because proofing gives yeast a head start, it's used in the following recipes. If you prefer not to proof, simply dissolve the yeast in the warm liquid called for in the recipe and continue making the bread.

To proof yeast: Dissolve the yeast and 1 teaspoon sugar in the warm liquid called for in the recipe. Let the mixture stand 5 to 10 minutes. If the mixture begins to swell and foam, the yeast is alive and active. If there's no activity, discard the mixture and begin again with new yeast. There's absolutely no way to revive dead yeast.

The sponge method The use of this technique adds a distinctive flavor and texture to breads and reduces kneading and rising times. Almost any yeast bread recipe can be adapted to this method. In a large bowl, dissolve the yeast in the warm liquid called for. Add any remaining liquid except eggs and any fat, such as butter or oil. Add as much as 1/4 cup sugar (but no more than the recipe calls for) and enough flour to make a medium-stiff batter. Beat with an electric mixer at least 3 minutes to help develop the gluten. Tightly cover with plastic wrap and set in a warm place free from drafts. Let rise until batter foams and bubbles to twice its original bulk, usually at least 1 hour. If a tangy flavor is desired, let the mixture stand overnight. Stir the sponge down and add the remaining ingredients. Follow recipe directions for kneading and rising, neither of which, because of initial beating and fermenting, will take as long as the recipe indicates.

The rapid-mix method Developed by the Fleischmann's yeast test kitchens for use with their active dry yeast, it doesn't require dissolving the yeast separately. Most recipes calling for quick-rising yeast also use this method. Begin by combining the yeast, about a third of the flour, and the other dry ingredients in a large bowl. Heat the liquids (except for eggs) until very warm (120 to 130F, 50 to 55C). Beating constantly, add the warm liquid to the dry ingredients. Beat for about 2 minutes. Add any eggs that are called for and beat 3 more minutes. Stir in enough flour to form a soft dough; knead as directed in recipe.

Quick-mix method Developed by the Betty Crocker kitchens, it is a quick, one-rise method of breadmaking that combines extra yeast with baking powder. Most plain yeast breads can be adapted to this method. For a basic recipe using 5 to 6 cups of flour and about 2 cups of liquid, use two (1/4-oz.) packages active dry yeast or quick-rising yeast and 2 teaspoons baking powder. Dissolve yeast as recipe directs. Add baking powder with remaining dry ingredients. Knead dough as directed in recipe. Shape into loaves and place in prepared pans. Cover with buttered waxed paper. Let rise until doubled in bulk. Bake as directed.

Mixing & Kneading the Dough

After dissolving and proofing the yeast, the dough can be mixed and kneaded by one of several methods—by hand, electric mixer, or food processor. (See page 19 for information on using bread machines.) The initial beating process used in the hand and electric mixer methods stimulates gluten development and shortens the kneading time.

By hand: Add the remaining ingredients to the dissolved yeast mixture as directed in the recipe, using the amount of flour indicated. Use a wooden spoon to beat 200 to 300 strokes. After beating, stir in enough flour to make a soft dough. Turn out dough onto a lightly floured work surface. Use a paper towel to wipe out the bowl in which the dough was mixed. Butter the bowl and set aside to use for the first rising.

The height of your work surface is critical for successful kneading. If the table or countertop is too high, you lose leverage and power; too low, and you're sure to finish with a tired back. The ideal height allows you to fully extend your arms downward, palms resting on the work surface.

Kneading is important because it strengthens and stretches the gluten strands so they can form the mesh that holds in the gas bubbles produced by the yeast. Everyone has their own style of kneading. Any way you do it is fine, as long as the end result is a smooth, elastic dough.

Basically, kneading is a push-fold-turn action. To begin, dust your hands with flour. Firmly press down on the dough with the heels of both hands, pushing away from you. Fold the dough and give it a quarter turn. Continue pushing, folding and turning, establishing your own pace, and developing a rhythm. Lean into the dough and let your body weight help. To give your wrists a rest, pick up the dough and slam it down hard on the work surface several times. It's great fun and a wonderful way to work off steam!

Too much flour on the work surface may result in a heavy dough. The amount of flour to use depends on the flour's basic characteristics and the humidity and temperature of the day. The more humidity, the more flour needed. If the dough is extremely soft and sticky when you begin to knead, use a pastry scraper to slowly work a little flour at a time into the dough until it's easy to handle. If you mistakenly add too much flour to the dough, use an atomizer to mist it lightly with lukewarm water. Gradually knead in enough water until the dough is once again pliable.

If layers of flour and dough begin to build up on the palms of your hands during kneading, rub your palms together over a sink or wastebasket. These particles should not be kneaded back into the dough. If you're interrupted during kneading, place a bowl over the dough to prevent it drying until you can continue.

Properly kneaded dough is smooth and elastic. Press on the dough with your fingers, making shallow indentations. If the dough springs back, it's been kneaded enough. Another indication is when tiny blisters form on the dough's surface. After just a few times, you'll know when the dough has been kneaded enough by how it feels.

By electric mixer: You need a heavy-duty mixer to mix and knead dough. After dissolving the yeast in the large mixing bowl, add the remaining ingredients as directed in the recipe. Use the beaters (a paddle for some machines) to beat batter for 2 to 3 minutes.

After beating, add enough flour to make a soft dough. Change to dough hook/s (some machines have a single hook); begin kneading according to the manufacturer's directions. Kneading by machine takes two-thirds to three-quarters as long as by hand. Finish kneading by hand the last minute or so. Machines may have muscle, but they can't tell you when the dough feels right.

By food processor: Always check your manufacturer's instruction booklet to make sure your food processor is strong enough to knead dough. In general, medium- to large-capacity food processors can handle 6 to 8 cups of flour and 2-1/2 cups of liquid. Smaller models can usually take up to 3 cups of flour and 1-1/2 cups of liquid.

To use your food processor, dissolve and proof yeast. If dissolving yeast in a small amount of warm liquid, use a measuring cup. Transfer yeast mixture to the work bowl fitted with the plastic or steel blade. Always use the plastic blade when the bread contains fruit or nuts, which the steel blade would chop into minuscule pieces. Add remaining ingredients, using the smaller amount of flour. Process until mixture comes away from the sides of work bowl. Continue to process about 30 seconds. Let dough stand 2 to 3 minutes to absorb the liquid completely. With the processor running, add more flour through feed tube, if necessary, until the dough forms a ball. Process 15 to 30 seconds longer, or until dough is smooth. Turn out onto a lightly floured surface; knead by hand for 1 to 2 minutes, or until smooth and elastic.

Setting the Dough to Rise

Now you're ready to place the dough in a bowl for the first rising. Form the dough into a ball. Place it in a buttered bowl, turning to coat all surfaces. This light coating of butter keeps the dough moist and prevents it from forming a skin that will inhibit the dough's expansion. Cover the bowl with a slightly damp towel to keep in the natural moisture. Set the bowl in a warm place free from drafts. Drafts are enemies of yeast and will cause dough to rise unevenly and slowly.

During the rising time, the yeast continues to grow, giving off gas that gently and slowly expands the dough. Rising times vary, depending on the temperature of the ingredients, the amount of yeast used, and where the dough is set to rise. The first rising will usually take 1 to 1-1/2 hours in a warm place, up to 2 hours at normal room temperature, and 8 to 12 hours in the refrigerator. Dough rises faster the second and third times around. Longer rising times at cooler temperatures create more flavorful breads.

Warm places for the dough to rise: Ideally, dough should rise at temperatures of 80 to 85F (25 to 30C), but will rise at 100F (45C) without killing the yeast. Dough rises nicely in a gas oven warmed only by the pilot light. Or in an electric oven that's been heated at 200F (95C) for 1 minute and then turned off (check the temperature with an oven thermometer to be safe). If your washer or dryer has been used recently and the room is still warm and humid, set the bowl of dough on top of the machine. Or, run the dryer for a minute on the heat cycle, then turn it off and place the dough inside. Never set dough on top of machines that are running; the vibration will affect the rising. You can set your dough on a rack set over a pan of hot water in a closed oven. If there's a special closet for your hot water heater, set the dough in there. Or bring 2 cups of water to a boil in a microwave oven. Turn off the power, place the dough in the oven with the water, and close the door.

Micro-rise method: Any form of quick rising means the dough won't have as much time to develop its full flavor. However, if time's short, micro-rising can be a lifesaver. Each microwave oven is different, so it is important that you thoroughly read the manufacturer's directions relating to raising bread dough. If you don't have the instruction booklet, take the safe route and don't raise dough at over 10 percent power. Higher settings can kill the yeast and cook the dough. One general point to keep in mind is that microwaves don't have as much room to bounce around in a small-capacity oven, which means they heat bread dough faster than larger ovens.

To micro-rise dough for two standard loaves: Set 1 cup of hot water at a back corner of your microwave oven. Place the dough in a large, buttered, microwave-safe bowl. Cover with plastic wrap or a damp towel. Set the power level at 10 percent; heat for 3 minutes. Let dough stand in oven for 3 minutes. Heat again for 3 minutes; let dough stand 8 minutes. If the dough has not doubled in bulk, repeat the 3-minute heating, 8-minute standing process. Doughs enriched with butter, fruits, and nuts will take longer to rise than plain doughs. The second rising can take place in the microwave oven (using the above technique), providing the dough is placed in microwave- and oven-safe pans.

Quick-rise method: If you don't have a microwave oven, the quick-rise method can be used. Knead the dough as usual; cover and let rest in a warm place 20 minutes. Knead 30 seconds, then shape into loaves and place in greased pans. Let rise until doubled in bulk, then bake as directed. The flavor of quick-rise bread won't be as developed as with conventional rising, but it will still be delicious.

Coolrise method: Dough is made one day, then baked the next with this method developed by the Robin

Hood flour test kitchens. It works best for basic white and wheat loaves that don't contain a lot of weighty ingredients such as fruits and nuts. Begin by kneading the dough as directed. Cover and let the dough rest in a warm place 20 minutes. Knead the dough 30 seconds; shape into loaves and place in greased pans. Use pans that can make fast temperature changes from cold to hot. Lightly brush the tops of the loaves with vegetable oil or melted butter. Cover loosely with waxed paper. Place each pan in a plastic bag large enough for the dough to expand without bursting the bag; seal tightly. Refrigerate for 2 to 24 hours. Remove loaves in their pans from the plastic bags. Slash tops of loaves as desired (page 16). Let stand at room temperature while preheating oven to 400F (205C). Bake 35 to 45 minutes, or until the bread tests done.

Testing the Dough After the First Rising

Except for the preceding quick-rise and coolrise methods, the first rising should increase dough to double its original bulk. To make sure it's risen enough, poke two of your fingers about 1/2 inch deep into the dough. Don't be timid—give it a good jab. If the indentations stay after you remove your fingers, the dough is ready.

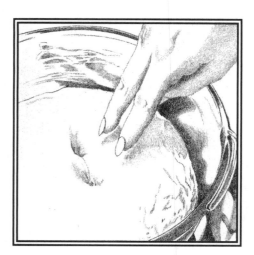 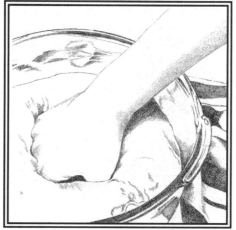

Punching Down & Shaping the Dough

Now comes the fun part. Give the dough a good sock in the middle with your fist. This is called *punching down the dough.* The air will release like a sigh as the dough collapses. On a lightly floured surface, gently knead the dough about 30 seconds. At this point, the dough can be returned to the bowl to rise again before shaping. The texture of the final loaf will become progressively finer each time the dough rises. Or, you can return the dough to the bowl, cover tightly, and refrigerate for up to two days.

The dough will continue to rise in the refrigerator and should be punched down once a day. Remove the dough from the refrigerator at least 3 hours before shaping for final rising and baking.

To shape the dough Begin by dividing the dough, if necessary, as indicated in the recipe. Covering and letting the dough rest for 10 minutes at this point makes it easier to shape. While the dough is resting, grease the required baking pans or sheets. For loaf pans, shape the dough into an oblong form that will fit the pan. Pull the sides of the dough to bottom; pinch to seal. Or, roll or pat the dough into a rectangle with the short side equal to the length of the pan. Roll up tightly, jelly-roll fashion. Pinch seams to seal. For round loaves, simply form the dough into a ball, pinching the bottom edges tightly to seal. Shape free-form loaves that are to rise and bake on baking sheets as directed in the recipe.

Placing Dough in Pans for Final Rising

The baking pans or sheets you use will affect how your bread will turn out. In general, dull metals are better heat conductors than shiny metals. Pans with a dark surface, including those with nonstick coatings, absorb and hold heat, thereby creating a crisp, evenly dark-brown crust. Glass, ceramic, and clay containers also retain heat well and produce beautiful, deep crusts. Reduce oven temperature 25F (15C) when using such bakeware. Bright metal finishes, such as aluminum, reflect heat, which results in breads with a soft, pale crust.

After the dough has been formed into loaves and placed in pans or on baking sheets, cover it with a dry towel. Set in a warm, draft-free place until doubled in bulk. This should take two-thirds to three-quarters the time of the first rising unless the dough contains fruits or nuts. Toward the end of the second rise, preheat the oven for 15 minutes.

Slashing & Finishing Loaf Tops

After the dough rises the final time, slash the top with a sharp knife, razor blade, or metal food processor blade. Make the slashes 1/4 to 1/2 inch deep. You can also use pointed scissors to clip loaf tops. Slashing the top of your loaf before baking not only gives it a professional look, but allows excess gas to escape during baking, preventing unsightly splitting. Brush loaf tops with a glaze as directed in recipe, or choose your own glaze (see The Upper Crust, page 23). If desired, sprinkle glazed loaves with seeds, grains, etc., before baking.

Baking & Cooling

Position the baking pans about 3 inches apart near the center of the middle rack in a preheated oven. Resist peeking the first 15 to 20 minutes so as not to lose oven heat and create a draft during this important initial baking period. It's not unusual for a loaf to increase in size by a third during the first 15 minutes of baking. This dramatic rising is known as *oven-spring* and will continue until the interior temperature of the bread reaches 140F (60C), killing the yeast.

Bread may also be started in a cold oven. This technique is most often used if you're in a hurry and trying to speed the last few minutes of rising time. However, it shouldn't be used to replace the second rising period. When the dough has almost doubled, place it in a cold oven. Set temperature 25F (5C) higher than called for in the recipe. Bake 5 minutes less than called for in the recipe before testing for doneness. The crust on a loaf started in a cold oven will be thicker and firmer than usual.

To test bread for doneness, cover your hands with hot pads or oven mitts. Turn the baked loaf out onto your covered hand and lightly tap the bottom with your fingertips—perfectly baked bread sounds hollow. If the bottom of your loaf isn't as firm or brown as you like, place it directly on the oven rack and bake 5 minutes longer.

Cool freshly baked bread by placing it top side up on a rack. For the best texture, cool breads about 2 hours before slicing. If you absolutely can't wait, and don't mind your bread a little doughy, wait 30 minutes, then have at it.

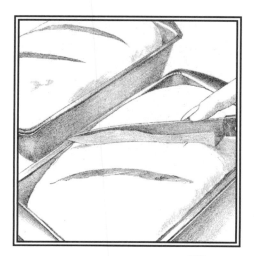

Bread Machines

There's no doubt about it—bread machines are here to stay. These Japanese inventions are computer-driven wonders that mix, knead, rise, punch down, bake, and sometimes cool bread—all in a single compartment. In the best of all worlds, all you do is measure and add the ingredients, press a button to specify the cycle, and let the machine do its thing. A bread machine can create a satisfying, flavorful yeast bread while you're busy doing something else. It enables you to create healthy, wholesome breads with minimum effort. An added bonus is the one-compartment mixing bowl–baking pan, which saves time on cleanup.

Among the bread machines currently on the market are the Panasonic (which is also marketed under the name of National), Zojirushi, Seiko, and Magic Mill. There's also the Hitachi, Regal, and Sanyo, which are basically the same machine, as are the Dak and Welbilt.

All bread machines are about the size of an old-fashioned bread box. Each contains a nonstick canister that serves as a mixing bowl and baking pan. A motor-driven blade at the bottom of this compartment mixes and kneads the dough. A heating coil handles the baking. Each function—mixing, rising, and baking—is controlled by a sophisticated microcomputer that regulates timing, temperature, and the motor.

There are three basic loaf shapes—vertical rectangle, horizontal rectangle, and cylindrical—depending on the brand and model of bread machine. Though the vertical rectangle is the shape most manufacturers use, it can be problematic. The top sometimes collapses, forming a slight hollow in the bread's top crust. The round loaves create slices that are fine for sandwiches, but they must be halved or quartered to fit in a standard toaster. Besides their unconventional shapes, bread-machine loaves have a singularly distinctive characteristic—a bottom hole created by the mixing blade. In addition to the blade, some machines have a kneading pin, which pulls at the dough and maximizes kneading. This removable pin creates a small hole in the side of the bread.

Most bread machines have a capacity for either 1 or 1-1/2 pounds. Machines that yield 1-pound loaves (about eight slices) use around 2 cups of dry ingredients and 1/2 cup liquid. Those that produce 1-1/2-pound loaves (about 12 slices) can hold 3 to 4 cups of dry ingredients and 1 to 1-1/2 cups of liquid. Dry ingredients include everything from flour to oats to bran, and liquids include foods like milk, water, and eggs.

The way ingredients are added to a bread machine depends on the model of bread machine. The instructions for some machines direct you to put the yeast in first, whereas others start with the liquid, followed by the dry ingredients and topped with the yeast. Several other bread machines have a separate yeast dispenser, which automatically adds the yeast according to the machine's software program. One thing all manufacturers agree on is using active dry yeast. Compressed fresh yeast or quick-rising yeast won't work with the programmed timing of most machines, although some manufacturers do give instructions for quick-rising yeast.

Timing for the various cycles differs from machine to machine. For instance, the basic bread setting takes 4-1/4 hours on one machine and only 3 hours and 10 minutes on another—with almost identical results. Some machines have a rapid-bake setting, which produces a loaf of bread in about 2-3/4 hours. Check the owner's manual for your particular machine to see how long each cycle is programmed to take.

A programmable timer is available on most machines. This allows you to delay the machine's starting time up to 9 hours. That means you can get up in the morning to the fragrance of freshly baked bread or walk into the house after a hard day's work to a well-deserved treat. Remember to calculate the time according to how long your machine takes to produce a finished loaf. Add an hour to that time so the bread has time to cool and set before serving. With delayed settings, never use ingredients like eggs or milk that could spoil during the waiting period.

All machines have a dough setting, which mixes the ingredients, kneads the dough, and takes it through its first rising. The dough can then be removed from the machine, shaped into loaves, rolls, coffeecakes, breadsticks, or whatever, and set to rise the second time outside the bread machine. Some machines have a timer that can be used with the dough setting, which means that when you get home from work the dough will be ready and waiting to be shaped into pizza, rolls, etc. Use the micro-rise method (page 14) for the second rise, and dinner's ready that much faster.

Several bread machines have a raisin-bread setting that sounds an alarm indicating the kneading will end in 5 minutes. This allows raisins, nuts, chopped dried fruit, etc., to be added to the dough with just enough time to be kneaded into it without the fruit being pulverized. At least one manufacturer offers a whole-wheat setting, engineered for use with heavy, whole-grain doughs. Some machines have a French bread mode, which is specially programmed for this sometimes difficult bread. One machine has a manual setting that allows you to bypass the computer's programming in order to personalize recipes. For instance, if your favorite bread has risen sufficiently and is ready to be baked, you simply turn the dial to the bake mode. With most machines, machine settings must never be changed while the machine is running.

Some bread machines have a viewing window through which you can see how the bread's developing. If your machine doesn't have a window, it won't hurt to lift the lid and check the dough's progress during the kneading cycle. (Don't lift the lid of a machine with a yeast dispenser until the yeast has been added.) Though bread-machine manuals warn against peeking, doing so will let you see whether or not the dough needs an extra tablespoon or two of flour or liquid. Breadmaking is not an exact science and flour is sensitive to atmospheric conditions, so the need for adjustments isn't unusual. And checking the dough during mixing could prevent a failed loaf of bread. Just don't open the lid during the rising or baking cycles.

Many bread machines have a cooling feature, a fan that circulates air, cooling the bread, and crisping the crust while it's still in the machine. Such a cycle is mandatory if the bread finishes baking while you're at work or before you get up in the morning. Otherwise, the hot bread would sit in the machine and steam in its own heat, creating a soggy crust and overly moist interior.

What are the drawbacks of bread machines? Some don't have removable containers, which increases the hazard of spilling ingredients onto the heating element—a mess to clean. All are extremely noisy—a problem that will undoubtedly be solved in future models. The machines can become very hot during the baking cycle, so caution is the byword. Some breads have a tendency to overrise in a bread machine, which causes the top to collapse slightly.

For sure success with bread machines, it's vital that you read your instruction manual thoroughly, and precisely follow the directions for ingredients and method. Only when you're experienced with your machine's idiosyncrasies and how certain doughs react in it should you begin experimenting. Even then, allow for normal trial and error. Only the brave will risk testing a new recipe the night company's coming.

Tips for Using Bread Machines

As with breads baked conventionally, those created in bread machines are susceptible to humidity, temperature (of the ingredients and the room), and the quality of the ingredients. See Basic Bread Ingredients (pages 3–9) for information on how basic breadmaking ingredients react in different situations.

Always follow the manufacturer's instructions for adding and layering ingredients.

When using the timer for a delayed starting time, it's vital that the yeast not touch the liquid.

The computer timing for most bread machines is programmed for the use of active dry yeast. Some machine manuals give directions for using quick-rising yeast. Compressed fresh yeast shouldn't be used for machine-baked breads.

Substituting 1/4 cup gluten flour for whole-wheat flour in whole-grain loaves will give them a better texture.

Unless the recipe calls for melted butter, always cut butter into pieces and soften it before adding to the mixture. This makes it easier for the butter to combine with the other ingredients.

Substituting honey or other liquid sweeteners for sugar can cause overbrowning, so make allowances when choosing the crust selection.

When employing the timer for delayed start times, don't use ingredients like eggs or fresh milk products that might spoil during the wait.

Bread machines with containers shaped like a horizontal rectangle sometimes have trouble blending ingredients in the corners. If that's the case, simply use a rubber spatula to move the ingredients from the corners toward the center.

Prevent an imperfect loaf by checking the dough's progress during the mixing/kneading period. The dough should be forming a soft, pliable mass around the blade. Dough that's lumpy or in chunks is too dry. Add a tablespoon of liquid and let it mix into the dough. Check after a minute or so and add a little more liquid if the dough isn't the right texture. An overly moist dough can be brought to the right consistency by adding flour, a tablespoon at a time, until the dough is soft but not sticky.

A dough that's too soft because of excess liquid can mushroom out of the pan, causing the baked loaf to fall. It can also create bread that is dense, moist, or with an uneven crumb.

Dough that's too dry won't rise properly and the resulting bread will be dense and heavy with a cracked top.

When converting your favorite recipe to the bread machine, remember that 1-1/2-pound machines can hold 3 to 4 cups of dry ingredients and 1 to 1-1/2 cups of liquid. That means that an average two-loaf yeast-bread recipe would have to be divided in half to fit in this machine. One-pound machines can hold about 2 cups of dry ingredients and 1/2 cup liquid. That means a conventional recipe would have to be altered drastically, reduced by about two-thirds.

Ingredients like raisins and nuts can be broken into minuscule pieces if they're added at the beginning of the mixing mode. Some machines beep 5 minutes before kneading is done so you can add such ingredients, thereby kneading them into the dough while keeping them whole. Don't worry if your machine doesn't have that feature. Simply check your user's manual to see how long mixing/kneading takes in your machine. Then set a timer to go off 5 minutes before the kneading finishes and add the ingredients. They should be evenly distributed by the time the dough is ready for the first rising.

To bake bread in a conventional oven rather than the bread machine, use the dough setting, then remove the dough from the machine after the first rising. Knead the dough for a minute; cover and set aside while you grease the pans. Dough from a 1-pound machine will fit into an 8" x 4" loaf pan or a 1-1/2-quart casserole dish. A 1-1/2-pound loaf needs a 9" x 5" loaf pan or a 2-quart casserole dish. Cover and let rise until doubled in bulk; micro-rise (page 14) if you're really in a hurry. Most breads can be baked at 375F (190C) for 30 to 40 minutes. For breads high in sugar or those baked in glass, reduce the temperature by 25F (5C).

When using the timer for delayed baking, don't forget to allow for the bread to finish baking about an hour before you want to serve it. This gives the bread a chance to cool and set, making it easier to slice.

If the mixing blade comes loose and gets stuck in the bottom of the baked loaf, simply wait for the loaf to cool, then pull the blade out with your fingers. Be careful not to scratch the blade's nonstick finish.

Unless your machine has a cooling cycle, immediately remove the bread from the machine when it's finished baking. Otherwise, the bread will have a soggy crust and overly moist interior.

If a bread is hard to remove from the container, gently rap the pan on the side of the counter. Or use a rubber mallet to tap lightly on the sides of the pan.

Bread-machine success will come with experience, so don't give up if you have a few failures. Every time a loaf doesn't turn out right, make a note to adjust the recipe the next time you use it. Before long, your bread machine will be turning out a successful loaf every time you use it.

The Upper Crust

The tops of unbaked loaves can be slashed (see page 16) before or after they're brushed with a glaze and sprinkled with seeds or other toppings. Slashing beforehand gives a uniformly colored and garnished final crust. Doing so afterwards creates a crust with both textural contrast and an attractive, two-tone effect. The slashes will be a lighter color and free of seeds or other topping.

Whether you like your crust tender, crisp, or chewy, you can achieve what you want with one of the following techniques. Before baking, brush the top of your loaf with one of the following.

For a crisp crust: Brush again with water 10 minutes before baking time is complete, or spray with an atomizer. For a lightly salted crust, brush with a solution of 2 teaspoons salt and 1/4 cup water. Placing a pan of hot water on an oven rack below the bread while baking will also create steam for a crispier crust. Remove water 10 minutes before baking time is complete to let crust dry.

For shine and holding seeds in place: Egg yolks give a dark-brown crust; egg whites a shiny crust; and whole eggs both shine and color. Mix 1 whole egg with 1 tablespoon cold water, 1 egg yolk, or 1 egg white with 2 teaspoons cold water. For added flavor, orange juice or other liquid can be substituted for water.

For a soft, tender crust: Use milk or melted butter.

For a soft, shiny, slightly sweet crust: Use honey, molasses, or maple syrup glaze. Any syrupy sweetener can be combined with water or melted butter to create a glaze. Mix 1 teaspoon honey, maple syrup, molasses, or other syrup with 2 to 3 teaspoons water or melted butter. Undiluted syrupy sweeteners may be used for a more concentrated flavor and sheen, but can cause overbrowning. If the crust begins to darken, cover it lightly with foil.

For a chewy crust: Use a cornstarch wash. In a small saucepan, dissolve 1/2 teaspoon cornstarch in 1/3 cup cold water. Bring mixture to a boil; cook, stirring constantly, for 30 seconds. Cool to lukewarm before brushing loaf tops.

For a crackled, flour-crunchy crust: Make a dutch-crunch topping. Dissolve three (1/4-oz.) packages active dry yeast and 1 teaspoon sugar in 3/4 cup warm water (110F, 45C). Let stand until foamy, 5 to 10 minutes. Add 1 tablespoon sugar, 1 teaspoon salt, 1 tablespoon vegetable oil, and 1 cup rice flour (not oriental sweet rice flour); beat until smooth. Cover and let rise in a warm place until bubbly and doubled in bulk, about 30 minutes. Spread over tops of loaves or rolls before second rising.

High-Altitude Adjustments

Altitudes above 3,500 feet have lower atmospheric pressure, which causes cooked or baked foods to react differently. For instance, water boils at 212F at sea level, but at an altitude of 7,500 feet it boils at 198F. That's because there's not as much air pressure to inhibit the boiling action. Foods stored at high altitudes dry out more quickly than those at low altitudes, which means that an ingredient such as flour is drier and will absorb more liquid. Therefore, slightly more liquid or less flour may be required for bread doughs and batters to reach the proper consistency.

At high altitudes, leavening must also be adjusted so baked goods don't overrise. Likewise, sugar adjustments are necessary in order to prevent a porous crumb with a heavy crust.

For baked goods leavened by baking powder or baking soda at an altitude of:

3,000 feet: Reduce leavening by 1/8 teaspoon for each teaspoon, reduce sugar by 1/2 to 1 tablespoon for each cup, and increase liquid by 1 to 2 tablespoons for each cup.

5,000 feet: Reduce leavening by 1/8 to 1/4 teaspoon for each teaspoon, reduce sugar by 1/2 to 2 tablespoons for each cup, and increase liquid by 2 to 4 tablespoons for each cup.

7,000 feet: Reduce leavening by 1/4 teaspoon for each teaspoon, reduce sugar by 1 to 3 tablespoons for each cup, and increase liquid by 3 to 4 tablespoons for each cup.

No recipe adjustment is suggested for yeast breads baked at high altitudes. However, letting the dough rise twice before the final pan rising allows it to develop a fuller flavor. Increase the baking temperature by 25F (5C)—this sets the crust faster so bread won't overrise during the first 10 to 15 minutes of baking.

For breads fried in deep fat, decrease the oil temperature by 3F for each 1,000 feet above sea level; fry foods for a longer time.

What Went Wrong?

Problem	Cause	Solution
Yeast Breads:		
Bread rose up and over sides of pan.	Pan was too small.	Do not fill pans more than 1/2 to 2/3 full.
Crust is too pale.	Oven temperature too low.	Place pan higher in oven.
Crust too dark.	Oven too hot.	Place a tent of foil over top after lightly browned.
	Too much sugar in dough.	Use amount of sugar stated in recipe.
Bread is crumbly and dry.	Not enough flour for liquid. Not enough kneading.	Follow recipe directions. Knead for longer time.
Top crust separates from rest of loaf.	Crust dried during rising. Loaf improperly shaped.	Cover rising dough with slightly damp towel. Knead excess air from dough after punching down. Use greater care in shaping.
Bread rose unevenly.	Oven temperature too low. Loaf improperly shaped.	Use an oven thermometer to determine oven temperature. Use greater care in shaping.
Pale bottom and side crusts.	Baked in shiny aluminum pans that deflect heat.	Remove from pans; bake directly on oven rack 5 minutes or until crust is nicely browned.
Large holes in bread.	Too much yeast. Overkneading. Inadequate punch down. Too long a rising time.	Reduce yeast 1 teaspoon. Knead only recommended time. Knead out excess air before shaping. Reduce rising time.
Loaf has crack on one side. (Doesn't affect flavor. Call loaf *country* or *peasant*, because of rugged appearance.)	Bread expanded after crust formed.	Slash top of loaf before baking.
Free-form loaf is flat.	Dough too soft.	Add extra flour for a firmer dough.
Bread is dense and soggy.	Too much liquid; not enough kneading.	Follow recipe directions for liquid and kneading.
Has nice crumb, but is slightly gummy.	Underbaked.	Test loaf for doneness before cooling.
One side higher than the other.	Uneven baking.	All ovens have hot spots. Rotate pans front to back; bottom shelf to top shelf.

Problem	Cause	Solution
Bread is flat and compact.	Rose too long in pans, then collapsed in oven heat.	Let rise a shorter time in pans.
Crust too thick and tough.	Oven temperature too low.	Raise oven temperature 25F (15C). Test doneness sooner.
Dense, close-textured crumb.	Not enough yeast. Too much salt. Insufficient rising time.	Add 1 to 3 teaspoons yeast. Measure salt carefully. Let dough rise until doubled in bulk or as directed.
Porous texture. Strong yeast flavor.	Too much yeast.	Use less yeast or as recipe directs.
Bread is chewy and dry.	Too little fat.	Use 2 tablespoons fat per loaf of bread.

Quick Breads:

Soggy and sunken in middle.	Too much liquid or sugar. Too little baking powder or baking soda.	Follow recipe directions.
Crack in top of loaf.	Characteristic of quick breads. Caused by escaping steam and gas.	Leave as is or, line pan with waxed paper, letting paper extend 3 inches over top. This deflects heat from top of loaf.
Dry crumb with bulge in center.	Not enough liquid. Not enough shortening.	Follow recipe directions.
Coarse, crumbly texture and bitter aftertaste.	Too much baking soda or baking powder.	Reduce baking soda or baking powder. See recipe directions. Make altitude adjustments.
Bread is greasy with crisp edges.	Too much shortening.	Measure shortening correctly.
Crust is thick, porous, and too brown.	Too much sugar.	Reduce sugar slightly.
Breads, muffins, or biscuits are tough.	Overhandling of batter or dough.	Stir ingredients together *only* until dry ingredients are moistened. Never beat batter or dough.

The Recipes

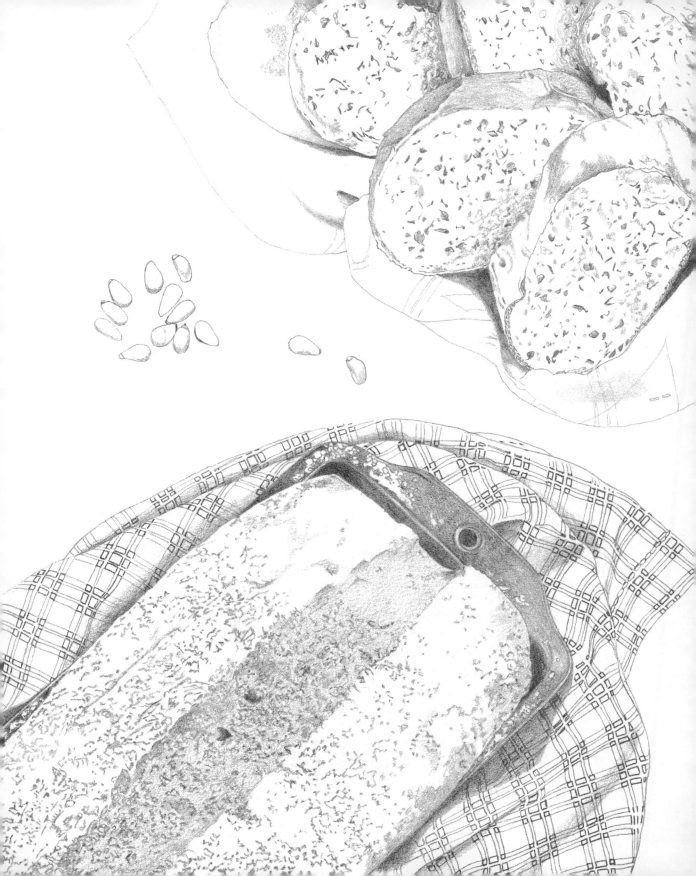

White-Flour Yeast Breads

Don't let the title of this chapter mislead you. It doesn't promise an ordinary assortment of cotton-textured, uninteresting loaves lacking flavor and character. Far from it! White flour—I use unbleached bread or all-purpose flour—forms the foundation for myriad flavor possibilities. It's like a blank canvas just waiting for inspiration. Ingredients like garlic, onions, fresh herbs, nuts, cheese, or potatoes can transform bread from plain to outstanding. It takes only a little creativity to produce white-flour breads that are anything but ordinary.

Certainly, no one ever called brioche "ordinary." *Au contraire!* This regal French member of the bread family is buttery-rich, finely textured, and suitable for the finest occasions. Another unique white-flour creation is the turban-shaped, cheese-filled Khachapuri, from Georgia, in the former USSR, where hawkers sell miniature, simplified versions of it on the streets to passersby who eat it on the run.

Living just across the majestic Golden Gate Bridge from San Francisco, I have a natural passion for yet another white-flour creation—tangy sourdough bread. Early American frontier families knew the value of a good sourdough starter and carried crocks of it with them on long, covered-wagon treks. It was a legacy to be treasured and passed on to family and good friends throughout the years. Why should we be any different?

White-flour breads can be enhanced with any number of your favorite foods and condiments. For instance, I love the fresh garlic-basil perfume of pesto, so I created Pesto–Pine Nut Bread. My husband Ron, coauthor of *Wine Lover's Companion*, came up with the idea for Wine & Cheese Bread, which uses wine for the liquid and adds chunks of cheese. The flavors of potatoes au gratin—a favorite comfort food—translate into a bread of the same name. Blue cheese added to a basic white-flour dough becomes Blue Cheese Baguettes. So, you see, white-flour breads never have to be plain or boring. The only limitation when working with white flour is your imagination!

Basil-Lemon Brioche

The classic shape of this butter-rich bread has a fluted base and a jaunty topknot. The large, classic loaf is called *brioche a tête*; individual rolls are called *petites brioches*. Special brioche molds are available in kitchenware shops or in the cookware section of most department stores. You don't need a special mold, however, because this bread is just as delicious when baked in a regular pan.

1 (1/4-oz.) package active dry yeast
1/4 cup warm water (110F, 45C)
2 tablespoons sugar
2 cups all-purpose flour
1-1/2 teaspoons salt
2 eggs
1 egg yolk
3/4 cup unsalted butter, softened
1/2 cup packed finely chopped fresh basil
Finely grated zest of 1 large lemon
1 egg yolk mixed with 1 teaspoon cream for glaze

In large bowl of electric mixer, dissolve yeast in warm water. Add a pinch of the sugar; let stand until foamy, 5 to 10 minutes. Add remaining sugar, flour, salt, eggs, egg yolk, butter, basil, and lemon zest. Beat at medium speed with electric mixer 4 to 6 minutes, or until shiny and pliable. Dough will be soft and sticky. If your mixer can't handle the dough, beat vigorously with a wooden spoon 10 to 15 minutes. Or grab the dough with your hands, lift it up about a foot, then slap it back down hard into bowl until shiny and pliable. Cover bowl tightly with plastic wrap and a slightly damp towel. Let rise in a warm place free from drafts until light, spongy, and tripled in bulk, about 3 hours.

Stir down dough; beat 1 minute. Cover tightly with plastic wrap; refrigerate overnight, or at least 6 hours.

Remove dough from refrigerator; punch down. For the large brioche, generously grease a 7- or 8-inch fluted brioche mold or 1-1/2-quart casserole or soufflé dish. Pinch off a piece of dough the size of an extra-large egg; set aside. Shape remaining dough into a smooth ball. Place seam side down in prepared mold or dish. Butter your thumb and press into center of dough ball, making an indentation about 3/4 inch deep. Shape remaining dough like a teardrop. Pressing lightly, insert small end into your thumb depression. Loosely cover with buttered waxed paper or plastic wrap. Let rise until doubled in bulk, 1-1/2 to 2 hours.

Preheat oven to 425F (220C). Gently brush brioche with egg-yolk glaze. Bake 5 minutes. Reduce heat to 375F (190C); bake additional 35 minutes, or until a wooden pick inserted in center comes out clean. Turn out onto a rack; cool at least 20 minutes before serving warm.

Makes 1 loaf.

Variation

Petites Brioches (Little Brioches):

Generously butter 16 individual brioche tins or muffin cups; set aside. Divide dough in half; cover and return one half to refrigerator. Separate remaining dough into 8 pieces. Pinch off about 1/5 of each piece and form into teardrop shape; refrigerate. Shape larger pieces into smooth balls. Place one ball in each prepared tin or muffin cup. Butter your little finger or the tip of a wooden spoon handle. Make a depression about 3/8 inch deep in center of each ball; insert refrigerated teardrop-shaped pieces, small ends down. Repeat with remaining dough. Place individual tins on baking sheet (unnecessary if using muffin pans). Lightly cover with buttered waxed paper. Let rise until doubled in bulk, about 1-1/2 hours.

Preheat oven to 450F (230C). Gently brush brioches with egg-yolk glaze. Bake 5 minutes. Reduce heat to 350F (175C); bake 6 to 7 minutes longer, or until a wooden pick inserted in the center comes out clean. Serve warm.

Makes 16 individual brioches.

Basic White Bread

A white bread that doesn't taste like cotton. Use one of the variations below to personalize it to your taste.

1 (1/4-oz.) package active dry yeast
1/4 cup warm water (110F, 45C)
2 tablespoons sugar
1 tablespoon salt
1-3/4 cups milk
1/4 cup vegetable oil
6 to 6-1/2 cups bread or all-purpose flour
1 egg white mixed with 1 tablespoon water for glaze

In large bowl of electric mixer, dissolve yeast in warm water. Add a pinch of the sugar; let stand until foamy, 5 to 10 minutes. Add remaining sugar, salt, milk, oil, and 1-1/2 cups of the flour. Beat at medium speed with electric mixer 2 minutes, or beat 200 vigorous strokes by hand. Stir in enough remaining flour to make a soft dough. Change to dough hook(s) if using mixer, or turn out dough onto a lightly floured surface.

Knead dough 8 to 10 minutes, or until smooth and elastic, adding only enough flour to prevent sticking. Clean and butter bowl. Place dough in bowl, turning to coat all surfaces. Cover with a slightly damp towel; set in a warm place free from drafts. Let rise until doubled in bulk, about 1 hour. Grease 2 (8" x 4") loaf pans; set aside.

Punch down dough; knead 30 seconds. Divide dough in half. Shape into loaves and place in prepared pans. Cover with a dry towel; let rise until doubled in bulk, about 1 hour.

Preheat oven to 375F (190C). Slash tops of loaves; brush with egg-white glaze. Bake 35 to 40 minutes, or until bread sounds hollow when tapped on the bottom. Remove from pans; cool on racks.
Makes 2 loaves.

Variations

Spiced Nut or Fruit Bread: Increase sugar to 1/2 to 3/4 cup, add 1-1/2 cups finely chopped nuts or dried fruit and 1 to 2 teaspoons ground spices such as cinnamon, nutmeg, and ginger.

Seeded Bread: Add 1 tablespoon caraway seeds, 1/4 cup poppy seeds, 1/3 cup toasted sesame seeds, or 1/2 cup chopped, hulled sunflower kernels to dough.

Herbed Bread: Add 1/4 to 1/2 cup minced fresh herbs (or 1-1/2 to 3 tablespoons dried herbs) to first addition of flour.

Garlic Bread: Substitute olive oil for vegetable oil; add 3 to 4 minced garlic cloves.

Egg Bread: Increase warm water to 3/4 cup, omit milk, and add 6 eggs, slightly beaten. Substitute fruit juice, vegetable juice, beer, wine, bouillon, etc. for milk.

Sun-dried Tomato-Fennel Focaccia

*F*ocaccia (foh-KAH-chee-ah) is like a pizza with the flavoring ingredients kneaded into the dough rather than adorning the top. Whereas pizza is usually considered a meal, focaccia is more commonly eaten as a soup or salad accompaniment, or as a snack. Don't add too much flour to this dough—it should be quite soft and pliable. You can make, bake, and enjoy this wonderful bread in about an hour by using quick-rising yeast and the microwave oven for rising.

1 (1/4-ounce) package active dry yeast
1/2 teaspoon sugar
3/4 cup warm water (110F, 45C)
2 to 2-1/2 cups bread or all-purpose flour
1 tablespoon fennel seeds
1 teaspoon salt
1/2 teaspoon freshly ground pepper
1/2 cup finely chopped (oil-packed) sun-dried tomatoes
1/4 cup plus 2 tablespoons olive oil
About 1-1/2 tablespoons yellow cornmeal
1/3 cup grated Parmesan cheese

In large bowl of electric mixer, dissolve yeast and sugar in warm water. Let stand until foamy, 5 to 10 minutes. Add 2 cups of the flour, the fennel seeds, salt, pepper, sun-dried tomatoes, and 1/4 cup of the oil. Beat at medium speed 2 minutes, or beat 200 vigorous strokes by hand. Change to dough hook(s) if using mixer, or turn dough out onto a lightly floured surface.

Knead dough 6 to 8 minutes, or until smooth and elastic. Add only enough flour to prevent sticking; the dough should be very soft. Clean and oil bowl. Place dough in oiled bowl, turning to coat all surfaces. Cover with a slightly damp towel; set in a warm place free from drafts. Let rise until doubled in bulk, about 1 hour.

Preheat oven to 450F (230C). Punch dough down; knead 30 seconds. Cover and set aside 10 minutes. Generously rub a 15" x 10" jelly-roll pan with 1 tablespoon of the remaining olive oil; sprinkle lightly and evenly with cornmeal. Press dough evenly over bottom of prepared pan. Use the tip of your little finger to dimple the dough at 2-inch intervals. Brush with remaining tablespoon olive oil; sprinkle with Parmesan cheese.

Bake 15 to 20 minutes, or until golden brown. Remove from oven; use kitchen shears to cut focaccia into 10 (5" x 3") pieces, cutting 2 strips lengthwise and 5 strips crosswise. Serve warm or at room temperature. Best if eaten the same day baked.

Makes 10 individual servings.

Variation

Herbed Focaccia: Add 1/2 cup minced fresh herbs (of your choice) during kneading process. Five minutes before focaccia is done, sprinkle with 2 more tablespoons minced fresh herbs.

Basic Sourdough Starter

Sourdough starter, the mother of all sourdough breads, has always been temperamental. A true old-fashioned starter relies on wild yeast spores to create its characteristically tart, tangy flavor. Some say the San Francisco Bay area has the perfect climate for these sometimes elusive yeast cells. Unfortunately, if enough of these important little spores aren't lurking in the atmosphere, your starter will be sluggish and flavorless. That's why most of today's sourdough starters are given a boost from yeast. Once you have a good starter, keep it fresh by replenishing it regularly (opposite). And, by all means, share it with a friend.

Before beginning, read the tips in "Working with Sourdough Starter" (opposite).

1 (1/4-oz.) package active dry yeast
2 tablespoons sugar or honey
2 cups warm water (110F, 45C)
1/3 cup nonfat milk powder
2 cups bread or all-purpose flour

In a large, nonmetallic container or bowl, dissolve yeast and sugar or honey in water. Let stand until foamy, 5 to 10 minutes. With a wooden or plastic spoon, stir in milk powder and flour. Small lumps in batter will be dissolved by fermentation process. Cover container with 2 to 3 layers of cheesecloth; secure with rubberband. Set in a warm place free from drafts. Let stand 3 to 5 days, stirring mixture several times each day, until starter has a pleasantly sour aroma and is full of bubbles.

Variations

Potato Starter: Substitute 2 cups warm potato water (water in which peeled potatoes have been cooked) for 2 cups regular water.

Whole-Wheat Starter: Substitute 2 cups whole-wheat flour for 2 cups bread or all-purpose flour.

Rye Starter: Substitute 2 cups rye flour for 2 cups bread or all-purpose flour.

⊠

Working with Sourdough Starter

Make a sourdough starter several days before baking bread so the characteristically tangy flavor can develop.

Always use glass or plastic containers, and plastic or wooden spoons when working with starters. Metal containers and utensils produce an undesirable flavor.

Containers for mixing starters should be large enough to allow mixture to double in bulk. Starters should ferment in a warm place (80 to 90F, 25 to 30C).

The clear liquid that rises to the top of a starter should be stirred back into it several times a day.

If a starter turns orange or pink and develops an unpleasant, acrid odor, undesirable bacteria have invaded it, and the mixture must be discarded.

To use starter, remove the amount called for in the recipe from the refrigerator; bring to room temperature before preparing sponge.

Once starter is made, it may be refrigerated indefinitely as long as it is replenished every 2 weeks.

To replenish starter, add equal amounts of flour and water. For instance, if you use 1 cup starter, replenish it by adding 1 cup flour and 1 cup water. Cover and let stand in a warm place overnight, then cover and refrigerate.

If refrigerated starter isn't used for 2 to 3 weeks, remove 1/2 cup and discard, or give to a friend. Replenish as directed above.

Freshly fed starter may be frozen for up to 2 months. Thaw at room temperature, then let stand in a warm place overnight, or until active and bubbly.

It's a good idea to wash your starter container occasionally to remove any caked-on residue.

Share your starter with a friend to start him or her on the road to sourdough success.

⊠

San Francisco Sourdough Bread

*T*his classic recipe takes time, but that won't deter true sourdough lovers. If your schedule is tight, try the quick sourdough variation below.

> **1-1/2 cups warm water (110F, 45C)**
> **1 teaspoon sugar**
> **1/3 cup nonfat milk powder**
> **1 cup Basic Sourdough Starter (page 34)**
> **6-3/4 to 7-1/4 cups bread or all-purpose flour**
> **2-1/2 teaspoons salt**
> **Cornmeal (optional)**
> **1 egg white mixed with 1 tablespoon water for glaze**

In a large, nonmetallic bowl, make sponge by combining water, sugar, milk powder, sourdough starter, and 2 cups of the flour. Cover with a double layer of cheesecloth; secure with rubber band. Let stand in a warm place free from drafts 24 to 48 hours, depending on sourness desired. Stir once or twice a day with a wooden or plastic spoon.

When sponge is fermented and bubbly, add salt and enough remaining flour to make a soft dough. Turn out dough onto a lightly floured surface. Knead dough 10 to 12 minutes, or until smooth and elastic, adding only enough flour to prevent sticking. Clean and butter bowl. Place dough in bowl, turning to coat all surfaces. Cover with a slightly damp towel; set in a warm place free from drafts. Let rise until doubled in bulk, 1-1/2 to 2 hours. Grease 2 large baking sheets or 2 (2-quart) casserole dishes. If desired, sprinkle baking sheets or bottoms of pans lightly with cornmeal.

Punch down dough; knead 30 seconds. Divide dough in half. Shape into narrow oblong loaves with tapered ends for baking sheets, round loaves for casserole dishes. Place on prepared pans or in casserole dishes. Cover with dry towel. Let rise until doubled in bulk, about 1-1/2 hours.

Adjust oven racks to two lowest positions. Place a shallow roasting pan on lower shelf; pour in 2 cups boiling water. Preheat oven to 425F (220C). Slash tops of oblong loaves diagonally; slash a tic-tac-toe design in tops of round loaves. Brush with egg-white glaze. Bake 15 minutes; brush again with egg glaze. Remove water from oven. Bake 15 to 20 minutes longer, or until bread sounds hollow when tapped on the bottom. Brush a third time with egg glaze 5 minutes before removing from oven. Remove from pans; cool on racks.

Makes 2 loaves.

Variations

Quick Sourdough Bread: Dissolve 1 (1/4-oz.) package active dry yeast and sugar in warm water.

Let stand until foamy, 5 to 10 minutes. Stir in milk powder, sourdough starter, and 2 cups flour. Cover and let ferment overnight, or at least 8 hours. Proceed with recipe as directed. Rising times will be less due to added yeast.

Sourdough Wheat Bread: Substitute 1 cup whole-wheat sourdough starter (page 34) for 1 cup basic sourdough starter, 2 cups whole-wheat flour for 2 cups bread or all-purpose flour, and add 1 cup cracked wheat to sponge. After sponge has fermented, stir in 1/4 cup honey, 2 tablespoons melted unsalted butter or margarine, and 1/2 cup toasted wheat germ.

Sourdough Rye Bread: Substitute 1 cup rye sourdough starter (page 34) for 1 cup basic sourdough starter. After sponge has fermented, substitute 1 more cup rye flour for 1 cup of bread or all-purpose flour. Stir in 1/4 cup dark molasses, 1 tablespoon freshly grated orange zest, 1 tablespoon vegetable oil, 1 tablespoon caraway seeds, and 1 cup rye flakes (optional). After brushing with egg glaze, sprinkle tops of loaves with additional caraway seeds or rye flakes.

Classic French Bread

An overnight sponge and lots of kneading are necessary—but, *ooh-la-la*, the flavor! French bread doesn't keep well because it's made without fat, so plan on using it within a day or two.

2 (1/4-oz.) packages active dry yeast
2-1/2 cups warm water (110F, 45C)
7-1/2 to 8 cups bread or all-purpose flour
1 tablespoon salt
1 egg white mixed with 1 tablespoon water for glaze

In large bowl of electric mixer, dissolve yeast in warm water. Add 2-1/2 to 3 cups flour; stir 1 minute. Batter will have consistency of soft pudding. Cover bowl tightly with plastic wrap; set in a warm place free from drafts. Let stand overnight or at least 8 hours. The longer the sponge ferments, the better the flavor will be. Stir in salt and 1 to 1-1/2 cups of remaining flour. Beat at medium speed with electric mixer 6 minutes or 600 vigorous strokes by hand. Stir in enough remaining flour to make a soft dough. Change to dough hook(s) if using mixer, or turn out dough onto a lightly floured surface.

Knead dough 15 to 20 minutes, or until velvety-smooth and elastic, adding only enough flour to prevent sticking. Clean and lightly flour bowl. Place dough in bowl; dust surface lightly with flour. Cover with a slightly damp towel; set in a warm place free from drafts. Let rise until tripled in bulk, about 1-1/2 hours. Grease 2 large baking sheets or four French bread pans; set aside.

Punch down dough; knead 2 minutes. Cover and let rest 10 minutes.

For oblong loaves, divide dough into 3 or 4 pieces, depending on desired thickness of loaves. On a lightly floured surface, roll each piece into a smooth log shape, gently tapering ends. Place on baking sheets.

For round loaves, divide dough in half. Shape each half into a smooth ball; place balls on baking sheets. Cover with a dry towel. Let rise until doubled in bulk, about 1 hour.

Adjust oven racks to 2 lowest positions. Place shallow roasting pan on lower shelf; pour in 2 cups hot water. Preheat oven to 425F (220C) 15 minutes. Slash tops of oblong loaves with 5 diagonal cuts; slash round loaves with tic-tac-toe design. Brush loaves lightly with cold water. Bake 15 minutes; brush with egg-white glaze. Bake another 10 minutes; brush again with egg glaze. Remove pan of water from oven. Bake additional 10 to 15 minutes longer, a total baking time of 35 to 40 minutes, or until bread sounds hollow when tapped on the bottom. Remove bread from pans and place directly on oven rack; bake 5 more minutes. Cool on racks.

Makes 2 to 4 loaves.

Variation

Wheat French Bread: Substitute whole-wheat flour for the bread or all-purpose flour added to the fermented sponge mixture.

Butterflake Bread

*I*nspired by the traditional butterflake rolls, this rich pull-apart bread doesn't need additional butter.

2 (1/4-oz.) packages active dry yeast
3/4 cup warm water (110F, 45C)
1/4 cup sugar
1-1/2 teaspoons salt
3 eggs
1/2 cup plus 1 tablespoon unsalted butter or margarine, melted
4-1/2 to 5 cups all-purpose flour
4 tablespoons unsalted butter or margarine, softened
4 teaspoons sesame seeds

In large bowl of electric mixer, dissolve yeast in warm water. Add a pinch of the sugar; let stand until foamy, 5 to 10 minutes. Add remaining sugar, salt, eggs, 1/2 cup melted butter or margarine, and 1-1/2 to 2 cups of the flour. Beat at medium speed with electric mixer 2 minutes, or beat 200 vigorous strokes by hand. Stir in enough remaining flour to make a soft dough. Change to dough hook(s) if using mixer, or turn out dough onto a lightly floured surface.

Knead dough about 5 minutes, or until smooth and resilient, adding only enough flour to prevent sticking. Clean and butter bowl. Place dough in bowl, turning to coat all surfaces. Cover with a slightly damp towel; set in a warm place free from drafts. Let rise until doubled in bulk, about 1 hour. Grease 2 (8" x 4") loaf pans; set aside.

Punch down dough; knead 30 seconds. Divide dough in half. Pat or roll out 1 piece of dough into a 12-inch square. Spread 2 tablespoons softened butter over two-thirds of rolled-out dough. Fold unbuttered third over center; fold remaining third over top, making a 12" x 4" rectangle. Cut dough into 12 (1-inch) slices. Arrange slices, cut side down and side by side, in prepared pan. Repeat with remaining dough. Brush tops of loaves with remaining 1 tablespoon melted butter; sprinkle each with 2 teaspoons sesame seeds. Cover with buttered waxed paper; set in a warm place free from drafts. Let rise until doubled in bulk, 45 to 60 minutes.

Preheat oven to 400F (205C). Bake 30 to 35 minutes, or until bread sounds hollow when tapped on the bottom. For a crisper bottom crust, remove bread from pans and bake directly on oven rack during final 5 minutes of baking time. Remove from pans; cool on racks about 30 minutes before serving warm.

Makes 2 loaves.

Peppered Walnut Bread

Pepper adds pizzazz to this earthy loaf flavored with walnuts and coffee. Walnut oil can be found in the gourmet section of many supermarkets and in specialty kitchen shops. Keep it refrigerated, or it can turn rancid in just a few months.

> 1 (1/4-oz.) package active dry yeast
> 1/4 cup warm water (110F, 45C)
> 2 tablespoons sugar
> 1-1/2 cups strong coffee
> 1 tablespoon salt
> 1 tablespoon freshly ground pepper
> 1/3 cup walnut oil or olive oil
> 6-1/2 to 7 cups bread or all-purpose flour
> 1 cup coarsely chopped toasted walnuts (Tip, page 262)
> 4 tablespoons finely chopped walnuts

In large bowl of electric mixer, dissolve yeast in warm water. Add a pinch of the sugar; let stand until foamy, 5 to 10 minutes. Add remaining sugar, coffee, salt, pepper, oil, and 1-3/4 to 2-1/4 cups of the flour. Beat at medium speed with electric mixer 2 minutes, or beat 200 vigorous strokes by hand. Stir in the 1 cup walnuts and enough remaining flour to make a soft dough. Change to dough hook(s) if using mixer, or turn out dough onto a lightly floured surface.

Knead dough 8 to 10 minutes, or until smooth and elastic, adding only enough flour to prevent sticking. Clean and butter bowl. Place dough in bowl, turning to coat all surfaces. Cover with a slightly damp towel; set in a warm place free from drafts. Let rise until doubled in bulk, about 1 hour. Grease 2 round 8-inch cake pans or 1-1/2-quart casserole dishes. Sprinkle bottom of each pan or dish with 1 tablespoon finely chopped walnuts.

Punch down dough; knead 30 seconds. Divide dough in half. Shape into round loaves; place in prepared pans. Sprinkle top of each loaf with 1 tablespoon remaining walnuts, pressing lightly into surface. Cover with a dry towel; let rise until doubled in bulk, about 45 minutes.

Preheat oven to 400F (205C). Slash tops of loaves as desired. Bake 35 to 40 minutes, or until bread sounds hollow when tapped on the bottom. Remove from pans; cool on racks.

Makes 2 loaves.

Wine & Cheese Bread

*T*his fragrant, wine-flavored bread is generously studded with cheese, apples, and sun-dried tomatoes. It's wonderful for roasted-meat sandwiches, and great as an adjunct to soup or salad. Choose a full-bodied, complex-flavored wine such as Chardonnay, Pouilly-Fuisse, or dry Alsatian Riesling.

2 (1/4-oz.) packages active dry yeast
1/2 teaspoon sugar
1/4 cup warm water (110F, 45C)
1-3/4 cups plus 1 tablespoon dry white wine
3 tablespoons vegetable oil
1-1/2 teaspoons salt
1/2 teaspoon dry mustard
6 to 6-1/2 cups bread or all-purpose flour
1 pound Gouda cheese, cut into 1/2-inch cubes
1-1/2 cups chopped unpeeled tart apple
1/2 cup minced (oil-packed) sun-dried tomatoes

In large bowl of electric mixer, dissolve yeast and sugar in warm water. Let stand until foamy, 5 to 10 minutes. Add the 1-3/4 cups wine, oil, salt, mustard, and 2 to 2-1/2 cups flour. Beat at medium speed with electric mixer 2 minutes, or beat 200 vigorous strokes by hand. Stir in cheese, apple, tomatoes, and enough remaining flour to make a soft dough. Change to dough hook(s) if using mixer, or turn out dough onto a lightly floured surface.

Knead dough 8 to 10 minutes, or until smooth and elastic, adding only enough flour to prevent sticking. Clean and butter bowl. Place dough in bowl, turning to coat all surfaces. Cover with a slightly damp towel; set in a warm place free from drafts. Let rise until doubled in bulk, about 1 hour. Grease 2 (9" x 5") loaf pans; set aside.

Punch down dough; knead 30 seconds. Divide dough in half. Shape into loaves and place in prepared pans. Cover with a dry towel; let rise until doubled in bulk, about 1 hour.

Preheat oven to 375F (190C). Slash tops of loaves as desired; brush with remaining 1 tablespoon wine. Bake 35 to 40 minutes, or until bread sounds hollow when tapped on the bottom. Remove from pans; cool on racks at least 30 minutes before slicing.

Makes 2 loaves.

Potatoes-au-Gratin Bread

*B*its of Cheddar cheese dot this moist potato bread, which is even better the second day. Leaving the peel on the potatoes gives the bread a flavor bonus.

2 (1/4-oz.) packages active dry yeast
1/2 cup warm water (110F, 45C)
2 tablespoons sugar
1 cup milk
4 tablespoons vegetable or olive oil
1 tablespoon salt
1/8 teaspoon red (cayenne) pepper
4 to 4-1/2 cups bread or all-purpose flour
2 cups grated peeled or unpeeled potatoes
1 cup shredded sharp Cheddar cheese (4 oz.)

In large bowl of electric mixer, dissolve yeast in warm water. Add a pinch of the sugar; let stand until foamy, 5 to 10 minutes. Add milk, 3 tablespoons of the oil, salt, cayenne, and 2 cups of the flour. Beat at medium speed with electric mixer 2 minutes, or beat 200 vigorous strokes by hand. Stir in potatoes and enough remaining flour to make a soft dough. Change to dough hook(s) if using mixer, or turn out dough onto a lightly floured surface.

Knead dough 6 minutes; add cheese. Knead 2 to 4 more minutes, or until dough is smooth and elastic. Because of the starch in the potatoes, dough will feel slightly sticky. Clean and butter bowl. Place dough in bowl, turning to coat all surfaces. Cover with a slightly damp towel; set in a warm place free from drafts. Let rise until doubled in bulk, about 1 hour. Grease and flour 2 round 9-inch cake pans or 1-1/2-quart casserole dishes; set aside.

Punch down dough; knead 30 seconds. Divide dough in half. Shape into round loaves and place in prepared pans. Cover with buttered waxed paper; set in a warm place free from drafts. Let rise until doubled in bulk, about 45 minutes.

Preheat oven to 400F (205C) or 375F (190C) if using glass baking containers. Slash tops of loaves as desired; brush with remaining tablespoon oil. Bake 35 to 40 minutes, or until bread sounds hollow when tapped on the bottom. Remove from pans; cool on racks.

Makes 2 loaves.

Blue Cheese Baguettes

Toast thin slices of this fragrant bread and serve with pâté for an appetizer. Or, split the baguettes lengthwise, spread with Blue Cheese Butter (page 257) and broil until toasty brown.

1 (1/4-oz.) package active dry yeast
1 teaspoon sugar
3/4 cup warm water (110F, 45C)
3 tablespoons olive oil
1 teaspoon salt
1/2 teaspoon white pepper
3 to 3-1/2 cups bread or all-purpose flour
4 ounces blue cheese, crumbled
1 egg white mixed with 2 teaspoons water for glaze

In large bowl of electric mixer, dissolve yeast and sugar in warm water. Let stand until foamy, 5 to 10 minutes. Add oil, salt, pepper, and 1 to 1-1/2 cups of the flour. Beat at medium speed with electric mixer 2 minutes, or beat 200 vigorous strokes by hand. Stir in cheese and enough remaining flour to make a soft dough. Change to dough hook(s) if using mixer, or turn out dough onto a lightly floured surface.

Knead dough 4 to 6 minutes, or until smooth and elastic, adding only enough flour to prevent sticking. Clean and butter bowl. Place dough in bowl, turning to coat all surfaces. Cover with a slightly damp towel; set in a warm place free from drafts. Let rise until doubled in bulk, about 1 hour. Grease 2 baking sheets; set aside.

Punch down dough; knead 30 seconds. Divide dough into 3 equal pieces. Shape each piece into a 12-inch-long loaf, slightly tapered at ends. Place 2 baguettes, 4 inches apart, on 1 baking sheet; place 1 baguette on the other. Cover with dry towels and set in a warm place free from drafts. Let rise until doubled in bulk, 30 to 45 minutes.

Preheat oven to 375F (190C). Slash tops of loaves as desired; brush with egg-white glaze. Bake 20 to 30 minutes, or until bread sounds hollow when tapped on the bottom. Remove from pans; cool on racks.

Makes 3 baguettes.

Khachapuri

*P*ronounced kah-chah-POOR-ee, this turban-shaped bread from Georgia (formerly of the USSR) is the Russian equivalent of pizza or, more accurately, calzone. Though it takes time, the end result is stunning. Khachapuri should be served at room temperature and is a great picnic food. Slice thick wedges of it to serve with marinated artichokes and mushrooms, cherry tomatoes, fresh fruit, and a perfectly chilled bottle of wine.

> 1 (1/4-oz.) package active dry yeast
> 1/4 cup warm water (110F, 45C)
> 2 tablespoons sugar
> 3/4 cup milk
> 1/2 cup unsalted butter or margarine, melted
> 1 teaspoon salt
> 3 to 3-1/2 cups bread or all-purpose flour
> Cheese Filling, see below
> 1 egg white mixed with 1 tablespoon water for glaze

Cheese Filling:
> 8 ounces feta cheese, crumbled
> 1/2 pound mozzarella cheese, shredded
> 1/2 pound sharp Cheddar cheese, shredded
> 2 eggs, lightly beaten
> 2 tablespoons finely chopped fresh parsley
> 1/4 teaspoon white pepper

In large bowl of electric mixer, dissolve yeast in warm water. Add a pinch of the sugar; let stand until foamy, 5 to 10 minutes. Add remaining sugar, milk, butter, salt, and 1-1/2 to 2 cups of the flour. Beat at medium speed with electric mixer 2 minutes, or beat 200 vigorous strokes by hand. Stir in enough remaining flour to make a soft dough. Change to dough hook(s) if using mixer, or turn out dough onto a lightly floured surface.

Knead dough 4 to 6 minutes, or until smooth, adding only enough flour to prevent sticking. Dough will be soft. Clean and butter bowl. Place dough in bowl, turning to coat all surfaces. Cover with a slightly damp towel; set in a warm place free from drafts. Let rise until doubled in bulk, about 1 hour. Prepare Cheese Filling. Grease a 9-inch springform pan or round 8- or 9-inch cake pan; set aside.

Punch down dough; knead 30 seconds. Shape into a smooth ball. On a lightly floured surface, roll out dough into a 20-inch circle. Gently ease dough into prepared pan, letting excess hang over edge. Spoon Cheese Filling on center of dough, forming a smooth mound. Bring dough up over filling, folding to make 8 to 10 evenly spaced pleats. Bring ends of pleats to center top. Twist and pinch ends together to form a rough knob. Cover with buttered waxed paper; set in a warm place free from drafts. Let rise until doubled in bulk, about 45 minutes.

Preheat oven to 375F (190C). Brush loaf with egg-white glaze. Bake 40 to 50 minutes, or until deep golden brown. Remove bread from pan; place directly on oven rack during final 5 minutes of baking time to brown bottom crust. Cool on rack 45 minutes before cutting into wedges, or serve at room temperature.

Makes 1 loaf.

Cheese Filling: Combine all ingredients in a large bowl. Cover and refrigerate.

TIP: Four ounces (1/4 lb.) of firm, semifirm, or semisoft cheese equals about 1 cup grated cheese. Such cheeses are easier to grate when cold. On the other hand, hard cheeses like Parmesan grate better if at room temperature.

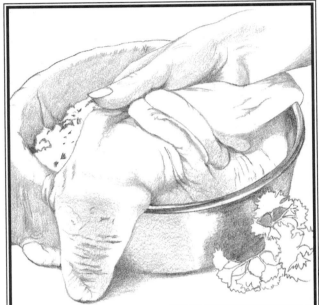

*Shaping Khachapuri,
pages 44–45.*

Pesto–Pine Nut Bread

*T*he ingredients of the classic pesto—basil, olive oil, garlic, Parmesan, and pine nuts—infuse this bread with a fragrance and flavor that's hard to beat.

> 1 (1/4-oz.) package active dry yeast
> 1 teaspoon sugar
> 1-3/4 cups warm water (110F, 45C)
> 1/4 cup olive oil
> 2 teaspoons salt
> 2 medium-size garlic cloves, minced
> 5-1/4 to 6 cups bread or all-purpose flour
> 1 cup finely chopped fresh basil
> 3/4 cup grated Parmesan cheese
> 3/4 cup toasted pine nuts

In large bowl of electric mixer, dissolve yeast and sugar in warm water. Let stand until foamy, 5 to 10 minutes. Add oil, salt, garlic, and 2 to 2-1/2 cups of the flour. Beat at medium speed with electric mixer 2 minutes, or beat 200 vigorous strokes by hand. Stir in basil, cheese, pine nuts, and enough remaining flour to make a soft dough. Change to dough hook(s) if using mixer, or turn out dough onto a lightly floured surface.

Knead dough 8 to 10 minutes, or until smooth and elastic, adding only enough flour to prevent sticking. Clean and butter bowl. Place dough in bowl, turning to coat all surfaces. Cover with a slightly damp towel; set in a warm place free from drafts. Let rise until doubled in bulk, about 1 hour. Grease 2 (8" x 4") loaf pans; set aside.

Punch down dough; knead 30 seconds. Divide dough in half. Shape into loaves and place in prepared pans. Cover with a dry towel and set in a warm place free from drafts. Let rise until doubled in bulk, 45 to 60 minutes.

Preheat oven to 375F (190C). Slash tops of loaves as desired. Bake about 30 minutes, or until bread sounds hollow when tapped on the bottom. Remove from pans; cool on racks.

Makes 2 loaves.

TIP: Bread will bake and brown more evenly if you rotate the loaves—from front to back and from top to bottom racks—during baking. Wait 20 minutes after beginning baking before moving the bread to allow it to set.

Gremolata Bread

*G*remolata (greh-moh-LAH-tah), a mixture of finely chopped lemon zest, garlic, and parsley, is classically used as a garnish for *osso bucco* and other dishes. Here it makes a lively bread that's as good toasted and served with eggs as it is used for sandwiches.

1 (1/4-oz.) package active dry yeast
2 teaspoons sugar
1/2 cup warm water (110F, 45C)
1 (12-oz.) can evaporated milk
2-1/2 tablespoons olive or vegetable oil
2 teaspoons salt
4-1/4 to 5-3/4 cups bread or all-purpose flour
1/3 cup finely chopped fresh parsley
4 medium-size garlic cloves, minced
Finely grated zest of 2 large lemons

In large bowl of electric mixer, dissolve yeast and sugar in warm water. Let stand until foamy, 5 to 10 minutes. Add milk, 2 tablespoons of oil, salt, and 1-1/2 to 2 cups of the flour. Beat at medium speed with electric mixer 2 minutes, or beat 200 vigorous strokes by hand. Stir in parsley, garlic, lemon zest, and enough remaining flour to make a soft dough. Change to dough hook(s) if using mixer, or turn out dough onto a lightly floured surface.

Knead dough about 8 minutes, or until smooth and elastic, adding only enough flour to prevent sticking. Clean and butter bowl. Place dough in bowl, turning to coat all surfaces. Cover with a slightly damp towel; set in a warm place free from drafts. Let rise until doubled in bulk, about 1 hour. Grease 2 (8" x 4") loaf pans; set aside.

Punch down dough; knead 30 seconds. Divide dough in half. Shape into loaves and place in prepared pans. Cover with a dry towel and set in a warm place free from drafts. Let rise until doubled in bulk, 45 to 60 minutes.

Preheat oven to 425F (220C). Slash tops of loaves as desired, brush with remaining 1/2 tablespoon oil. Bake 10 minutes. Reduce heat to 350F (175C); bake 20 to 25 minutes more, or until bread sounds hollow when tapped on the bottom. Remove from pans; cool on racks.

Makes 2 loaves.

Sesame-Saffron Bread

*S*affron, the yellow-orange stigmas from a small purple crocus, is the world's most expensive spice. That's because each flower provides only three stigmas, and it takes 14,000 of them for each ounce of saffron. Saffron threads (the stigmas) are usually more reliable than saffron powder, which loses its flavor rapidly and can easily be adulterated with imitations. Because saffron's so expensive, many markets keep it under lock and key; ask the store manager for it.

1/2 teaspoon saffron threads
1 tablespoon hot water
2 (1/4-oz.) packages active dry yeast
1/3 cup warm water (110F, 45C)
2 tablespoons sugar
1-1/2 cups sour cream
1/4 teaspoon baking soda
2-1/2 teaspoons salt
4 to 4-1/2 cups bread or all-purpose flour
1/2 cup plus 1 tablespoon toasted sesame seeds (Tip, page 262)
1 egg white mixed with 1 tablespoon water for glaze

In a small bowl, combine saffron and hot water; let stand 10 minutes. In large bowl of electric mixer, dissolve yeast in warm water. Add a pinch of the sugar; let stand until foamy, 5 to 10 minutes. Add remaining sugar, sour cream, baking soda, salt, saffron mixture, and 1-1/2 cups of the flour. Beat at medium speed with electric mixer 2 minutes, or beat 200 vigorous strokes by hand. Stir in 1/2 cup sesame seeds and enough remaining flour to make a soft dough. Change to dough hook(s) if using mixer, or turn out dough onto a lightly floured surface.

Knead dough 6 to 8 minutes, or until smooth and elastic, adding only enough flour to prevent sticking. Clean and butter bowl. Place dough in bowl, turning to coat all surfaces. Cover with a slightly damp towel; set in a warm place free from drafts. Let rise until doubled in bulk, 45 to 60 minutes. Grease 2 (8" x 4") loaf pans or 1-1/2-quart casserole dishes; set aside.

Punch down dough; knead 30 seconds. Divide dough in half. Shape into loaves and place in prepared pans. Cover with a dry towel; let rise until doubled in bulk, 30 to 45 minutes.

Preheat oven to 375F (190C). Slash tops of loaves as desired. Brush with egg-white glaze; sprinkle with remaining 1 tablespoon sesame seeds. Bake 25 to 35 minutes, or until bread sounds hollow when tapped on the bottom. Cool on racks.

Makes 2 loaves.

Onion-Poppy Bread

*Sautéed onions and crunchy poppy seeds make this bread the perfect choice for ham, meatloaf, or bacon, lettuce, and tomato sandwiches.

About 1/2 cup olive oil
1 cup finely chopped onion
2 (1/4-oz.) packages active dry yeast
1-1/2 cups warm beer (110F, 45C)
1/4 cup sugar
1 egg
1 tablespoon salt
1/2 teaspoon freshly ground pepper
1/2 teaspoon dry mustard
1/2 teaspoon paprika
6-3/4 to 7-1/4 cups bread or all-purpose flour
1/3 cup plus 1 tablespoon poppy seeds
1 egg yolk mixed with 2 teaspoons water for glaze

In a medium-size skillet over medium heat, heat 2 tablespoons olive oil. Add onions and sauté, stirring often, about 5 minutes, or until they begin to brown. Remove from heat; set aside to cool. In large bowl of electric mixer, dissolve yeast in warm beer. Add a pinch of the sugar; let stand until foamy, 5 to 10 minutes. Add remaining sugar, 1/3 cup olive oil, egg, salt, pepper, dry mustard, paprika, and 2-1/2 to 3 cups of the flour. Beat at medium speed with electric mixer 2 minutes, or beat 200 vigorous strokes by hand. Stir in cooked onions, including any residual oil, 1/3 cup poppy seeds, and enough remaining flour to make a soft dough. Change to dough hook(s) if using mixer, or turn out dough onto a lightly floured surface.

Knead dough 8 to 10 minutes, or until smooth and elastic, adding only enough flour to prevent sticking. Clean and butter bowl. Place dough in bowl, turning to coat all surfaces. Cover with a slightly damp towel; set in a warm place free from drafts. Let rise until doubled in bulk, 45 to 60 minutes. Grease 2 (9" x 5") loaf pans; set aside.

Punch down dough; knead 30 seconds. Divide dough in half. Shape into loaves and place in prepared pans. Cover with a dry towel; let rise until doubled in bulk, about 45 minutes.

Preheat oven to 375F (190C). Slash tops of loaves as desired. Brush with egg-yolk glaze; sprinkle with remaining 1 tablespoon poppy seeds. Bake 30 to 35 minutes, or until bread sounds hollow when tapped on the bottom. Remove from pans; cool on racks.

Makes 2 loaves.

TIP: Cooked food to be added to bread dough will cool more rapidly if transferred from skillet to a bowl or plate and stirred occasionally.

Roasted Garlic Bread

*D*on't be put off by the amount of garlic in this bread—roasted garlic is much milder than its raw form. This bread is great with pasta. Or, slice it, brush with olive oil, and grill it. Fantastico!

1 head Roasted Garlic (page 256)
1 (1/4-oz.) package active dry yeast
1 tablespoon sugar
1/3 cup warm water (110F, 45C)
1 cup milk
1/2 cup olive oil
2 teaspoons salt
4-1/4 to 4-3/4 cups bread or all-purpose flour
About 2/3 cup grated Parmesan cheese

Squeeze the soft garlic out of the skin. Use a fork to mash the garlic; set aside. In large bowl of electric mixer, dissolve yeast and a pinch of sugar in warm water. Let stand until foamy, 5 to 10 minutes. Add remaining sugar, garlic puree, milk, 1/4 cup oil, salt, and 2 to 2-1/2 cups of the flour. Beat at medium speed with electric mixer 2 minutes, or beat 200 vigorous strokes by hand. Stir in enough remaining flour to make a soft dough. Change to dough hook(s) if using mixer, or turn out dough onto a lightly floured surface.

Knead dough 6 to 8 minutes, or until smooth and elastic, adding only enough flour to prevent sticking. Clean and butter bowl. Place dough in bowl, turning to coat all surfaces. Cover with a slightly damp towel; set in a warm place free from drafts. Let rise until doubled in bulk, about 1 hour. Grease 2 (9" x 5") loaf pans; set aside. Place Parmesan in one small bowl and remaining 1/4 cup oil in another; set aside.

Punch down dough; knead 30 seconds. Divide dough in half; divide each half into 6 equal pieces. Form each piece into a smooth ball. Roll balls in oil, then in cheese. Arrange 6 balls, zig-zag fashion, in each prepared pan. Sprinkle with any remaining cheese. Cover with buttered waxed paper and set in a warm place free from drafts. Let rise until doubled in bulk, about 1 hour.

Preheat oven to 375F (190C). Bake 30 to 35 minutes or until bread sounds hollow when tapped on top. Carefully remove from pans; cool on racks.

Makes 2 loaves.

Whole-Grain & Rye Yeast Breads

The comfort factor in biting into a slice of whole-grain bread, full-flavored and chewy, is incredibly high. And today it's so much easier for those who love making such breads to find the ingredients. Oat and wheat brans, buckwheat flour, cornmeal, oats, rye flour, wheat germ, and whole-wheat flour are commonly available in most supermarkets. Items like cracked wheat, whole-wheat berries, gluten flour, graham flour, rice flour, rye and wheat flakes, triticale flour, and soy flour will more likely be found in natural food stores.

Many natural food stores and some supermarkets sell whole-grain products in bulk. To avoid the risk of rancid bulk products, buy only from stores that have rapid turnover. Always check bulk items carefully for bugs and other detritus. Most packaged whole-grain products are wholesome.

Because whole-grain products are susceptible to rancidity, buy them in small quantities. For maximum storage life, wrap them airtight and refrigerate for up to six months, freeze for up to a year. Always bring chilled flours and grains to room temperature before using in baked goods. In general, breads made with all whole-grain flours are heavier and denser than white-flour loaves. For a medium-weight loaf, use half whole-grain flour and half bread flour (see Flours, pages 4–5).

Many whole-grain breads have roots in early America. Squaw bread, with its hearty combination of rye and wheat flours, is said to have originated with Native Americans. A New England pioneer farmer is credited with creating anadama bread, which gets its heartiness from cornmeal. Rye breads conjure visions of the old country. Certainly, Russian Black Bread evokes visions of heavy-booted Russian peasants tromping in from the snow to thick slices of dense, dark bread slathered with homemade butter. The more delicate Swedish Limpa is a traditional Scandinavian rye bread heady with orange peel, fennel, and anise seed.

Whatever their origin, homebaked whole-grain breads are a delicious and satisfying way to add fiber and nutrition to your diet. The bonus for all involved is the fabulous wholesome flavor in every bite.

Toasted Polenta Bread

Polenta is simply coarsely ground yellow cornmeal. If you can't find it in your market, regular cornmeal can be substituted. The combination of beer and toasted polenta gives this bread a nutty nuance that's irresistible. It's wonderful for sandwiches and French toast, or simply toasted and spread with Honey Butter (page 260).

> 3/4 cup plus 3 tablespoons polenta
> 1 cup beer or water
> 2 teaspoons salt
> 2 (1/4-oz.) packages active dry yeast
> 1/4 cup honey
> 1/2 cup warm water (110F, 45C)
> 2 eggs
> 4 tablespoons olive oil
> 4-3/4 to 5-1/4 cups bread or all-purpose flour

In a large, dry skillet over medium heat, toast polenta, stirring often, until golden brown. Or, sprinkle polenta in an even layer over the bottom of a 13" x 9" baking pan. Bake at 350F (175C) about 10 minutes, or until golden brown. Set aside. In a small saucepan, combine beer or water and salt; bring to a simmer. Remove from heat. Slowly whisk in 3/4 cup polenta, stirring until smooth. Set aside until mixture is lukewarm.

In large bowl of electric mixer, dissolve yeast and 1 teaspoon of the honey in the 1/2 cup warm water. Let stand until foamy, 5 to 10 minutes. Add remaining honey, eggs, 3 tablespoons of the oil, cooled polenta mixture, and 1 to 1-1/2 cups flour. Beat at medium speed with electric mixer 2 minutes, or beat 200 vigorous strokes by hand. Stir in enough remaining flour to make a soft dough. Change to dough hook(s) if using mixer, or turn out dough onto a lightly floured work surface.

Knead dough 8 to 10 minutes, or until smooth and elastic, adding only enough flour to prevent sticking. Clean and butter bowl. Place dough in bowl, turning to coat all surfaces. Cover with a slightly damp towel; set in a warm place free from drafts. Let rise until doubled in bulk, about 1 hour. Grease 2 (9" x 5") loaf pans or 2-quart casserole dishes. Sprinkle 1 tablespoon of the remaining polenta over bottom and sides of each pan; set aside.

Punch down dough; knead 30 seconds. Divide dough in half. Shape into loaves and place in prepared pans. Cover with a dry towel; let rise until doubled in bulk, 30 to 45 minutes.

Preheat oven to 375F (190C). Brush tops of loaves with remaining 1 tablespoon oil, sprinkle with remaining polenta, and slash as desired. Bake 30 to 35 minutes, or until bread sounds hollow when tapped on the bottom. Remove from pans; cool on racks.

Makes 2 loaves.

Wheaty Greek Olive Bread

*F*eta is a dry, crumbly Greek cheese that can be made from sheep, goat, or cow milk. It's important that the feta be cold, so the heat of your hands doesn't start melting it during kneading.

>   2 (1/4-oz.) packages active dry yeast
>   1 tablespoon sugar
>   1/3 cup warm water (110F, 45C)
>   1 cup milk
>   1/3 cup plus 1 tablespoon olive oil
>   2 teaspoons salt
>   2-1/4 to 2-3/4 cups bread or all-purpose flour
>   2 cups whole-wheat flour
>   4 ounces cold feta cheese, crumbled
>   2 cups pitted kalamata olives, coarsely chopped

In large bowl of electric mixer, dissolve yeast and a pinch of the sugar in warm water. Let stand until foamy, 5 to 10 minutes. Add remaining sugar, milk, 1/3 cup oil, salt, and 2 to 2-1/2 cups of the bread flour. Beat at medium speed with electric mixer 2 minutes, or beat 200 vigorous strokes by hand. Stir in the whole-wheat flour and enough remaining bread flour to make a soft dough. Change to dough hook(s) if using mixer, or turn out dough onto a lightly floured surface.

Knead dough 6 to 8 minutes, or until smooth and elastic, adding only enough flour to prevent sticking. Clean and butter bowl. Place dough in bowl, turning to coat all surfaces. Cover with a slightly damp towel; set in a warm place free from drafts. Let rise until doubled in bulk, about 45 minutes. Grease 2 (9" x 5") loaf pans; set aside.

Punch down dough. Pat out into a rectangle about 1/2 inch thick. Sprinkle feta and olives over dough; lightly press into surface. Knead dough until cheese and olives are evenly distributed. Divide dough in half. Shape into loaves; place in prepared pans. Cover with a dry towel. Let rise until doubled in bulk, about 1 hour.

Preheat oven to 375F (190C). Slash tops of loaves. Bake 30 to 35 minutes or until bread sounds hollow when tapped on the top. Remove from pans; cool on racks. Brush tops of warm loaves with remaining 1 tablespoon olive oil.

Makes 2 loaves.

Malted Multigrain Bread

A quartet of grains gives a power punch of nutrition to this wholesome bread. Malt syrup (extracted from sprouted barley) has a rich flavor that enhances the flavor of grains. Buy plain malt syrup rather than hop-flavored style, which is bitter. Malt syrup and wheat and rye flakes can be found at natural food stores, whereas wheat germ and oat bran are commonly available in most supermarkets. Honey or molasses can be substituted for the malt syrup, though there'll be a slight flavor variation.

1 cup wheat flakes
1 cup rye flakes
1/3 cup plus 1 teaspoon malt syrup
2 cups very hot water (200F, 95C)
2 (1/4-oz.) packages active dry yeast
1/3 cup warm water (110F, 45C)
1 cup nonfat milk powder
1/2 cup unprocessed oat or wheat bran flakes
1/2 cup wheat germ
1/4 cup vegetable oil
1 tablespoon salt
4-3/4 to 5-1/4 cups bread or all-purpose flour
1-1/2 cups whole-wheat flour
1 egg white mixed with 2 teaspoons water for glaze
Wheat or rye flakes for garnish

In large bowl of electric mixer, combine wheat flakes, rye flakes, 1/3 cup malt syrup, and hot water. Stir to combine; cool to room temperature. Dissolve yeast and remaining teaspoon malt syrup in warm water. Let stand until foamy, 5 to 10 minutes. Add milk powder, bran flakes, wheat germ, oil, salt, and 1 to 1-1/2 cups of the bread flour. Beat at medium speed with electric mixer 2 minutes, or beat 200 vigorous strokes by hand. Stir in wheat flour and enough remaining bread flour to make a soft dough. Change to dough hook(s) if using mixer, or turn out dough onto a lightly floured surface.

Knead dough 10 to 12 minutes, or until smooth and elastic, adding only enough flour to prevent sticking. Clean and butter bowl. Place dough in bowl, turning to coat all surfaces. Cover with a slightly damp towel; set in a warm place free from drafts. Let rise until doubled in bulk, about 1 hour. Grease 2 (9" x 5") loaf pans or 2-quart casserole dishes; set aside.

Punch down dough; knead 30 seconds. Divide dough in half. Shape into loaves and place in prepared pans. Cover with a dry towel; let rise until doubled in bulk, about 45 minutes.

Preheat oven to 375F (190C). Brush tops of loaves with egg glaze. Sprinkle with wheat flakes; slash tops as desired. Bake 30 to 35 minutes, or until bread sounds hollow when tapped on the bottom. Remove from pans; cool on racks.

Makes 2 loaves.   .

Variations

Substitute 2 cups rolled oats for 1 cup each wheat flakes and rye flakes.

Fruited Multigrain Bread: Add 1-1/2 cups raisins or other chopped, dried fruit with whole-wheat flour.

TIP: Give a nutritional boost to any bread with the Cornell Enrichment Formula. Before measuring the flour, spoon 1 teaspoon wheat germ and 1 tablespoon each soy flour and nonfat milk powder into the measuring cup. Spoon in flour and level off. Repeat for each cup of flour used in recipe.

Sprouted Wheat Berry Bread

⋙⋘

Wheat sprouts give this bread a hearty, nutty flavor and satisfyingly chewy texture. Begin growing the sprouts two to four days before making the bread. Wheat berries (also called whole-grain wheat) can be found at natural food stores.

1/2 cup wheat berries
2 (1/4-oz.) packages active dry yeast
1 tablespoon brown sugar
2 cups warm water (110F, 45C)
2/3 cup nonfat milk powder
1/4 cup honey
1 tablespoon salt
1/4 cup vegetable oil
3-1/2 cups whole-wheat flour
4-3/4 to 5-1/4 cups bread or all-purpose flour
2 to 2-1/2 cups wheat berry sprouts
1/2 cup wheat germ
1 teaspoon honey mixed with 2 teaspoons water for glaze

To make sprouts, place wheat berries in a large glass jar or square casserole dish. Cover with lukewarm water. Place a double layer of cheesecloth over top of container; secure with an elastic band. Place container in a warm dark place (about 70F, 20C). Let stand 12 hours or overnight. Remove cheesecloth. Drain off water. Rinse berries with fresh lukewarm water; drain thoroughly. Turn jar sideways and gently shake berries to distribute evenly, or spread them evenly over bottom of casserole. Re-cover with cheesecloth. Set container in a warm, dark place. Repeat rinsing and draining two to three times a day for 2 to 4 days, or until sprouts are about 3/4 inch long. Blot sprouts thoroughly on paper towel before using in bread. If sprouts tangle, coarsely chop before adding to bread. Sprouts may be covered and refrigerated for up to 3 days.

In large bowl of electric mixer, dissolve yeast and brown sugar in warm water. Let stand until foamy, 5 to 10 minutes. Add milk powder, honey, salt, oil, 1 cup whole-wheat flour, and 2-1/2 to 3 cups of the bread flour. Beat at medium speed with electric mixer 2 minutes, or beat 200 vigorous strokes by hand. Stir in wheat berry sprouts, remaining 2-1/2 cups wheat flour, wheat germ, and enough remaining bread flour to make a soft dough. Change to dough hook(s) if using mixer, or turn out dough onto a lightly floured surface.

Knead dough 10 to 12 minutes, or until smooth and elastic, adding only enough flour to prevent sticking. Clean and butter bowl. Place dough in bowl, turning to coat all surfaces. Cover with a slightly damp towel; set in a warm place free from drafts. Let rise until doubled in bulk, 1 to 1-1/2 hours.

Grease 2 (9" x 5") loaf pans or 2-quart casserole dishes; set aside.

Punch down dough; knead 30 seconds. Divide dough in half. Shape into loaves and place in prepared pans. Cover with a dry towel; let rise until doubled in bulk, 45 to 60 minutes.

Preheat oven to 375F (190C). Slash tops of loaves as desired; brush with honey glaze. Bake 25 minutes; brush again with honey glaze. Bake 5 to 10 minutes longer, or until bread sounds hollow when tapped on the bottom. Remove from pans; cool on racks.

Makes 2 loaves.

TIP: To prevent foods like wheat germ, bran flakes, and shelled nuts from becoming rancid, wrap them airtight and store in the freezer. Warm such ingredients to room temperature before adding to breads.

Cracked-Wheat Bread

*C*racked wheat, which can be found in natural food stores and some supermarkets, gives this bread a soul-satisfying flavor and chewiness.

2 cups boiling water
2 cups cracked wheat
2 (1/4-oz.) packages active dry yeast
1 tablespoon sugar
1/2 cup warm water (110F, 45C)
1 tablespoon salt
2 tablespoons vegetable oil
4-1/2 to 5 cups bread or all-purpose flour
1 egg white mixed with 1 tablespoon water for glaze

In large bowl of electric mixer, combine boiling water and cracked wheat; cool to room temperature. In a 1-cup liquid measure, dissolve yeast and sugar in 1/2 cup warm water. Let stand until foamy, 5 to 10 minutes. Add to wheat mixture, along with salt, oil, and 1 cup of the flour. Beat at medium speed with electric mixer 2 minutes, or beat 200 vigorous strokes by hand. Stir in enough remaining flour to make a soft dough. Change to dough hook(s) if using mixer, or turn out dough onto a lightly floured surface.

Knead dough 10 to 12 minutes, or until smooth and elastic, adding only enough flour to prevent sticking. Clean and butter bowl. Place dough in bowl, turning to coat all surfaces. Cover with a slightly damp towel; set in a warm place free from drafts. Let rise until doubled in bulk, about 1 hour. Grease 2 (8" x 4") loaf pans or 1-1/2-quart casserole dishes; set aside.

Punch down dough; knead 30 seconds. Divide dough in half. Shape into loaves and place in prepared pans. Cover with a dry towel; let rise until doubled in bulk, about 45 minutes.

Preheat oven to 400F (205C). Slash tops of loaves as desired; brush with egg-white glaze. Bake 20 minutes; brush again with egg glaze. Bake 10 to 15 minutes longer, or until bread sounds hollow when tapped on the bottom. Remove from pans; cool on racks.

Makes 2 loaves.

Triticale Bread

*T*riticale (trih-tih-KAY-lee) is an extremely nutritious hybrid of wheat and rye. It has more protein and less gluten than wheat and a nutty-sweet flavor. Triticale flour can be found in natural food stores and some supermarkets. If you prefer, honey or malt syrup (see page 56) can be substituted for the molasses.

> **2 (1/4-oz.) packages active dry yeast**
> **1/3 cup molasses**
> **2 cups warm water (110F, 45C)**
> **1/3 cup vegetable oil**
> **1 egg**
> **1/2 cup nonfat milk powder**
> **1 tablespoon salt**
> **4 cups triticale flour**
> **4 to 4-1/2 cups bread or all-purpose flour**
> **1 egg white mixed with 1 teaspoon molasses for glaze**

In large bowl of electric mixer, dissolve yeast and 1 teaspoon of the molasses in warm water. Let stand until foamy, 5 to 10 minutes. Add remaining molasses, oil, egg, milk powder, salt, 1-1/2 cups triticale flour, and 2 to 2-1/2 cups of the bread flour. Beat at medium speed with electric mixer 2 minutes, or beat 200 vigorous strokes by hand. Stir in remaining 2-1/2 cups triticale flour and enough remaining bread flour to make a soft dough. Change to dough hook(s) if using mixer, or turn out dough onto a lightly floured surface.

Knead dough 8 to 10 minutes, or until smooth and elastic, adding only enough flour to prevent sticking. Clean and butter bowl. Place dough in bowl, turning to coat all surfaces. Cover with a slightly damp towel; set in a warm place free from drafts. Let rise until doubled in bulk, about 1 hour. Grease 2 (9" x 5") loaf pans; set aside.

Punch down dough; knead 30 seconds. Divide dough in half. Shape into loaves and place in prepared pans. Cover with a dry towel; let rise until doubled in bulk, about 45 minutes.

Preheat oven to 350F (175C). Slash tops of loaves as desired; brush with egg-white glaze. Bake 35 to 40 minutes, or until bread sounds hollow when tapped on the bottom. Remove from pans; cool on racks.

Makes 2 loaves.

Brown Rice Bread

*T*his dense, moist bread is flavorful with cooked brown rice as well as brown-rice flour. You can use regular or quick brown rice, just be sure not to overcook it. The rice should be *al dente*, tender, but firm to the bite. Because of the rice flour and whole-wheat flour, this dough is very sticky. Generously oiling your hands will make handling easier.

1 (1/4-oz.) package active dry yeast
2 tablespoons honey
1 cup warm water (110F, 45C)
3 tablespoons vegetable or walnut oil
1 teaspoon pure vanilla extract
2 teaspoons salt
1/2 teaspoon ground nutmeg
1/2 teaspoon ground cinnamon
1-3/4 to 2-1/4 cups bread or all-purpose flour
1 cup whole-wheat flour
1 cup uncooked brown rice, ground until floury
1/2 cup chopped toasted walnuts (Tip, page 262)
1 cup plus 2 tablespoons cooked brown rice
1 egg white mixed with 1 teaspoon water for glaze

In large bowl of electric mixer, dissolve yeast and 1 teaspoon of the honey in warm water. Let stand until foamy, 5 to 10 minutes. Add remaining honey, oil, vanilla, salt, nutmeg, cinnamon, and 1-3/4 cups of the bread flour. Beat at medium speed with electric mixer 2 minutes, or beat 200 vigorous strokes by hand. Stir in whole-wheat flour, ground rice, and enough remaining bread flour to make a soft dough. Change to dough hook(s) if using mixer, or turn out dough onto a lightly floured surface.

Knead dough 8 to 10 minutes, or until smooth and elastic, adding only enough flour to prevent sticking. Pat out dough into a square. Sprinkle with nuts and 1 cup cooked rice; knead until evenly distributed throughout dough. Clean and butter bowl. Place dough in bowl, turning to coat all surfaces. Cover with a slightly damp towel; set in a warm place free from drafts. Let rise until doubled in bulk, about 1 hour. Generously grease a 9" x 5" loaf pan; set aside.

Punch down dough; knead 30 seconds. Dough will be sticky; oil hands, if necessary, to facilitate handling. Shape dough into a loaf; place in prepared pan. Cover with a dry towel; let rise until doubled in bulk, about 45 minutes.

Preheat oven to 375F (190C). Generously brush top of loaf with egg-white glaze. Sprinkle with remaining 2 tablespoons cooked rice. Brush again with egg-white glaze. Bake 40 minutes, or until bread sounds hollow when tapped on the bottom. Remove from pan; cool on rack.

Makes 1 loaf.

Seeded Squaw Bread

*T*his Native American original is a hearty wheat-and-rye loaf naturally sweetened with honey and ground raisins. Adding the seeds is a modern enhancement.

2 (1/4-oz.) packages active dry yeast
1/4 cup honey
1/2 cup warm water (110F, 45C)
1/4 cup packed brown sugar
1/3 cup raisins
1-3/4 cups milk, room temperature
1/3 cup unsalted butter or margarine, melted
1 tablespoon salt
2 tablespoons each poppy, fennel, and toasted sesame seeds (Tip, page 262)
2-1/2 cups bread or all-purpose flour
1-1/2 cups medium rye flour
2-1/2 to 3 cups whole-wheat flour
1-1/2 tablespoons yellow cornmeal

In large bowl of electric mixer, dissolve yeast and 1 teaspoon of the honey in warm water. Let stand until foamy, 5 to 10 minutes. In a blender or food processor fitted with a metal blade, combine brown sugar, raisins, 1/2 cup milk, and remaining honey. Process 30 to 45 seconds, or until raisins are finely ground. To yeast mixture, add raisin mixture, remaining 1-1/4 cups milk, butter, salt, poppy, fennel, and sesame seeds, and bread flour. Beat at medium speed with electric mixer 2 minutes, or beat 200 vigorous strokes by hand. Stir in rye flour and enough whole-wheat flour to make a soft dough. Change to dough hook(s) if using mixer, or turn out dough onto a lightly floured surface.

Knead dough 10 to 12 minutes, or until smooth and elastic, adding only enough flour to prevent sticking. Clean and butter bowl. Place dough in bowl, turning to coat all surfaces. Cover with a slightly damp towel; set in a warm place free from drafts. Let rise until doubled in bulk, about 1-1/2 hours. Grease 2 (2-quart) soufflé or casserole dishes; sprinkle lightly with cornmeal; set aside.

Punch down dough; knead 30 seconds. Divide dough in half. Shape into loaves; place in prepared pans. Cover with a dry towel; let rise until doubled in bulk, about 1 hour.

Preheat oven to 375F (190C). Bake 35 to 40 minutes, or until bread sounds hollow when tapped on the bottom. Remove from pans; cool on racks.

Makes 2 large or 4 small loaves.

Triple-Treat Wheat Bread

*C*racked wheat, whole-wheat flour, and toasted wheat germ form the triumvirate that gives this bread its country-good flavor. Cracked wheat, the whole berry broken into fragments, is available in natural food stores.

2 cups buttermilk
3 tablespoons vegetable oil
1/4 cup honey
1 tablespoon salt
1 cup cracked wheat
2 (1/4-oz.) packages active dry yeast
1 teaspoon brown sugar
1/2 cup warm water (110F, 45C)
1/2 teaspoon baking soda
3-1/4 to 3-3/4 cups bread or all-purpose flour
3 cups whole-wheat flour
1/2 cup toasted wheat germ
1 tablespoon butter, melted

In a medium-size saucepan, combine buttermilk, oil, honey, and salt; bring to a simmer. Remove from heat; stir in cracked wheat. Set aside until lukewarm. In large bowl of electric mixer, dissolve yeast and sugar in warm water. Let stand until foamy, 5 to 10 minutes. Add cooled cracked wheat mixture, baking soda, and 1 to 1-1/2 cups bread flour. Beat at medium speed with electric mixer 2 minutes, or beat 200 vigorous strokes by hand. Stir in whole-wheat flour, wheat germ, and enough remaining bread flour to make a soft dough. Change to dough hook(s) if using mixer, or turn out dough onto a lightly floured surface.

Knead dough 8 to 10 minutes, or until smooth and elastic, adding only enough flour to prevent sticking. Clean and butter bowl. Place dough in bowl, turning to coat all surfaces. Cover with a slightly damp towel; set in a warm place free from drafts. Let rise until doubled in bulk, about 1 hour. Grease 2 (8" x 4") loaf pans; set aside.

Punch down dough; knead 30 seconds. Divide dough in half. Shape into loaves and place in prepared pans. Cover with a dry towel; let rise until doubled in bulk, about 45 minutes.

Preheat oven to 375F (190C). Slash tops of loaves as desired; brush with melted butter. Bake 30 to 35 minutes, or until bread sounds hollow when tapped on the bottom. Brush again with melted butter. Remove from pans; cool on racks.

Makes 2 loaves.

Whole-Earth Date Bread

If you don't like dates, substitute the same amount of chopped, dried fruit (such as apples or apricots), toasted nuts, or raisins.

1-1/2 cups finely chopped dates
5 to 5-1/2 cups bread or all-purpose flour
2 (1/4-oz.) packages active dry yeast
1/3 cup honey
2 cups warm water (110F, 45C)
1/4 cup vegetable oil
1/2 cup nonfat milk powder
1 tablespoon salt
1-1/2 cups whole-wheat flour
1/2 cup medium rye flour
1/2 cup wheat germ
1/2 cup oat or wheat bran flakes
1/4 cup plus 1 tablespoon toasted sesame seeds (Tip, page 262)
1 teaspoon honey mixed with 1 tablespoon milk for glaze

In a small bowl, combine dates with 1/2 cup bread flour. Toss to coat and separate; set aside. In large bowl of electric mixer, dissolve yeast and 1 teaspoon of the honey in warm water. Let stand until foamy, 5 to 10 minutes. Add remaining honey, oil, milk powder, salt, whole-wheat flour, and 1-1/2 cups of the bread flour. Beat at medium speed with electric mixer 2 minutes, or beat 200 vigorous strokes by hand. Stir in rye flour, wheat germ, bran flakes, 1/4 cup sesame seeds, reserved date-flour mixture, and enough remaining bread flour to make a soft dough. Change to dough hook(s) if using mixer, or turn out dough onto a lightly floured surface.

Knead dough 8 to 10 minutes, or until smooth and elastic, adding only enough flour to prevent sticking. Clean and butter bowl. Place dough in bowl, turning to coat all surfaces. Cover with a slightly damp towel; set in a warm place free from drafts. Let rise until doubled in bulk, about 1-1/2 hours. Grease 2 (8" x 4" or 9" x 5") loaf pans; set aside.

Punch down dough; knead 30 seconds. Divide dough in half. Shape into loaves and place in prepared pans. Cover with a dry towel; let rise until doubled in bulk, about 45 minutes.

Preheat oven to 375F (190C). Slash tops of loaves as desired. Brush with honey glaze; sprinkle with remaining sesame seeds. Bake 30 to 35 minutes, or until bread sounds hollow when tapped on the bottom. Remove from pans; cool on racks.

Makes 2 loaves.

Sunflower Bread

You get a double whammy of sunflower kernels—ground and whole—in this orange-scented bread. It's great for ham, turkey, or bacon, avocado, and tomato sandwiches!

> **About 2 cups raw hulled sunflower kernels, toasted (Tip, page 262)**
> **2 (1/4-oz.) packages active dry yeast**
> **1 cup warm orange juice (110F, 45C)**
> **1 (8-oz.) carton plain yogurt (1 cup)**
> **1/4 cup honey**
> **1/4 cup vegetable oil**
> **1 egg**
> **1 egg yolk**
> **1 tablespoon salt**
> **5 to 5-1/2 cups bread or all-purpose flour**
> **1-1/2 cups whole-wheat flour**
> **1 egg white mixed with 2 teaspoons water for glaze**

In a blender or food processor fitted with a metal blade, grind 1/2 cup sunflower kernels until very fine; set aside. In large bowl of electric mixer, dissolve yeast in orange juice. Let stand until foamy, 5 to 10 minutes. Add yogurt, honey, oil, egg, egg yolk, salt, and 2-1/2 to 3 cups of the bread flour. Beat at medium speed with electric mixer 2 minutes, or beat 200 vigorous strokes by hand. Stir in whole-wheat flour, ground sunflower kernels, 1-1/4 cups whole sunflower kernels, and enough remaining bread flour to make a soft dough. Change to dough hook(s) if using mixer, or turn out dough onto a lightly floured surface.

Knead dough 8 to 10 minutes, or until smooth and elastic, adding only enough flour to prevent sticking. Clean and butter bowl. Place dough in bowl, turning to coat all surfaces. Cover with a slightly damp towel; set in a warm place free from drafts. Let rise until doubled in bulk, about 1 hour. Generously grease 2 (8" x 4" or 9" x 5") loaf pans. Sprinkle bottom and sides of each pan with 2 tablespoons sunflower kernels; set aside.

Punch down dough; knead 30 seconds. Divide dough in half. Shape into loaves and place in prepared pans. Cover with a dry towel; let rise until doubled in bulk, 30 to 45 minutes.

Preheat oven to 375F (190C). Slash tops of loaves as desired; brush with egg-white glaze and sprinkle each loaf with 2 teaspoons sunflower kernels. Bake 30 to 35 minutes, or until bread sounds hollow when tapped on the bottom. Remove from pans; cool on racks.

Makes 2 loaves.

TIP: The amount of flour required for a yeast bread may vary from day to day, depending on humidity, temperature, and brand of flour. For perfect results, learn to judge the dough by feel rather than strictly relying on the amount of flour called for in a recipe.

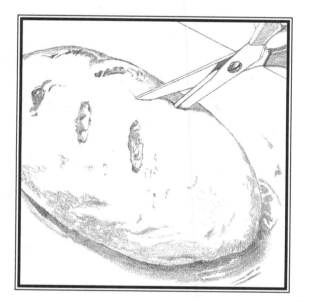

Apple Anadama Bread

*L*egend has it that this early American bread was created by a New England farmer plagued by a lazy wife who served him the same cornmeal and molasses gruel, day after day. Finally, in desperation, the disgusted farmer grabbed the bowl of gruel, tossed in some flour and yeast, and began stirring like crazy—all the while muttering angrily, "Anna, damn 'er!" Polite society later changed the name of this irritated farmer's inspiration to anadama.

> 1 cup plus 1 tablespoon yellow cornmeal
> 2 teaspoons salt
> 1 cup water
> 1 cup milk
> 1/4 cup vegetable oil
> 1/2 cup dark molasses
> 1 (1/4-oz.) package active dry yeast
> 1 teaspoon sugar
> 1/4 cup warm water (110F, 45C)
> 5-1/2 to 6 cups bread or all-purpose flour
> 1 cup chopped tart apple
> 1 tablespoon butter, melted

In large bowl of electric mixer, combine 1 cup cornmeal and salt; set aside. In a medium-size saucepan, combine water, milk, and oil; bring to a boil over medium heat. Slowly pour hot liquid over cornmeal, whisking constantly until smooth. Stir in molasses; cool to lukewarm. In a 1-cup liquid measure, dissolve yeast and sugar in warm water. Let stand until foamy, 5 to 10 minutes. Stir yeast mixture and 2 to 2-1/2 cups flour into cornmeal mixture. Beat at medium speed with electric mixer 2 minutes, or beat 200 vigorous strokes by hand. Stir in apples and enough remaining flour to make a soft dough. Change to dough hook(s) if using mixer, or turn out dough onto a lightly floured surface.

Knead dough 10 to 12 minutes, or until smooth and elastic, adding only enough flour to prevent sticking. Clean and butter bowl. Place dough in bowl, turning to coat all surfaces. Cover with a slightly damp towel; set in a warm place free from drafts. Let rise until doubled in bulk, about 1-1/2 hours. Grease 2 (8" x 4") loaf pans or 1-1/2-quart casserole dishes. Sprinkle 1/2 tablespoon of remaining cornmeal over bottom of each pan or dish.

Punch down dough; knead 30 seconds. Divide dough in half. Shape into loaves and place in prepared pans. Cover with a dry towel; let rise until doubled in bulk, 45 to 60 minutes.

Preheat oven to 375F (190C). Bake 35 to 40 minutes, or until bread sounds hollow when tapped on the bottom. Remove from pans; brush tops with melted butter. Cool on racks.

Makes 2 loaves.

Molasses Bran Bread

*B*ran adds nutrition and molasses lends a hearty character to this wholesome bread. Spread it with Molasses Butter (page 261) for a great day's start.

2 (1/4-oz.) packages active dry yeast
1/2 cup dark molasses
2-1/3 cups warm water (110F, 45C)
2/3 cup nonfat milk powder
1/3 cup unsalted butter or margarine, melted
2-1/2 teaspoons salt
3/4 teaspoon ground ginger
6-3/4 to 7-1/4 cups bread or all-purpose flour
About 1-1/4 cups unprocessed oat or wheat bran flakes
1 cup whole-wheat flour
1 teaspoon molasses mixed with 1 tablespoon melted butter for glaze

In large bowl of electric mixer, dissolve yeast and 1 teaspoon of the molasses in warm water. Let stand until foamy, 5 to 10 minutes. Add remaining molasses, milk powder, butter, salt, ginger, and 4 to 4-1/2 cups cups bread flour. Beat at medium speed with electric mixer 2 minutes, or beat 200 vigorous strokes by hand. Stir in 1-1/4 cups bran flakes, whole-wheat flour, and enough remaining bread flour to make a soft dough. Change to dough hook(s) if using mixer, or turn out dough onto a lightly floured surface.

Knead dough 8 to 10 minutes, or until smooth and elastic, adding only enough flour to prevent sticking. Clean and butter bowl. Place dough in bowl, turning to coat all surfaces. Cover with a slightly damp towel; set in a warm place free from drafts. Let rise until doubled in bulk, about 1 hour. Grease 2 large baking sheets; set aside.

Punch down dough; knead 30 seconds. Divide dough in half. Shape into oval loaves and place on prepared baking sheets. With pointed scissors, cut diagonal notches every 1-1/2 inches in a zig-zag pattern in tops of loaves. Cover with a dry towel; let rise until doubled in bulk, 45 to 60 minutes.

Preheat oven to 375F (190C). Brush loaves with molasses-butter glaze; lightly sprinkle with additional bran flakes. Bake 30 to 35 minutes, or until bread sounds hollow when tapped on the bottom. Remove from baking sheets; cool on racks.

Makes 2 loaves.

Bunny Bread

*Y*ou don't have to be a rabbit to love this carroty bread, naturally sweetened with honey, raisins, and wheat germ. What a sneaky (and delicious) way to add nutrition to sandwiches. Unless the carrots are old, leave the skin on them (just give them a good scrub).

2 (1/4-oz.) packages active dry yeast
1/4 cup honey
1 cup warm water (110F, 45C)
2 eggs
1/4 cup vegetable oil
1 tablespoon finely chopped gingerroot
1 teaspoon pure vanilla extract
2 teaspoons salt
1/2 teaspoon ground ginger
1/2 teaspoon ground nutmeg
1/3 cup nonfat milk powder
4-3/4 to 5-1/4 cups bread or all-purpose flour
1 cup whole-wheat flour
1/2 cup wheat germ
1-1/2 cups shredded carrots, blotted dry
1 cup raisins
3/4 cup chopped toasted walnuts (Tip, page 262)
1 egg yolk mixed with 2 teaspoons water for glaze

In large bowl of electric mixer, dissolve yeast and 1 teaspoon of the honey in warm water. Let stand until foamy, 5 to 10 minutes. Add remaining honey, eggs, oil, gingerroot, vanilla, salt, ginger, nutmeg, milk powder, and 2-1/2 to 3 cups bread flour. Beat at medium speed with electric mixer 2 minutes, or beat 200 vigorous strokes by hand. Stir in whole-wheat flour, wheat germ, carrots, raisins, nuts, and enough remaining bread flour to make a soft dough. Change to dough hook(s) if using mixer, or turn out dough onto a lightly floured surface.

Knead dough 8 to 10 minutes, or until smooth and elastic, adding only enough flour to prevent sticking. Clean and butter bowl. Place dough in bowl, turning to coat all surfaces. Cover with a slightly damp towel; set in a warm place free from drafts. Let rise until doubled in bulk, about 1-1/2 hours. Grease 2 (8" x 4") loaf pans; set aside.

Punch down dough; knead 30 seconds. Divide dough in half. Shape into loaves and place in pre-pared pans. Cover with a dry towel; let rise until doubled in bulk, about 1 hour.

Preheat oven to 375F (190C). Slash tops of loaves as desired; brush with egg-yolk glaze. Bake 35 to 40 minutes or until bread sounds hollow when tapped on the bottom. Remove from pans; cool on racks.

Makes 2 loaves.

Oatmeal-Apple Bread

The raisins can be soaked in apple or orange juice instead of rum or brandy. Turn this bread into Oatmeal-Raisin Bread by omitting the apples and substituting the same amount of raisins. Try golden raisins for a beautiful pale-colored loaf.

1/3 cup raisins
2 tablespoons rum or brandy
2 (1/4-oz.) packages active dry yeast
1/3 cup packed brown sugar
1/2 cup warm water (110F, 45C)
1-1/2 cups regular or quick-cooking rolled oats
1 tablespoon salt
1/2 teaspoon ground cinnamon
1-1/3 cups unsweetened apple juice
1/4 cup vegetable oil
5-1/2 to 6 cups bread or all-purpose flour
1 cup finely chopped unpeeled tart apple
1/2 cup chopped walnuts
1 egg white mixed with 1 tablespoon water for glaze

In a small bowl, combine raisins and rum; cover with plastic wrap. Microwave on HIGH 30 seconds; let stand 5 minutes. Or, combine raisins and rum in a small saucepan; bring to a simmer. Cover and remove from heat; let stand 10 minutes. In large bowl of electric mixer, dissolve yeast and 1 teaspoon of the sugar in warm water. Let stand until foamy, 5 to 10 minutes. Add remaining brown sugar, oats, salt, cinnamon, apple juice, oil, and 2 to 2-1/2 cups of the flour. Beat at medium speed with electric mixer 2 minutes, or beat 200 vigorous strokes by hand. Stir in raisins and rum, apples, nuts, and enough remaining flour to make a soft dough. Turn dough out onto a lightly floured surface.

Knead dough 8 to 10 minutes, or until smooth and elastic, adding only enough flour to prevent sticking. Clean and butter bowl. Place dough in buttered bowl, turning to coat all surfaces. Cover with a slightly damp towel; set in a warm place free from drafts. Let rise until doubled in bulk, about 1 hour. Grease 2 (9" x 5") loaf pans or 2-quart casserole dishes; set aside.

Punch down dough; knead 30 seconds. Divide dough in half. Shape into loaves and place in prepared pans. Cover with a dry towel; let rise until doubled in bulk, about 45 minutes.

Preheat oven to 375F (190C). Slash tops of loaves as desired; brush with egg-white glaze. Bake 35 to 40 minutes, or until bread sounds hollow when tapped on the bottom. Remove from pans; cool on racks.
Makes 2 loaves.

TIP: Adding too much flour to a dough while kneading creates a dense, heavy loaf. It's better for the dough to feel slightly tacky than dry to the touch.

Dilly-of-a-Rye Bread

*ill seed or weed may be used in this light rye bread with the scent of summer.

    2 (1/4-oz.) packages active dry yeast
    2 tablespoons sugar
    1/2 cup warm water (110F, 45C)
    1 (16-oz.) carton cottage cheese (2 cups)
    1/4 cup olive or vegetable oil
    4 eggs
    1 tablespoon salt
    3 tablespoons finely minced fresh dill weed or 4 teaspoons dried dill weed or seed
    5 to 5-1/2 cups bread or all-purpose flour
    2 cups medium rye flour
    1 egg white mixed with 1 tablespoon water for glaze
    1 to 2 teaspoons dill seed for garnish

In large bowl of electric mixer, dissolve yeast and a pinch of the sugar in warm water. Let stand until foamy, 5 to 10 minutes. Add remaining sugar, cottage cheese, oil, eggs, salt, dill weed or seed, and 2-1/2 to 3 cups of the bread flour. Beat at medium speed with electric mixer 2 minutes, or beat 200 vigorous strokes by hand. Stir in rye flour and enough remaining bread flour to make a soft dough. Change to dough hook(s) if using mixer, or turn out dough onto a lightly floured surface.

Knead dough 8 to 10 minutes, or until smooth and elastic, adding only enough flour to prevent sticking. Clean and butter bowl. Place dough in bowl, turning to coat all surfaces. Cover with a slightly damp towel; set in a warm place free from drafts. Let rise until doubled in bulk, about 1 hour. Grease 2 (9" x 5") loaf pans or 2-quart casserole dishes; set aside.

Punch down dough; knead 30 seconds. Divide dough in half. Shape into loaves and place in prepared pans. Cover with a dry towel; let rise until doubled in bulk, about 45 minutes.

Preheat oven to 375F (190C). Brush tops of loaves with egg-white glaze and sprinkle with dill seed; slash as desired. Bake 30 to 35 minutes, or until bread sounds hollow when tapped on the bottom. Remove from pans; cool on racks.

Makes 2 loaves.

Variation

Cheese-Dilly Rye Bread: After first rising, knead in 1 cup grated Cheddar or Swiss cheese.

Mighty Wheat Bread

*U*sing 100 percent whole-wheat flour produces a whole-grain flavor that's especially delicious toasted.

2 (1/4-oz.) packages active dry yeast
1/4 cup malt syrup or honey
1/2 cup warm water
1 cup cottage cheese (8 oz.)
2 tablespoons molasses
5 to 5-1/2 cups whole-wheat flour
1/4 cup vegetable oil
2 eggs, slightly beaten
2-1/2 teaspoons salt
1/2 cup plus 3 tablespoons wheat germ
2 teaspoons malt syrup or honey mixed with 1 tablespoon water for glaze

In large bowl of electric mixer, dissolve yeast and 1 teaspoon of the malt syrup in warm water. Let stand until foamy, 5 to 10 minutes. Add cottage cheese, remaining malt syrup, molasses, and 1 to 1-1/2 cups flour. Beat at medium speed with electric mixer 2 minutes, or beat 200 vigorous strokes by hand. Scrape down sides of bowl. Cover tightly with plastic wrap. Let stand in a warm place, free from drafts, until bubbly and tripled in bulk, about 45 to 60 minutes. Stir in oil, eggs, salt, 1/2 cup wheat germ, and enough remaining flour to make a soft dough. Change to dough hook(s) if using mixer, or turn out dough onto a lightly floured surface.

Knead dough 10 to 12 minutes or until smooth and elastic. Place dough in buttered bowl, turning to coat all surfaces. Cover with a slightly damp towel. Let rise in a warm place, free from drafts, until tripled in bulk, about 1 hour. Grease 2 (8" x 4") loaf pans. Sprinkle bottom and sides of each pan with 1 tablespoon wheat germ; set aside.

Punch down dough; knead 30 seconds. Divide dough in half; shape into loaves and place in prepared pans. Cover with a dry towel. Let rise until doubled in bulk, about 45 minutes. Slash tops of loaves as desired. Brush with malt-syrup glaze; sprinkle with remaining 1 tablespoon wheat germ.

Place bread in cold oven. Set oven temperature at 375F (190C). Bake 30 to 35 minutes or until bread sounds hollow when tapped on bottom. Remove from pans; cool on racks.

Makes 2 loaves.

Swedish Limpa

This distinctive Scandinavian legacy is redolent with orange zest, fennel, and anise. My nontraditional addition of beer contributes both fragrance and flavor to this bread. Choose a beer that's full-bodied, but not too dark. If you don't want to use beer, substitute 1-1/2 cups milk.

2 (1/4-oz.) packages active dry yeast
1/4 cup packed brown sugar
1 cup warm water (110F, 45C)
1-1/2 cups flat beer
1/4 cup molasses
1/4 cup unsalted butter or margarine, melted
2 teaspoons anise seeds, crushed
2 teaspoons fennel seeds, crushed
1/2 teaspoon ground cardamom
1 tablespoon salt
Finely grated zest of 2 medium-size oranges
6 to 6-1/2 cups bread or all-purpose flour
3 cups medium rye flour
1 egg white mixed with 2 teaspoons water for glaze

In large bowl of electric mixer, dissolve yeast and a pinch of the brown sugar in warm water. Let stand until foamy, 5 to 10 minutes. Add remaining brown sugar, beer, molasses, butter, anise seeds, fennel seeds, cardamom, salt, orange zest, and 3-1/2 to 4 cups of the bread flour. Beat at medium speed with electric mixer 2 minutes, or beat 200 vigorous strokes by hand. Stir in rye flour and enough remaining bread flour to make a soft dough. Change to dough hook(s) if using mixer, or turn out dough onto a lightly floured surface.

Knead dough 10 to 12 minutes, or until smooth and elastic, adding only enough flour to prevent sticking. Dough should be slightly tacky, but not sticky. Place dough in buttered bowl, turning to coat all surfaces. Cover with a slightly damp towel; set in a warm place free from drafts. Let rise until doubled in bulk, about 1 hour. Grease 2 large baking sheets; set aside.

Punch down dough; turn out onto a lightly floured work surface. Knead 2 minutes, flouring surface as necessary to prevent sticking. Divide dough in half. Shape into 2 round balls about 6 inches in diameter; place on prepared baking sheets. Use the tip of a wooden spoon handle to poke about 12 indentations, 1/2 inch deep, in tops of loaves. Cover with a dry towel; let rise until doubled in bulk, about 45 minutes.

Preheat oven to 375F (190C). Brush tops of loaves with egg-white glaze. Bake 30 to 40 minutes, or until bread sounds hollow when tapped on the bottom. Remove from pans; cool on racks.

Makes 2 loaves.

Storing & Freezing Baked Bread

Bread must be completely cooled before storing or freezing. If bread will be used within three to four days, simply wrap it airtight in heavy-duty foil or plastic wrap. Store in a dry place at room temperature—a traditional bread box is ideal. Bread can also be wrapped airtight and stored in the refrigerator (a must if it contains meat) for up to seven days. Croissants and Danish pastries should be refrigerated because of their high butter content. Breads enriched with eggs, butter, fruits, and nuts will keep longer than plain breads because of the added fat and moisture content. Breads with little or no fat, such as French bread, won't stay fresh for over a day or two.

To freeze baked bread: Most breads freeze well if wrapped airtight in heavy-duty foil and sealed in a freezer bag. Label each package with the contents and date frozen. If you can't use a loaf of bread within three to four days, consider freezing half of it. Most yeast breads can be frozen for up to three months, quick breads for up to six months. Add icings or glazes to frozen coffeecakes and sweet breads after thawing.

To defrost bread: Thaw bread at room temperature. Reheat in a 350 to 375F (175 to 190C) oven, using same foil in which bread was frozen. Breads with soft crusts may be heated with foil sealed. Open foil for hard-crusted loaves, or place bread directly on oven rack. For warm bread, heat rolls 8 to 12 minutes, loaves 15 to 25 minutes.

Beer-Rye Bread

ss≫⋈≪ss

*B*ock beer is perfect for this hearty bread. Barring that, use porter or other full-bodied dark brew.

> 2 (1/4-oz.) packages active dry yeast
> 2 cups warm dark beer (110F, 45C)
> 1/3 cup molasses
> 3 tablespoons vegetable oil
> 2-1/2 teaspoons salt
> 1-1/2 tablespoons caraway seeds
> 3/4 teaspoon cumin seeds, crushed
> 1 tablespoon freshly grated orange zest
> 4-1/2 to 5 cups bread or all-purpose flour
> 2 cups medium rye flour
> 1/2 cup wheat germ
> 2 teaspoons cornmeal
> 1 egg white mixed with 1 tablespoon water for glaze

In large bowl of electric mixer, dissolve yeast in beer. Let stand until foamy; 5 to 10 minutes. Add molasses, oil, salt, 1 tablespoon caraway seeds, cumin seeds, orange zest, and 3 to 3-1/2 cups bread flour. Beat at medium speed with electric mixer 2 minutes, or beat 200 vigorous strokes by hand. Stir in rye flour, wheat germ, and enough remaining bread flour to make a soft dough. Change to dough hook(s) if using mixer, or turn out dough onto a lightly floured surface.

Knead dough 10 to 12 minutes, or until smooth and elastic, adding only enough flour to prevent sticking. Clean and butter bowl. Place dough in bowl, turning to coat all surfaces. Cover with a slightly damp towel; set in a warm place free from drafts. Let rise until doubled in bulk, about 1 hour. Grease 2 baking sheets or 2 (8" x 4") loaf pans. Sprinkle baking sheets or bottom of loaf pans with cornmeal; set aside.

Punch down dough; knead 30 seconds. Divide dough in half. Shape into loaves and place on prepared baking sheets or in prepared pans. Cover with a dry towel; let rise until doubled in bulk, about 45 minutes. Brush tops of loaves with egg-white glaze. Sprinkle each loaf with remaining caraway seeds; slash as desired.

Place bread in cold oven; set temperature to 400F (205C). Bake 30 to 40 minutes, or until bread sounds hollow when tapped on the bottom. Remove from pans; cool on racks.

Makes 2 loaves.

Spicy Raisin Rye Bread

A delightfully fragrant rye bread laced with spices, orange, and raisins—wonderful with cream cheese. If you don't have semisweet chocolate on hand, substitute 3 tablespoons unsweetened cocoa, adding with the first addition of flour.

2 (1/4-oz.) packages active dry yeast
2 tablespoons molasses
2 cups warm water (110F, 45C)
2 tablespoons vegetable oil
1 ounce semisweet chocolate, melted
1 teaspoon ground allspice
1/2 teaspoon ground ginger
1/2 teaspoon ground nutmeg
1/4 teaspoon ground cloves
1 tablespoon freshly grated orange zest
1 tablespoon salt
4 to 4-1/2 cups bread or all-purpose flour
2 cups medium rye flour
2 teaspoons caraway seeds
1 cup raisins

In large bowl of electric mixer, dissolve yeast and 1 tablespoon molasses in warm water. Let stand until foamy; 5 to 10 minutes. Add remaining molasses, oil, chocolate, allspice, ginger, nutmeg, cloves, orange zest, salt, and 2-1/2 to 3 cups bread flour. Beat at medium speed with electric mixer 2 minutes, or beat 200 vigorous strokes by hand. Stir in rye flour, caraway seeds, raisins, and enough bread flour to make a soft dough. Change to dough hook(s) if using mixer, or turn dough out onto a lightly floured surface.

Knead dough 8 to 10 minutes, or until smooth and elastic, adding only enough flour to prevent sticking. Clean and butter bowl. Place dough in bowl, turning to coat all surfaces. Cover with a slightly damp towel; set in a warm place free from drafts. Let rise until doubled in bulk, about 1 hour. Grease 2 (8" x 4") loaf pans or 1-1/2-quart casserole dishes; set aside.

Punch down dough; knead 30 seconds. Divide dough in half. Shape into loaves and place in prepared pans. Cover with a dry towel and set in a warm place free from drafts. Let rise until doubled in bulk, 30 to 45 minutes.

Preheat oven to 375F (190C). Slash tops of loaves as desired. Bake 30 to 35 minutes, or until bread sounds hollow when tapped on the bottom. Cool on racks.

Makes 2 loaves.

Russian Black Bread

The addition of blackened caramel, unsweetened chocolate, and powdered coffee not only adds a rich, deep color, but gives this Russian classic its characteristically robust flavor. This dark, chewy loaf is wonderful for sandwiches and as an accompaniment for hearty soups.

1/2 cup plus 2 teaspoons sugar
2 cups boiling water
1/4 cup vinegar
1/4 cup vegetable oil
1-1/2 ounces unsweetened chocolate, coarsely chopped
3 (1/4-oz.) packages active dry yeast
1/2 cup warm water (110F, 45C)
3 cups medium or dark rye flour
1 cup whole-bran cereal
1/2 cup wheat germ
1 tablespoon instant coffee
1 tablespoon salt
2 teaspoons caraway seeds, crushed
1/2 teaspoon fennel seeds, crushed
4 to 4-1/2 cups bread or all-purpose flour
1 teaspoon molasses mixed with 1 tablespoon water for glaze

In a large, heavy saucepan, stir 1/2 cup sugar over medium-high heat until melted. Continue to cook until sugar smokes and is almost black. Slowly and carefully stir in boiling water. This will cause mixture to smoke and sugar to lump and harden. Continue cooking and stirring until sugar is completely dissolved. Remove from heat; stir in vinegar, oil, and chocolate. Set aside to cool, stirring occasionally to dissolve chocolate.

In large bowl of electric mixer, dissolve yeast and remaining 2 teaspoons sugar in 1/2 cup warm water. Let stand until foamy, 5 to 10 minutes. Add 1 cup rye flour, bran cereal, wheat germ, instant coffee, salt, caraway seeds, fennel seeds, cooled blackened caramel mixture, and 2 to 2-1/2 cups of the bread flour. Beat at medium speed with electric mixer 2 minutes, or beat 200 vigorous strokes by hand. Stir in remaining rye flour and enough remaining bread flour to make a stiff dough. Turn out onto a lightly floured surface.

Knead dough 10 to 12 minutes, or until smooth and elastic, adding only enough flour to prevent sticking. Clean and butter bowl. Place dough in bowl, turning to coat all surfaces. Cover with a slightly damp towel; set in a warm place free from drafts. Let rise until doubled in bulk, about 1 hour. Grease 2 medium-size baking sheets or 2 round 8-inch cake pans; set aside.

Punch down dough; knead 2 minutes. Divide dough in half; cover and let rest 10 minutes. Shape into two round loaves and place on prepared baking sheets or in prepared pans. Cover with dry towel; let rise until doubled in bulk, about 1 hour.

Preheat oven to 375F (190C). Slash tops of loaves as desired; brush with molasses-water glaze. Bake 30 to 35 minutes; brush again with molasses glaze. Bake 10 minutes longer, or until bread sounds hollow when tapped on the bottom. Remove from pans; cool on racks.

Makes 2 loaves.

Storing & Freezing Unbaked Dough

Although not generally recommended, unbaked dough can be frozen before or after the first rise. For best results, don't freeze dough longer than two or three weeks.

To freeze before first rise: Knead dough; cover and let rest 15 minutes. Lightly oil surface of dough. Wrap in heavy plastic wrap or freezer wrap. Freeze until solid, then wrap airtight in heavy-duty foil or other freezerproof wrapping. Return to freezer.

To defrost: Let frozen dough stand at room temperature 5 to 7 hours. Unwrap and place in large bowl; cover and let rise according to recipe directions. Punch down dough, shape into loaves, and let rise again in pans before baking.

To freeze after first rise: Punch down dough; knead 30 seconds to expel excess air. Line baking pans with heavy plastic wrap long enough to extend 3 inches over edges of pan. Shape loaves; coat lightly with oil. Place loaves in lined pans; fold plastic wrap loosely over dough. Freeze until solid. Remove frozen dough from pan by lifting with edges of plastic wrap. Tightly seal plastic wrap around dough. Wrap airtight in heavy-duty foil or other freezerproof wrapping. Return to freezer.

To defrost: Remove frozen dough from wrappings; place in same baking pan in which it was frozen. Cover lightly with plastic wrap; let stand at room temperature 5 to 6 hours. Let rise until doubled in bulk; bake as directed.

Sweet Yeast Breads & Coffeecakes

For centuries, cooks have been serving sweetened yeast breads both to begin and to end the day, and even for snacks. With their pretty shapes and decorative glazes, sweet breads and coffeecakes always look so inviting. And, unlike most of their store-bought counterparts, homemade sweet breads deliver the taste that's promised by the appearance.

Sweet yeast breads are usually enriched with butter and eggs. Eggs supply structure, strengthening protein, while butter relaxes the gluten and generates a softer crumb. Both imbue the final bread with a rich flavor and pale golden hue. Eggs and butter also produce soft, pliable doughs that are wonderful to work with. It's immensely satisfying to watch the malleable dough take shape as you form fanciful braids, twisted spirals, plaited rectangles, swirled loaves—whatever strikes your fancy.

In general, sweet yeast doughs take longer to rise than savory doughs, as do those containing large amounts of fruit and nuts. Caution is the byword when adding extra sugar to a yeast dough. Too much sugar overpowers the yeast's leavening action and produces a bread that doesn't rise as well as it should. Substituting liquid sweeteners like honey and maple syrup for granulated or brown sugar may take a little experimentation. Because of all the variables in breadmaking, there's no absolute formula. In general, for each 1/2 cup of granular sugar, substitute 1/3 cup liquid sweetener and reduce the total liquid used in the recipe by 2 tablespoons.

If you only try one of the following recipes, make it the Basic Sweet Yeast Dough, enriched with butter, eggs, and sour cream. This versatile dough can be used to produce myriad creations, including Mocha-Macadamia Coffeecake, Old-Fashioned Cinnamon Rolls, and Raised Doughnuts. This basic recipe makes one large coffeecake, two medium-size loaves, or twenty-four rolls. Let imagination be your key to creating your own sweet breads with this rich, easy-to-handle dough.

Whether you prefer breads sweetened lightly with fruit or nuts, or more boldly with chocolate or marzipan, you're bound to find a recipe on the following pages that appeals to you. Anyone with even the tiniest sweet tooth won't be able to resist these beautiful breads.

Basic Sweet Yeast Dough

This rich and easy sour cream dough can be used for dozens of breads, coffeecakes, and rolls.

> 1 (1/4-oz.) package active dry yeast
> 1/3 cup sugar
> 1/4 cup warm water (110F, 45C)
> 2 eggs
> 1/3 cup unsalted butter or margarine, melted
> 1/2 cup sour cream
> 1 teaspoon pure vanilla extract
> 1 teaspoon salt
> 3-1/2 to 4 cups bread or all-purpose flour

In large bowl of electric mixer, dissolve yeast and 1 teaspoon of the sugar in warm water. Let stand until foamy, 5 to 10 minutes. Add remaining sugar, eggs, butter, sour cream, vanilla, salt, and 1-1/2 to 2 cups of the flour. Beat at medium speed with electric mixer 2 minutes, or beat 200 vigorous strokes by hand. Stir in enough remaining flour to make a soft dough. Change to dough hook(s) if using mixer, or turn out dough onto a lightly floured surface.

Knead dough 4 to 6 minutes, or until smooth. Dough should feel soft and buttery, but not sticky. Clean and butter bowl. Place dough in bowl, turning to coat all surfaces. Cover with a slightly damp towel; set in a warm place free from drafts. Let rise until doubled in bulk, about 1-1/2 hours. Or, cover bowl tightly with plastic wrap; let rise in refrigerator overnight. Shape and bake as directed in specific recipes.

Makes 1 large or 2 small loaves, or 24 rolls.

Use to make: Granola Crunch Twist (page 83); Mocha-Macadamia Ring (page 86); Golden Ginger-Pear Coffeecake (page 84); Hazelnut Pinwheel Bread (page 91); Chocolate Chipper Loaf (page 103); Old-Fashioned Cinnamon Rolls (page 126); Linzer Spirals (page 137); Sweetheart Bread (page 211); Candy Cane Bread (page 231); Fried Bread Dough (page 253); and Raised Doughnuts (page 245).

Variation

Overnight Sweet Dough: Shape and place in pan according to recipe. Cover tightly with plastic wrap; refrigerate overnight. Uncover and let stand at room temperature 30 minutes before baking.

Granola Crunch Twist

Toasted-style granolas have more flavor and crunch than untoasted styles. Granolas with bits of fruit are also great in this recipe—choose your favorite.

1 recipe Basic Sweet Yeast Dough (opposite)
1-1/2 cups granola cereal, crushed
1/2 cup dry-roasted sunflower kernels
1/2 cup finely chopped toasted walnuts (Tip, page 262)
1/4 cup packed brown sugar
1/2 cup unsalted butter, melted

Prepare Basic Sweet Yeast Dough through first rising. Grease a large baking sheet; set aside.

Punch down dough; knead 30 seconds. Cover and let rest 10 minutes. In a medium bowl, stir together crushed granola, sunflower kernels, nuts, sugar, and butter; set aside. On a lightly floured surface, roll dough out into a 15-inch square. Sprinkle evenly with granola mixture to within 1/2 inch of edges. Lightly press granola into dough. Roll up tightly, jelly-roll fashion. Firmly pinch seam and ends to seal. Form roll into a circle; pinch ends together to join. Using a sharp knife, make cuts around outside of circle 1 inch apart and two-thirds of the way to the center. Twist each cut piece in the same direction, turning so filling faces upwards. Cover with a dry towel; let rise until doubled in bulk, about 1 hour.

Preheat oven to 350F (175C). Bake 30 to 40 minutes or until golden brown. Carefully remove from baking sheet; cool on rack at least 20 minutes before serving. Serve coffeecake warm or at room temperature.

Makes 1 large coffeecake.

Golden Ginger-Pear Coffeecake

Cheddar cheese adds golden flavor and color to a pear, ginger, raisin, and walnut filling. You can freeze one of these coffeecakes (page 75) for a future almost-instant breakfast. Tart, chopped apples can be substituted for the pears if you prefer that combination.

Basic Sweet Yeast Dough (page 82)
2 tablespoons unsalted butter, melted
1-1/2 cups finely chopped peeled pears
2 tablespoons all-purpose flour
1 cup grated Cheddar cheese (4 oz.)
1/3 cup packed brown sugar
1/3 cup raisins
1/3 cup chopped walnuts
1 tablespoon finely chopped crystallized ginger
1 egg white mixed with 2 teaspoons water for glaze

Prepare Basic Sweet Yeast Dough through first rising. Grease 2 baking sheets; set aside.

Punch down dough; knead 30 seconds. Cover and let rest 10 minutes. Divide dough in half; cover one piece. On a lightly floured surface, roll out remaining dough into a 15" x 10" rectangle. Brush with 1 tablespoon melted butter. In a medium bowl, toss pears and flour. Stir in cheese, sugar, raisins, walnuts, and ginger; stir to combine. Spoon half of pear mixture lengthwise down center of dough. Using a sharp knife, cut dough on each side of filling into 15 (1-inch-wide) strips. Cut straight, not diagonally. Starting at 1 end, alternately fold 7 strips from each side over filling at an angle, creating a braided effect. Repeat, starting from opposite end, with 7 pairs of strips. Bring remaining 2 center strips together; tie loosely, arranging ends attractively over filling. Repeat with remaining dough and filling. Place coffeecakes on prepared baking sheets. Cover with a dry towel; let rise until doubled in bulk, 1 to 1-1/2 hours.

Preheat oven to 350F (165C). Brush coffeecakes with egg-white glaze. Bake 20 to 30 minutes, or until golden brown. Remove from baking sheets; cool on racks 30 minutes before serving. Serve warm or at room temperature.

Makes 2 coffeecakes.

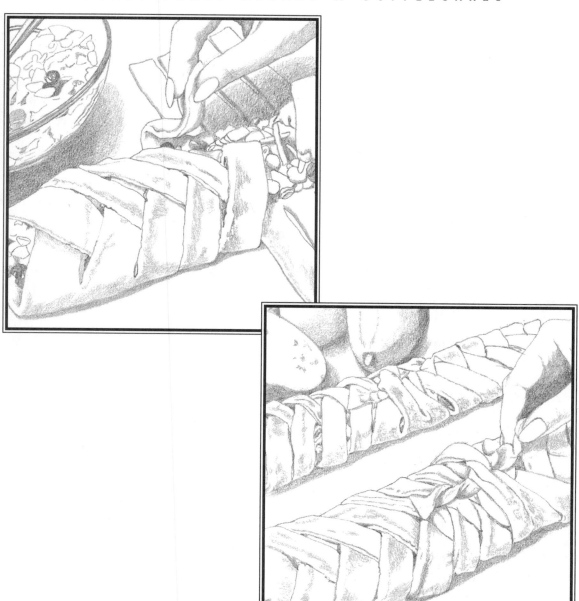

Mocha-Macadamia Ring

*C*offee and chocolate unite to create a delicious mocha meringue filling for this morning treat. Take a shortcut by making the dough the night before and letting it rise overnight in the refrigerator. A few minutes of kneading in the morning will help warm the dough for the second rising. To achieve maximum volume in the meringue, be sure the egg whites are at room temperature.

> 1 recipe Basic Sweet Yeast Dough (page 82)
> 2 egg whites
> 1-1/2 teaspoons instant coffee granules
> 1/8 teaspoon salt
> 1/2 cup sugar
> 1 cup finely chopped macadamia nuts
> 2 ounces semisweet chocolate, melted and cooled
> Candy coffee beans for garnish (optional)

Mocha Glaze:
> 1 teaspoon instant coffee granules
> 1 to 2 tablespoons milk
> 1 teaspoon pure vanilla extract
> 1 cup powdered sugar

Prepare Basic Sweet Yeast Dough through first rising. Generously grease a 1-cup Bundt pan or fluted tube pan; set aside.

Punch down dough; knead 30 seconds. Cover and let rest 10 minutes. In small bowl of electric mixer, beat 2 egg whites, instant coffee, and salt together until soft peaks form. Beating constantly, gradually add sugar, 2 tablespoons at a time. Beat until meringue is firm and glossy. Fold in nuts and cooled chocolate; set aside. On a lightly floured surface, roll out dough into a 20" x 16" rectangle. Spread meringue over dough to within 1 inch of edges. Beginning on long side, roll up dough tightly, jelly-roll fashion. Pinch seam and ends to seal. Place roll in prepared pan, seam side up. Overlap ends slightly; pinch together to join. Cover with a dry towel; let rise until doubled in bulk, about 1 hour. If seam pulls apart during rising, pinch together lightly to reseal.

Preheat oven to 350F (175C). Bake 35 to 45 minutes, or until bread sounds hollow when tapped on the top. Remove from pan; cool on rack. Prepare Mocha Glaze; drizzle over top of cooled coffeecake. If desired, garnish top with candy coffee beans.

Makes 1 coffeecake.

Mocha Glaze: In a small bowl, dissolve coffee granules in 1 tablespoon milk. Stir in pure vanilla, powdered sugar, and enough additional milk to make a thick and creamy glaze of drizzling consistency.

Coconut Sugar Crunch Coffeecake

*T*oasted coconut plus coconut milk give this bread an exotic flavor. Canned, unsweetened coconut milk can be found in Asian markets and many supermarkets. Don't confuse it with the intensely sweet cream of coconut, which is commonly used for desserts and mixed drinks.

> **2 (1/4-oz.) packages active dry yeast**
> **1/3 cup sugar**
> **1/3 cup warm water (110F, 45C)**
> **1-1/4 cups unsweetened coconut milk**
> **2 eggs**
> **Finely grated zest of 2 medium-size oranges**
> **1 teaspoon pure vanilla extract**
> **1-1/2 teaspoons salt**
> **1-1/2 cups toasted shredded coconut**
> **5-1/2 to 6 cups bread or all-purpose flour**
> **1 egg white mixed with 1 teaspoon water for glaze**

In large bowl of electric mixer, dissolve yeast and 1 teaspoon of the sugar in warm water. Let stand until foamy, 5 to 10 minutes. Add remaining sugar, coconut milk, eggs, orange zest, vanilla, salt, 1-1/2 cups coconut, and about 3 cups of the flour. Beat at medium speed with electric mixer 2 minutes, or beat 200 vigorous strokes by hand. Stir in enough remaining flour to make a soft dough. Change to dough hook(s) if using mixer, or turn out dough onto a lightly floured surface.

Knead dough 6 to 8 minutes, or until smooth and elastic, adding only enough flour to prevent sticking. Clean and butter bowl. Place dough in bowl, turning to coat all surfaces. Cover with a slightly damp towel; set in a warm place free from drafts. Let rise until doubled in bulk, about 1 hour. Grease 2 (9" x 5") loaf pans; set aside.

Punch down dough; knead 30 seconds. Divide dough in half. Shape into loaves and place in prepared pans. Cover with a dry towel; let rise until doubled in bulk, 45 to 60 minutes.

Preheat oven to 350F (175C). Slash tops of loaves; brush with egg-white glaze. Bake 35 to 45 minutes, or until bread sounds hollow when tapped on the bottom. Remove from pans; cool on racks.

Makes 2 loaves.

Two-Timin' Cinnamon Bread

*O*rdinary cinnamon bread is never spicy enough for me, so I added cinnamon and nutmeg to the dough in this recipe. That plus the cinnamon-nut filling make this bread doubly delicious. The fragrance of this bread is incredibly inviting. I have a real estate friend who swears if she could bottle its essence to spray around her open houses, she'd sell them on the first day. If your ground cinnamon is over six months old, it will most likely be lackluster in flavor. Either buy new cinnamon or increase the amount used by half.

> 2 (1/4-oz.) packages active dry yeast
> 1/3 cup packed brown sugar
> 1/3 cup warm water (110F, 45C)
> 1-1/4 cups milk
> 2 eggs
> 1/2 cup unsalted butter or margarine, melted
> 1 teaspoon pure vanilla extract
> 1 tablespoon ground cinnamon
> 1/2 teaspoon ground nutmeg
> 1-1/2 teaspoons salt
> 6 to 6-1/2 cups bread or all-purpose flour
> 2 tablespoons unsalted butter or margarine, melted
> 1 egg yolk mixed with 1 teaspoon cream for glaze
> 2 teaspoons sugar mixed with 1/4 teaspoon ground cinnamon for topping

Cinnamon-Nut Filling:

> 3/4 cup packed brown sugar
> 2-1/2 teaspoons ground cinnamon
> 1/2 teaspoon ground nutmeg
> 1/2 cup finely chopped walnuts or pecans

In large bowl of electric mixer, dissolve yeast and a pinch of the sugar in warm water. Let stand until foamy, 5 to 10 minutes. Add remaining sugar, milk, eggs, butter, vanilla, cinnamon, nutmeg, salt, and 3-1/2 to 4 cups flour. Beat at medium speed with electric mixer 2 minutes, or beat 200 vigorous strokes by hand. Stir in enough remaining flour to make a soft dough. Change to dough hook(s) if using mixer, or turn out dough onto a lightly floured surface.

Knead dough 8 to 10 minutes, or until smooth and elastic, adding only enough flour to prevent sticking. Clean and butter bowl. Place dough in bowl, turning to coat all surfaces. Cover with a slightly damp towel; set in a warm place free from drafts. Let rise until doubled in bulk, about 1 hour. Grease 2 (9" x 5") loaf pans; set aside. Prepare Cinnamon-Nut Filling.

Punch down dough; knead 30 seconds. Divide dough in half; cover 1 piece. On a lightly floured surface, roll out remaining dough into a 14" x 8" rectangle. Brush with 1 tablespoon melted butter. Sprinkle half of Cinnamon-Nut Filling evenly over dough to within 1/2 inch of edges. Lightly press filling mixture into dough with back of spoon. Beginning on a short side, roll up tightly, jelly-roll fashion. Firmly pinch seam and ends to seal. Turn loaf seam side down. Tuck ends under; pinch again. Place in a prepared pan. Repeat with remaining dough. Cover with a dry towel; let rise until doubled in bulk, about 45 minutes.

Preheat oven to 350F (175C). Brush tops of loaves with egg-yolk glaze; sprinkle with cinnamon-sugar topping. Bake 45 to 50 minutes, or until bread sounds hollow when tapped on the bottom. Remove from pans; cool on racks.

Makes 2 loaves.

Cinnamon-Nut Filling: Combine all ingredients in a small bowl; set aside.

Variations

Cinnamon-Wheat Bread: Substitute 3 cups whole-wheat flour for 3 cups bread or all-purpose flour; add 1/2 cup wheat germ.

Cinnamon-Raisin Bread: Add 1 to 1-1/2 cups raisins (golden or dark) with the second addition of flour (just before you start kneading).

Cinnamon-Orange Bread: Substitute 1-1/4 cups orange juice for 1-1/4 cups milk. Add 1 to 2 tablespoons finely grated orange zest.

TIP: Store brown sugar in a thick plastic bag in a cool dry place. If sugar begins to harden, add an apple wedge to the bag; seal, and let stand two days. Or, place hardened sugar in a covered dish and microwave at HIGH 30 to 40 seconds (depending on the amount of sugar). Or, place sugar in a pie plate and heat in a 250F (120C) oven about 5 minutes.

Maple Butter Bread

*T*his maple-scented bread is absolutely heavenly toasted, or when used to make French toast. Maple Butter (page 261) is the natural accompaniment. I urge you to use pure maple syrup, the maple-tree sap that's been boiled until most of the water has evaporated. Its flavor is far superior to so-called pancake syrup, which is nothing more than corn syrup flavored with artificial maple extract.

2 (1/4-oz.) packages active dry yeast
3/4 cup pure maple syrup
1/3 cup warm water (110F, 45C)
1/2 cup butter, melted
1/3 cup packed brown sugar
2 eggs
2 teaspoons salt
1 teaspoon pure vanilla extract
1/2 teaspoon ground nutmeg
1/2 teaspoon ground cinnamon
4-1/2 to 5 cups bread or all-purpose flour
1 cup finely chopped pecans

In large bowl of electric mixer, dissolve yeast and 1 teaspoon of the maple syrup in warm water. Let stand until foamy, 5 to 10 minutes. Add 1/2 cup maple syrup, butter, brown sugar, eggs, salt, vanilla, nutmeg, cinnamon, and 2-1/2 to 3 cups of the flour. Beat at medium speed with electric mixer 2 minutes, or beat 200 vigorous strokes by hand. Stir in nuts and enough remaining flour to make a soft dough. Turn dough out onto a lightly floured surface.

Knead dough 6 to 8 minutes, or until smooth and elastic, adding only enough flour to prevent sticking. Clean and butter bowl. Place dough in bowl, turning to coat all surfaces. Cover with a slightly damp towel; set in a warm place free from drafts. Let rise until doubled in bulk, about 1 hour. Generously grease 2 (8" x 4") loaf pans; set aside.

Punch dough down; knead 30 seconds. Divide dough in half. Shape into loaves and place in prepared pans. Cover with a dry towel and set in a warm place free from drafts. Let rise until doubled in bulk, about 1 hour.

Preheat oven to 350F (175C). Slash tops of loaves; brush generously with some of the remaining maple syrup. Bake 20 minutes; brush again with maple syrup. Bake 10 to 15 minutes longer, or until bread sounds hollow when tapped on the bottom. If tops begin to overbrown, cover loosely with foil. Remove from pans; cool on racks.

Makes 2 loaves.

Hazelnut Pinwheel Bread

1 recipe Basic Sweet Yeast Dough (page 82)
1 cup finely chopped toasted hazelnuts (Tip, page 262)
1/3 cup plus 1 tablespoon honey
1 (3-oz.) package cream cheese, softened
Finely grated zest from 1 medium-size orange

Prepare Basic Sweet Yeast Dough, adding 1/2 cup hazelnuts with flour, through first rising. Grease a 9" x 5" loaf pan; set aside.

Punch down dough; knead 30 seconds. Cover and let rest 10 minutes. In a medium bowl, stir together 1/3 cup honey, cream cheese, orange zest, and remaining 1/2 cup hazelnuts; set aside. On a lightly floured surface, roll out dough into a 14" x 8" rectangle. Spread evenly with hazelnut-honey mixture to within 1/2 inch of edges. Lightly press filling mixture into dough with back of spoon. Beginning on a short side, roll up tightly, jelly-roll fashion. Firmly pinch seam and ends to seal. Turn loaf seam side down; place in prepared pan. Cover with a dry towel; let rise until doubled in bulk, about 1 hour.

Preheat oven to 350F (175C). Brush top of loaf with remaining tablespoon honey. Bake 40 to 50 minutes, or until bread sounds hollow when tapped on the bottom. Remove from pan; cool on rack.

Makes 1 loaf.

TIP: Every baker's *batterie de cuisine* should include an oven thermometer, ruler, and thermometer for reading liquid temperatures.

Ricotta-Orange Twist

*T*his coffeecake doubles your pleasure with its creamy ricotta filling inside a ricotta-enriched dough. If you're watching calories, use low-fat or nonfat instead of whole-milk ricotta.

 1 (1/4-oz.) package active dry yeast
 1/4 cup sugar
 1/4 cup warm water (110F, 45C)
 1 egg
 1 (8-oz.) container ricotta cheese (1 cup)
 3 tablespoons unsalted butter or margarine, melted
 1 teaspoon salt
 3 tablespoons freshly grated orange zest
 2-1/2 to 3 cups bread or all-purpose flour
 Creamy Ricotta Filling, see below
 1 egg white mixed with 1 teaspoon orange juice for glaze
 Orange Glaze, see below

Creamy Ricotta Filling:
 1/2 cup ricotta cheese
 2 (3-oz.) packages cream cheese, softened
 1 tablespoon all-purpose flour
 1/4 cup sugar
 1 egg yolk
 2 teaspoons finely grated orange zest
 1/4 teaspoon ground nutmeg
 1/8 teaspoon salt

Orange Glaze:
 1 cup powdered sugar
 1/4 teaspoon ground nutmeg
 1 to 2 tablespoons orange juice

In large bowl of electric mixer, dissolve yeast and 1 teaspoon of the sugar in warm water. Let stand until foamy, 5 to 10 minutes. Add remaining sugar, egg, ricotta, butter, salt, 2-1/2 tablespoons orange zest, and 1 to 1-1/2 cups of the flour. Beat at medium speed with electric mixer 2 minutes, or beat 200 vigorous strokes by hand. Stir in enough remaining flour to make a soft dough. Change to dough hook(s) if using mixer, or turn out dough onto a lightly floured surface.

Knead dough 6 to 8 minutes, or until smooth and elastic, adding only enough flour to prevent sticking. Dough will be soft and pliable. Clean and butter bowl. Place dough in bowl, turning to coat all surfaces. Cover with a slightly damp towel; set in a warm place free from drafts. Let rise until doubled in bulk, about 1 hour. Grease a 9-inch springform pan with center tube or a 10-inch tube pan. Prepare Creamy Ricotta Filling; set aside.

Punch down dough; knead 30 seconds. On a lightly floured surface, roll dough out into a 20" x 8" rectangle. Cut rectangle in half lengthwise, forming 2 (20" x 4") strips. Spread half the filling down the center of each strip, to within 1/2 inch of edges. Working with 1 rectangle at a time, bring long sides up; pinch together tightly to seal. Pinch ends to seal; tuck under and pinch again. Turn filled rolls seam side down; place side by side. Keeping seam sides down, twist rolls together, pinching ends to secure. Place twist in prepared pan, overlapping ends slightly. Cover with a dry towel; let rise until doubled in bulk, about 1 hour.

Preheat oven to 350F (175C). Brush top of ring with egg-white glaze. Bake 35 to 45 minutes, or until a deep golden brown. Run knife around outside and inner edges to loosen bread from pan. Carefully remove pan; cool on rack. Prepare Orange Glaze. Drizzle cooled ring with Orange Glaze and garnish with remaining orange zest.

Makes 1 loaf.

Creamy Ricotta Filling: In small bowl of electric mixer, beat all ingredients until creamy.

Orange Glaze: In a small bowl, combine powdered sugar and nutmeg. Stir in enough orange juice to make a smooth, creamy glaze of drizzling consistency.

Swirled Orange-Poppy Loaves

*T*he unique, double-swirl design of these loaves makes this bread perfect for special occasions. Augment the flavor of poppy seeds by toasting them in a dry skillet over medium heat until they begin to lightly brown. Poppy seeds go rancid quickly but will keep for up to six months if refrigerated in a tightly sealed container.

     2 (1/4-oz.) packages active dry yeast
     1/3 cup sugar
     1/3 cup warm water (110F, 45C)
     1 cup orange juice
     1/4 cup unsalted butter or margarine, melted
     2 eggs
     2 egg yolks
     Finely grated zest of 1 medium-size orange
     1 teaspoon pure vanilla extract
     1 teaspoon salt
     5-1/2 to 6 cups bread or all-purpose flour
     Poppy Seed Filling, see below
     1 egg white mixed with 2 teaspoons honey for glaze
     Poppy seeds for garnish

Poppy Seed Filling:
     1-1/2 cups water
     3/4 cup poppy seeds
     1 cup toasted slivered almonds
     1/4 cup honey
     1/3 cup sugar
     1/4 teaspoon salt
     3 tablespoons orange juice
     1 teaspoon freshly grated orange zest
     1 teaspoon pure vanilla extract
     1/4 teaspoon almond extract
     1 egg white, beaten until stiff but not dry

In large bowl of electric mixer, dissolve yeast and 1 teaspoon of the sugar in warm water. Let stand until foamy, 5 to 10 minutes. Add remaining sugar, orange juice, butter, eggs, egg yolks, orange zest, vanilla, salt, and 2-1/2 to 3 cups of the flour. Beat at medium speed with electric mixer 2 minutes, or beat 200 vigorous strokes by hand. Stir in enough remaining flour to make a soft dough. Change to dough hook(s) if using mixer, or turn out dough onto a lightly floured surface.

Knead dough 6 to 8 minutes, or until smooth and elastic, adding only enough flour to prevent sticking. Clean and butter bowl. Place dough in bowl, turning to coat all surfaces. Cover with a slightly damp towel; set in a warm place free from drafts. Let rise until doubled in bulk, about 1 hour. Prepare Poppy Seed Filling; set aside. Grease 2 (9" x 5") loaf pans; set aside.

Punch down dough; knead 30 seconds. Divide dough in half. Cover and let rest 10 minutes. Roll out half of dough into an 18" x 10" rectangle. Spread with half of filling to within 1/2 inch of edges. Beginning on a long side, roll up tightly, jelly-roll fashion. Pinch seam and ends to seal. With seam side down, fold roll in half in a tight U shape. Place in prepared pan with halves side by side, seam side down. Repeat with remaining dough. Cover with a dry towel; let rise until doubled in bulk, 45 to 60 minutes.

Preheat oven to 350F (175C). Brush with egg-white glaze; sprinkle with poppy seeds. Bake 35 to 45 minutes, or until bread sounds hollow when tapped on the top. Remove from pans; cool on racks.

Makes 2 loaves.

Poppy Seed Filling: In a small saucepan, bring water and poppy seeds to a boil. Remove from heat; cover and set aside 30 minutes. Thoroughly drain poppy seeds. In a blender or a food processor fitted with a metal blade, combine drained poppy seeds and almonds. Process until almonds are coarsely ground. Transfer to a medium bowl. Stir in honey, sugar, salt, orange juice, orange zest, vanilla, and almond extract. Fold in egg white.

BREADS

Rise 'n' Shine Bread

*O*range juice gives this raisin-studded bread a sunshine flavor. For a beautifully golden loaf, use golden raisins. This versatile loaf can be changed by adding nuts, or substituting other dried fruits, or using part wheat flour (see variations opposite).

    1 (1/4-oz.) package active dry yeast
    1/3 cup packed brown sugar
    1/4 cup warm water (110F, 45C)
    Freshly grated zest of 1 large orange
    1-1/4 cups orange juice
    2 eggs
    1/3 cup vegetable oil
    1/2 cup nonfat milk powder
    1-1/2 teaspoons salt
    1 teaspoon ground allspice
    1/2 teaspoon ground cardamom
    5-1/2 to 6 cups bread or all-purpose flour
    1 to 1-1/2 cups dark or golden raisins
    Orange Glaze, see below

Orange Glaze:
    1 cup powdered sugar
    1 tablespoon unsalted butter or margarine, melted
    2 to 4 tablespoons orange juice

In large bowl of electric mixer, dissolve yeast and 1 teaspoon of the sugar in warm water. Let stand until foamy, 5 to 10 minutes. Add remaining sugar, orange zest, orange juice, eggs, oil, milk powder, salt, allspice, cardamom, and 2-1/2 to 3 cups of the flour. Beat at medium speed with electric mixer 2 minutes, or beat 200 vigorous strokes by hand. Stir in raisins and enough remaining flour to make a soft dough. Change to dough hook(s) if using mixer, or turn out dough onto a lightly floured surface.

Knead dough 8 to 10 minutes, or until smooth and elastic, adding only enough flour to prevent sticking. Clean and butter bowl. Place dough in bowl, turning to coat all surfaces. Cover with a slightly damp towel; set in a warm place free from drafts. Let rise until doubled in bulk, about 1 hour. Grease 2 (8" x 4") loaf pans or 1-1/2-quart casseroles; set aside.

Punch down dough; knead 30 seconds. Divide dough in half. Shape into loaves; place in prepared pans. Cover with a dry towel; let rise until doubled in bulk, about 45 minutes.

Preheat oven to 375F (190C). Slash tops of loaves as desired. Bake 30 to 35 minutes, or until bread sounds hollow when tapped on the bottom. Remove from pans; cool on racks over waxed paper. When bread is cool, prepare Orange Glaze. Drizzle over tops of loaves. Let glaze set at least 10 minutes before slicing bread.

Makes 2 loaves.

Orange Glaze: In a small bowl, combine sugar and butter. Stir in enough orange juice to make a smooth, creamy glaze of drizzling consistency.

Variations

Wheaty Rise 'n' Shine Bread: Substitute 2 cups whole-wheat flour for 2 cups all-purpose flour; add 1/4 cup wheat germ with flour.

Raisin-Nut Bread: Use only 1 cup raisins; add 1 cup chopped toasted walnuts, pecans, or almonds.

Fruit 'n' Nut Bread: Substitute 1/2 cup chopped dried prunes, 1/2 cup chopped dried apricots, and 1/2 cup dried cherries or cranberries for the raisins. Add 1/2 cup chopped toasted walnuts, pecans, or almonds.

TIP: In general, sweet yeast doughs take longer to rise because, though sugar encourages yeast's growth, too much sugar overpowers the leavening action and slows rising.

Chocolate Lover's Coffeecake

A chocolate-chip swirl inside a dark chocolate–flavored bread, embellished with a white-chocolate glaze—truly a chocoholic's dream. You can substitute dark chocolate for white chocolate in the glaze, but the white makes a better contrast against the dark bread.

1/2 cup milk
3 ounces semisweet chocolate, coarsely chopped
1/3 cup plus 2 tablespoons butter, softened
2 (1/4-oz.) packages active dry yeast
1/3 cup granulated sugar
1/3 cup warm water (110F, 45C)
2 eggs
2 teaspoons salt
1 teaspoon pure vanilla extract
4-1/4 to 4-3/4 cups bread or all-purpose flour
3/4 cup packed brown sugar
1 cup chopped toasted walnuts or pecans (Tip, page 262)
1 (6-oz.) package semisweet or white chocolate chips
2 tablespoons butter, softened
White Chocolate Glaze, see below

White Chocolate Glaze:
2 ounces white chocolate, chopped
2 tablespoons butter

In a small saucepan over medium-low heat, bring milk to a simmer. Remove from heat. Add chocolate; stir until melted. Add 1/3 cup butter; stir to melt. Set aside until lukewarm. In large bowl of electric mixer, dissolve yeast and 1 teaspoon of the granulated sugar in warm water. Let stand until foamy; 5 to 10 minutes. Add remaining granulated sugar, eggs, salt, vanilla, cooled chocolate mixture, and 2 to 2-1/2 cups of the flour. Beat at medium speed with electric mixer 2 minutes, or beat 200 vigorous strokes by hand. Stir in enough remaining flour to make a soft dough. Turn dough out onto a lightly floured surface.

Knead dough 8 to 10 minutes, or until smooth and elastic, adding only enough flour to prevent sticking. Clean and butter bowl. Place dough in bowl, turning to coat all surfaces. Cover with a slightly damp towel; set in a warm place free from drafts. Let rise until doubled in bulk, about 1 hour. Grease 2 large baking sheets; set aside. In a medium bowl, combine brown sugar, nuts, and semisweet or white chocolate chips; set aside.

Punch down dough; knead 30 seconds. Divide dough in half; cover 1 half. On a lightly floured surface, roll out remaining dough into a 17" x 9" rectangle. Spread 1 tablespoon softened butter to within 1/2 inch of edges. Sprinkle buttered area with half the chocolate-chip mixture. Use the back of a spoon to press mixture lightly into dough. Beginning on a long side, roll tightly in jelly-roll fashion. Pinch seam and ends firmly to seal. Place on prepared baking sheet; form into a horseshoe shape with the ends almost touching. With pointed scissors, snip top of dough crosswise, forming notches that are about 1/2 inch deep, 1-1/2 inches wide, and 1 to 1-1/2 inches apart. Repeat with second half of dough. Cover with dry towels and set in a warm place free from drafts. Let rise until doubled in bulk, 45 to 60 minutes.

Preheat oven to 375F (190C). Bake 25 to 35 minutes, or until coffeecake sounds hollow when tapped on the top. Remove from baking sheets; cool on racks. Prepare chocolate glaze. Drizzle cooled coffeecake with chocolate glaze.

Makes 2 coffeecakes.

White Chocolate Glaze: In a small saucepan over medium-low heat, stir chocolate and butter until melted.

TIP: Did you know that white chocolate isn't truly chocolate? That's because it doesn't contain chocolate liquor—the thick, dark paste left after the cocoa butter is extracted from the nibs. Instead, white chocolate is usually a mixture of sugar, cocoa butter, milk solids, lecithin, and vanilla. No wonder it doesn't really taste like chocolate!

Marzipan Coffee Ring

Impressive and delicious, this petal-topped bread encloses a delectable marzipan swirl. Definitely worth the time.

    1 (1/4-oz.) package active dry yeast
    1/4 cup sugar
    1/4 cup warm water (110F, 45C)
    1 cup sour cream
    2 eggs
    1 teaspoon salt
    1/2 teaspoon almond extract
    4-1/4 to 4-3/4 cups bread or all-purpose flour
    Marzipan Filling, see below
    3/4 cup finely chopped toasted almonds (Tip, page 262)
    1 egg white mixed with 2 teaspoons water for glaze
    Almond Glaze, see below

Marzipan Filling:
    1/2 cup packed almond paste
    1/4 cup packed brown sugar
    1 tablespoon unsalted butter or margarine, softened
    1 egg white
    1/4 teaspoon ground nutmeg
    1/2 teaspoon almond extract
    1/8 teaspoon salt

Almond Glaze:
    1 cup powdered sugar
    1/2 teaspoon pure vanilla extract
    1/4 teaspoon almond extract
    1 to 2 tablespoons Amaretto liqueur or milk

In large bowl of electric mixer, dissolve yeast and 1 teaspoon of the sugar in warm water. Let stand until foamy, 5 to 10 minutes. Add remaining sugar, sour cream, eggs, salt, almond extract, and 1 to 1-1/2 cups of the flour. Beat at medium speed with electric mixer 2 minutes, or beat 200 vigorous strokes by hand. Stir in enough remaining flour to make a soft dough. Change to dough hook(s) if using mixer, or turn out dough onto a lightly floured surface.

Knead dough 6 to 8 minutes, or until smooth and elastic, adding only enough flour to prevent sticking. Clean and butter bowl. Place dough in bowl, turning to coat all surfaces. Cover with a slightly damp towel; set in a warm place free from drafts. Let rise until doubled in bulk, about 1 hour. Grease a 10-inch tube pan; set aside. Prepare Marzipan Filling; set aside.

Punch down dough; knead 30 seconds. Pinch off one-fourth of the dough; cover and set aside. On a lightly floured surface, roll out remaining dough into a 20" x 12" rectangle. Spread evenly with Marzipan Filling to within 1 inch of edges. Sprinkle with 1/2 cup chopped almonds. Beginning on a long side, roll up tightly, jelly-roll fashion. Pinch seam and ends to seal. Place seam side down in prepared pan, overlapping ends slightly. Brush surface lightly with water. Roll remaining piece of dough into a 24-inch rope. Lay rope around outside edge of dough in pan. Overlap and pinch ends together to seal. Holding pointed scissors almost parallel to rope, make cuts in rope, 1 inch apart and to within 1/4 inch of outside edge. Twist each pointed piece of dough sharply toward center of pan, to resemble petals. Cover with a dry towel; let rise until doubled in bulk, about 1 hour.

Preheat oven to 350F (175C). Brush top of dough with egg-white glaze. Bake 30 to 40 minutes, or until bread sounds hollow when tapped on top. Carefully remove from pan; cool on rack. Prepare Almond Glaze. Drizzle ring with Almond Glaze; sprinkle with remaining 1/4 cup chopped almonds.

Makes 1 coffeecake.

Marzipan Filling: In small bowl of electric mixer, beat all ingredients at medium speed until smooth.

Almond Glaze: In a small bowl, combine powdered sugar with vanilla and almond extracts. Stir in enough liqueur or milk to make a smooth, creamy glaze of drizzling consistency.

TIP: Almond paste freezes well for up to a year if double-wrapped and tightly sealed. Thaw at room temperature before using.

Viennese Striezel

This classic Austrian bread is as light and lovely as a Viennese waltz. It's a braided three-tiered spectacle perfumed with lemon zest and generously studded with golden raisins. The secret of keeping the stacked braids in place is making a depression in the bottom braid in which to position successive braids. For a festive look, tuck glaceed cherry halves randomly in the folds of the braids.

1 (1/4-oz.) package active dry yeast
1/3 cup sugar
1/4 cup warm water (110F, 45C)
3/4 cup milk
1 egg
2 egg yolks
1/3 cup unsalted butter or margarine, melted
Freshly grated zest from 1 medium lemon
3/4 teaspoon salt
4-1/2 to 5 cups bread or all-purpose flour
1 cup golden raisins
1 egg white mixed with 1 teaspoon sugar for glaze
2 tablespoons slivered or sliced almonds
Sugar

In large bowl of electric mixer, dissolve yeast and 1 teaspoon of the sugar in warm water. Let stand until foamy, 5 to 10 minutes. Add remaining sugar, milk, egg, egg yolks, butter, lemon zest, salt, and 2 to 2-1/2 cups of the flour. Beat at medium speed with electric mixer 2 minutes, or beat 200 vigorous strokes by hand. Stir in raisins and enough remaining flour to make a soft dough. Change to dough hook(s) if using mixer, or turn out dough onto a lightly floured surface.

Knead dough 8 to 10 minutes, or until smooth and elastic, adding only enough flour to prevent sticking. Clean and butter bowl. Place dough in bowl, turning to coat all surfaces. Cover with a slightly damp towel; set in a warm place free from drafts. Let rise until doubled in bulk, about 1 hour. Grease a large baking sheet; set aside.

Punch down dough; knead 30 seconds. Divide dough in half. Cover one piece; set aside. Divide remaining dough into 3 equal pieces. On a lightly floured surface, roll each piece into a 15-inch rope. Place 3 ropes side by side; braid, starting from center. Pinch ends together to seal; tuck under and pinch again. Center braid on prepared baking sheet. Pinch off one-third of remaining dough. Divide into 3 pieces; roll each piece into an 8-inch rope. Braid and set aside. Shape remaining dough into 3 (12-inch) ropes; braid. With the side of your hand, make a depression, 1/2 inch deep, down center of large braid on baking sheet. Brush depression with egg-white glaze. Center next-largest braid lengthwise on top; press down lightly. Make a depression down center of second braid; brush with egg-white glaze. Center smallest braid on top; press down lightly. Cover with a dry towel; let rise until doubled in bulk, about 1 hour. Refrigerate egg-white glaze.

Preheat oven to 350F (175C). Brush loaf with egg-white glaze; sprinkle with almonds and a little sugar. Wipe off any sugar that gets on baking sheet or it will burn. Bake 30 to 40 minutes, or until bread sounds hollow when tapped on the bottom. Remove from baking sheet; cool on rack.

Makes 1 large loaf.

Chocolate Chipper Loaf

*T*his super loaf is great toasted, and kids (of all ages) love it for peanut butter sandwiches. Gild the lily by serving it with Chocolate Butter (page 258).

1 recipe Basic Sweet Yeast Dough (page 82)
1 (6-oz.) package semisweet chocolate chips
1 cup toasted chopped walnuts
1 egg white mixed with 2 tablespoons sugar for glaze

Prepare Basic Sweet Yeast Dough through first rising. Grease a 9" x 5" loaf pan; set aside.

Punch down dough. Add chocolate chips and nuts; knead into dough. Shape into loaf; place in prepared pan. Cover with a dry towel; let rise until doubled in bulk, about 1 hour.

Preheat oven to 350F (175C). Brush top of loaf with egg-white glaze; slash as desired. Bake 20 minutes; brush with glaze again. Bake 15 to 25 minutes longer, or until bread sounds hollow when tapped on the bottom. Remove from pan; cool on rack.

Makes 1 loaf.

TIP: You eat with your eyes first. Always finish your breads attractively with a sprinkling of seeds, unusual slashing, or glazes.

✳

Braiding Dough

Many breads can be braided—all you need is to know how. For the most uniform braid, always start from the middle and braid toward each end. For a pretty effect, slightly taper ends of braid. The lengths indicated in the following braids are based on an average yeast-bread recipe containing about five cups of flour.

In the following directions, rope positions in a braid are numbered from left to right, beginning with 1, and including however many ropes are to be braided. Numbers refer to positions, not the ropes themselves. Therefore, if rope 1 is crossed over rope 2, the former rope 2 becomes rope 1, and the former rope 1 becomes rope 2.

Three-Rope Braid:

Divide dough into three equal pieces; roll each piece into a 12-inch rope. Lay three ropes side by side. Braid as follows:
- 1 over 2
- 3 over 2
- 1 over 2
- 3 over 2
- Repeat until braid is completed.

Pinch ends to seal; tuck ends under and pinch again.

Four-Rope Braid:

Divide dough into four equal pieces; roll each piece into a 12-inch rope. Lay four ropes side by side. Braid as follows:
- 1 over 4 (This is the only time you'll do this.)
- 3 over 1
- 4 over 3
- 2 over 4
- 1 over 2
- Repeat, beginning with 3 over 1, until braid is complete.

Pinch ends to seal; tuck ends under and pinch again.

Five-Rope Braid:

Divide dough into five equal pieces; roll each piece into a 10- to 12-inch rope. Lay five ropes side by side. Braid as follows:

- 2 over 3
- 5 over 2
- 1 over 3
- Repeat until braid is completed.

Pinch ends of completed braid to seal; tuck ends under and pinch again.

Six-Rope Braid:

Divide dough into six equal pieces; roll each piece into a 10-inch rope. Lay six ropes side by side. Braid as follows:

- 5 over 1
- 6 over 4
- 2 over 6
- 1 over 3
- Repeat until braid is completed.

(Braid may appear to be unbraiding, but it isn't.) Pinch ends of completed braid to seal; tuck ends under and pinch again.

Piggyback Braid:

Pinch off one-third of dough; divide into three equal pieces. Roll each piece into an 8-inch rope. Braid in a three-rope braid. Pinch ends; tuck under and pinch again to seal. Divide remaining two-thirds dough into three pieces. Roll each piece into a 12-inch rope; braid in a three-rope braid. With the side of your hand, make a depression, 1/2 inch deep, down center of large braid. Brush depression with lightly beaten egg white. Position small braid lengthwise on top; press down lightly.

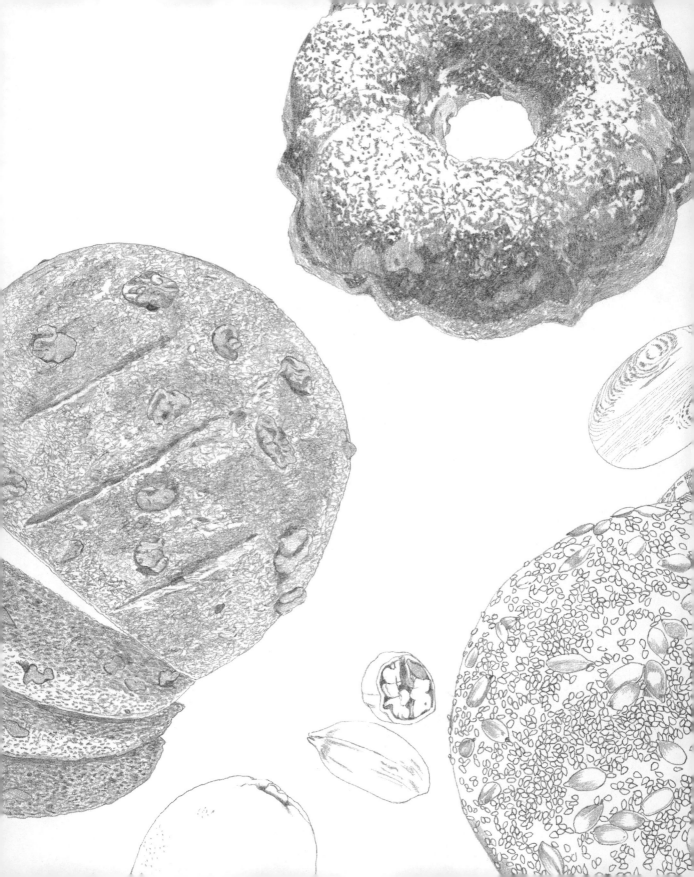

Batter Breads

There's no need to knead batter breads—one of my favorite members of the bread family. Extra yeast and vigorous beating are all it takes to create an easy and delicious loaf of bread. Because the flour's gluten isn't completely developed by a long kneading process, a batter bread's texture is more open and coarse. The flavor is slightly more yeasty because of the extra yeast. But, as far as I'm concerned, these differences only add to a batter bread's earthy charm.

The batter for this type of bread can be beaten with an electric mixer or with a wooden spoon and a little muscle. A food processor fitted with the plastic blade can sometimes be used, although some models can't handle the viscous, heavy batter. The end result should be a batter stiff enough for a spoon to stand up in. After beating, the batter's allowed to rise once in the bowl. It's then spooned into a baking pan and allowed to rise again before baking. You can butter your fingers or the back of a spoon to smooth the surface of the batter before the second rising. In theory, almost any yeast-bread recipe can be converted to a batter bread by simply using less flour and beating like crazy.

For times when speed is of the essence, the batter can be turned into the baking pan right after beating and allowed to rise only once before baking. The texture of the finished bread won't be as refined as with two risings, but your friends and family will be so delighted with homemade bread, I guarantee you won't hear any complaints!

Don't think, because of their easy beginnings, that batter breads can't be elegant. The regal, cakelike Kugelhopf—abundant with butter, eggs, rum-soaked raisins, and toasted almonds—can compete with the best of the kneaded yeast breads. It's so popular in Europe that Austrian, Alsatian, German, and Polish bakers all claim credit for its creation.

Because of their easy-going nature, batter breads lend themselves beautifully to adaptation and experimentation. Before you know it, you'll soon be creating your own favorites.

Peaches & Cream Coffeecake

※─────────────※

*T*his easy upside-down coffeecake can be started the night before to save time. Nectarines or plums can be substituted for the peaches, if you prefer.

1 (1/4-oz.) package active dry yeast
1/2 cup granulated sugar
1/4 cup warm water (110F, 45C)
1/2 cup peach puree (about 1 large peach)
1/2 cup milk
2 eggs
1/3 cup vegetable oil
1 tablespoon pure vanilla extract
1-1/2 teaspoons salt
1 teaspoon ground nutmeg
1 teaspoon ground cinnamon
3-3/4 to 4-1/4 cups all-purpose flour
3/4 cup toasted chopped pecans
1/2 cup packed brown sugar
1/4 cup unsalted butter or margarine, melted
2 ripe, firm medium-size peaches, peeled and sliced

In large bowl of electric mixer, dissolve yeast and 1 teaspoon of the sugar in warm water. Let stand until foamy, 5 to 10 minutes. Add remaining sugar, peach puree, milk, eggs, oil, vanilla, salt, 1/2 teaspoon nutmeg, 1/2 teaspoon cinnamon, and 2-1/2 to 3 cups of the flour. Beat at medium speed with electric mixer 4 minutes, or 400 vigorous strokes by hand. Stir in pecans and enough remaining flour to make a stiff batter. Cover with a slightly damp towel; set in a warm place free from drafts. Let rise until doubled in bulk, 1 to 1-1/2 hours. Liberally grease a 10-inch Bundt or tube pan. In a small bowl, combine brown sugar with remaining 1/2 teaspoon each cinnamon and nutmeg. Sprinkle evenly over bottom of prepared pan; drizzle with melted butter. Arrange peach slices decoratively on top.

Stir down batter. Spoon over peaches in pan, smoothing top. If desired, sprinkle top with additional chopped pecans. Cover with buttered waxed paper or plastic wrap. Let rise until almost doubled in bulk, about 45 minutes.

Preheat oven to 350F (175C). Bake 40 to 50 minutes, or until a metal skewer inserted in center comes out clean. Carefully invert onto a serving plate. Spoon any topping remaining in pan over coffeecake. Let stand 20 minutes before serving warm.

Makes 1 coffeecake.

TIP: Let batter breads rise overnight in the refrigerator. The next morning, transfer the batter to a baking pan for the second rise. If batter is refrigerated, the second rise will take longer than the recipe indicates.

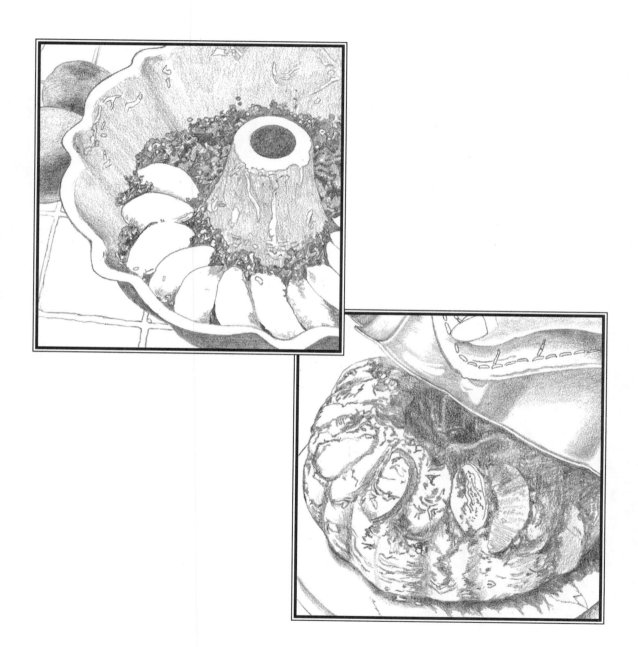

Kugelhopf

Kugelhopf (KOO-guhl-hopf), also called *gugelhopf*, is traditionally baked in a special fluted kugel-hopf ring mold, though a Bundt pan is a perfectly acceptable substitution. According to the noted English food writer Elizabeth David, the tiny town of Ribeauville in Alsace-Lorraine so loves kugelhopf that it sets aside a special day each year to celebrate its beginnings. The festivities include a marching brass band and local baking contest for the best kugelhopf.

1 cup golden raisins
1/3 cup light rum
3/4 cup finely chopped toasted almonds (Tip, page 262)
1 (1/4-oz.) package active dry yeast
1/2 cup sugar
1/4 cup warm water (110F, 45C)
3/4 cup unsalted butter or margarine, softened
4 eggs
3/4 cup milk
1 tablespoon freshly grated lemon zest
1 teaspoon salt
3-3/4 to 4-1/4 cups all-purpose flour
Powdered sugar for garnish

In a small bowl, combine raisins and rum; cover with plastic wrap. Microwave on HIGH 30 seconds; let stand 5 minutes. Or, combine raisins and rum in a small saucepan; bring to a simmer. Cover, remove from heat, and let stand 10 minutes. Generously grease a large kugelhopf mold or 10-cup Bundt pan. Sprinkle bottom and sides with 1/4 cup almonds; set aside. In a small bowl, dissolve yeast and 1 teaspoon of the granulated sugar in warm water. Let stand until foamy, 5 to 10 minutes. In large bowl of electric mixer, cream butter and remaining granulated sugar until light. Add eggs, one at a time, beating well after each addition. Slowly beat in yeast mixture and milk. Add lemon zest, salt, and 2-1/2 to 3 cups of the flour. Beat at medium speed with electric mixer 4 minutes, or 400 vigorous strokes by hand. Stir in raisins and rum, remaining 1/2 cup almonds, and enough remaining flour to make a stiff batter.

Turn batter into pan, smoothing top. Cover with buttered waxed paper or plastic wrap. Let rise until batter comes to within 1/2 inch of top of pan, about 2 hours.

Preheat oven to 375F (190C). Bake 50 to 60 minutes, or until a metal skewer inserted in center comes out clean. Remove from pan, inverting onto a rack. Cool at least 30 minutes. Just before serving, dust lightly with powdered sugar. Serve warm or at room temperature.

Makes 1 loaf.

Amaretto Bread

I won a professional cooking competition with this fragrant, crunchy almond bread. It's equally wonderful using toasted hazelnuts and Frangelico (hazelnut-flavored liqueur). Experiment to create your own favorite combination.

2 (1/4-oz.) packages active dry yeast
1/2 cup honey
1/2 cup warm water (110F, 45C)
2/3 cup milk
1/3 cup Amaretto (or other almond-flavored) liqueur
6 tablespoons unsalted butter or margarine, melted
2 eggs
1 teaspoon salt
2 teaspoons pure vanilla extract
Grated zest of 1 large lemon
4-1/4 to 4-3/4 cups bread or all-purpose flour
1 cup golden raisins
1-1/2 cups finely chopped toasted almonds (Tip, page 262)
2 tablespoons sugar

In large bowl of electric mixer, dissolve yeast and a teaspoon of the honey in warm water. Let stand until foamy, 5 to 10 minutes. Add remaining honey, milk, liqueur, butter, eggs, salt, vanilla, lemon zest, and 2 to 2-1/2 cups of the flour. Beat at medium speed with electric mixer 4 minutes, or 400 vigorous strokes by hand. Stir in raisins, 1 cup chopped almonds, and enough remaining flour to make a stiff batter. Cover with a slightly damp towel; set in a warm place free from drafts. Let rise until doubled in bulk, about 1-1/2 hours. Generously grease 2 (8" x 4") loaf pans or a 10-cup Bundt pan. Sprinkle bottom and sides of pan(s) with remaining 1/2 cup chopped almonds.

Stir down batter. Turn into prepared pan(s), smoothing top. Sprinkle 1 tablespoon sugar over top of batter in each loaf pan (not necessary for batter in Bundt pan). Cover pan(s) with buttered waxed paper or plastic wrap. Let rise until doubled in bulk, about 1 hour.

Preheat oven to 350F (175C). Bake 40 to 45 minutes for loaf pans, 45 to 50 minutes for Bundt pan, or until bread sounds hollow when tapped on the top. Remove from pans; cool on rack.

Makes 1 large or 2 medium loaves.

Variation

Honeyed Hazelnut Bread: Substitute 1/3 cup Frangelico liqueur for the Amaretto, and 1-1/2 cups chopped toasted hazelnuts for the almonds.

Toasted Oat Bran Bread

*Y*ou can use regular oat bran in this recipe, but toasting it gives the bread a wholesome, nutty flavor. Simply put the oat bran in a large, ungreased skillet and cook over medium heat 2 to 3 minutes, stirring often, until golden brown.

> **2 (1/4-oz.) packages active dry yeast**
> **1/3 cup honey**
> **1 cup warm water (110F, 45C)**
> **1/3 cup nonfat milk powder**
> **1 egg**
> **2 tablespoons unsalted butter or margarine, melted**
> **1-1/2 teaspoons salt**
> **3/4 cup plus 3 tablespoons toasted oat bran**
> **2-1/4 to 2-3/4 cups bread or all-purpose flour**

In large bowl of electric mixer, dissolve yeast and 1 teaspoon honey in warm water. Let stand until foamy, 5 to 10 minutes. Add remaining honey, milk powder, egg, butter, salt, 3/4 cup oat bran, and 1 to 1-1/2 cups of the flour. Beat at medium speed with electric mixer 4 minutes, or 400 vigorous strokes by hand. Stir in enough remaining flour to make a stiff batter. Cover with a slightly damp towel; set in a warm place free from drafts. Let rise until doubled in bulk, 1 to 1-1/2 hours. Generously grease a 9" x 5" loaf pan or 2-quart casserole dish. Sprinkle bottom and sides of pan with 2 tablespoons oat bran; set aside.

Stir down batter. Turn into prepared pan. Smooth top and sprinkle with remaining tablespoon oat bran. Cover with buttered waxed paper or plastic wrap. Let rise until doubled in bulk, about 45 minutes. Preheat oven to 375F (190C). Bake 35 to 40 minutes, or until bread sounds hollow when tapped on the bottom. Remove from pans; cool on rack.

Makes 1 loaf.

Reuben Rye

*S*auerkraut gives this hearty loaf a delicious tang that makes it a great partner with smoked meats and a natural for Reuben sandwiches. If you want even more zip, substitute 1/2 cup sauerkraut juice for 1/2 cup of the beer.

2 (1/4-oz.) packages active dry yeast
2-1/2 tablespoons molasses
1/2 cup warm water (110F, 45C)
1-1/2 cups beer, room temperature
1 cup well-drained, chopped sauerkraut
1 egg
3 tablespoons vegetable oil
1 tablespoon caraway or fennel seeds
1 teaspoon salt
1/2 teaspoon freshly ground pepper
2-3/4 to 3-1/4 cups bread or all-purpose flour
2 cups medium rye flour

In large bowl of electric mixer, dissolve yeast and 1/2 tablespoon of the molasses in warm water. Let stand until foamy, 5 to 10 minutes. Add remaining 2 tablespoons molasses, beer, sauerkraut, egg, oil, caraway or fennel seeds, salt, pepper, and 2 to 2-1/2 cups of the bread flour. Beat at medium speed with electric mixer 4 minutes, or 400 vigorous strokes by hand. Stir in rye flour and enough remaining bread flour to make a stiff batter. Cover with a slightly damp towel; set in a warm place free from drafts. Let rise until doubled in bulk, about 1-1/2 hours. Grease 2 (9" x 5") loaf pans or 2-quart casserole dishes; set aside.

Stir down batter. Divide evenly between prepared pans, smoothing tops. Cover with buttered waxed paper or plastic wrap. Let rise until doubled in bulk, about 45 minutes.

Preheat oven to 400F (205C). Bake 35 to 45 minutes, or until bread sounds hollow when tapped on the bottom. Remove from pans; cool on racks.

Makes 2 loaves.

Sun-Kissed Prune Bread

*T*he sunny flavors of orange and lemon make this bread a great eye-opener. Toast it and spread with Orange Cream (page 263) or use for French toast—what a treat! Sticky dried fruits like prunes are easier to handle if they're first tossed with a little flour to separate the pieces. If you absolutely detest prunes, substitute an equal amount of chopped dried apricots.

> 2 (1/4-oz.) packages active dry yeast
> 1/2 cup packed brown sugar
> 1-1/2 cups warm orange juice (110F, 45C)
> 2/3 cup nonfat milk powder
> 1/4 cup vegetable oil
> 2 teaspoons freshly grated lemon zest
> 2 teaspoons freshly grated orange zest
> 1-1/2 teaspoons ground cinnamon
> 1/2 teaspoon ground nutmeg
> 2 teaspoons salt
> About 4-3/4 cups bread or all-purpose flour
> 1 cup chopped pitted prunes
> 3/4 cup toasted chopped walnuts
> 1 tablespoon unsalted butter, melted

In large bowl of electric mixer, dissolve yeast and 1 tablespoon of the sugar in orange juice. Let stand until foamy, 5 to 10 minutes. Add remaining sugar, milk powder, oil, lemon and orange zest, cinnamon, nutmeg, salt, and 2-1/2 to 3 cups of the flour. Beat at medium speed with electric mixer 4 minutes, or 400 vigorous strokes by hand. Stir in enough remaining flour to make a very stiff batter. Cover with a slightly damp towel; set in a warm place free from drafts. Let rise until doubled in bulk, about 1 hour. In a medium-size bowl, combine prunes with 2 tablespoons of the flour. Toss to separate and thoroughly coat prunes with flour, discarding excess flour; set aside. Grease and flour 2 (1-pound) coffee cans or 1-1/2-quart casserole or soufflé dishes; set aside.

Stir down batter. Add floured prunes and nuts; stir until evenly distributed. Turn into prepared cans or dishes. Smooth tops; brush with melted butter. Cover with buttered waxed paper or plastic wrap. Let rise until doubled in bulk, about 1 hour.

Preheat oven to 375F (190C). Bake 35 to 40 minutes, or until bread sounds hollow when tapped on the surface with your fingertips. Remove from pans. Brush melted butter over top. Cool on racks.

Makes 2 loaves.

Wheaty Waldorf Bread

*T*his satisfying bread was inspired by the classic Waldorf salad, which combines apples, walnuts, and mayonnaise. The mayo is the only fat in this bread and since fat makes bread tender, it's important that you don't use nonfat mayonnaise. It's not necessary to peel the apples here—leaving the peel on adds color and texture.

 2 (1/4-oz.) packages active dry yeast
 1/3 cup packed brown sugar
 1/3 cup warm water (110F, 45C)
 1 (12-oz.) can evaporated milk
 1/4 cup mayonnaise
 1-1/2 teaspoons salt
 1/2 teaspoon ground nutmeg
 1/2 teaspoon ground cinnamon
 1-1/2 cups whole-wheat flour
 2-1/2 to 3 cups bread or all-purpose flour
 1 cup finely chopped apples
 3/4 cup toasted chopped walnuts
 1 teaspoon mayonnaise or butter, melted

In large bowl of electric mixer, dissolve yeast and a teaspoon of the sugar in warm water. Let stand until foamy, 5 to 10 minutes. Add remaining sugar, milk, mayonnaise, salt, nutmeg, cinnamon, whole-wheat flour, and 1 to 1-1/2 cups of the bread flour. Beat at medium speed with electric mixer 4 minutes, or 400 vigorous strokes by hand. Stir in apples, nuts, and enough remaining flour to make a stiff batter. Cover with a slightly damp towel; set in a warm place free from drafts. Let rise until doubled in bulk, 1-1/2 to 2 hours. Grease 2 (8" x 4") loaf pans or 1-1/2-quart casserole dishes; set aside.

Stir down batter. Spoon equally into prepared pans, smoothing tops. Cover with buttered waxed paper or plastic wrap. Let rise until doubled in bulk, about 1 hour.

Preheat oven to 375F (190C). Gently brush melted mayonnaise or butter over tops of loaves. Bake 30 to 40 minutes, or until bread sounds hollow when tapped on the bottom. Remove from pans; cool on racks.

Makes 2 loaves.

Jalapeño Nacho Bread

*T*his bread is great served with chili and immensely satisfying for snacks. The amount of jalapeños you use depends on how much heat your palate can take. Either canned or fresh jalapeños are suitable for this bread. Canned are by far the quickest form because they come already diced. Caution is the watchword when handling fresh jalapeños because their seeds and membranes contain oils that can severely irritate skin and eyes. Either wear rubber gloves or don't touch your face after cutting chiles until you thoroughly wash your hands.

1 (1/4-oz.) package active dry yeast
2 teaspoons sugar
1/4 cup warm water (110F, 45C)
2 cups milk
2 tablespoons vegetable oil
1 to 3 tablespoons diced jalapeño chiles
1-1/2 teaspoons salt
3/4 cup cornmeal
3-1/2 to 4 cups bread or all-purpose flour
1/2 cup finely crushed tortilla chips
1 cup coarsely crushed tortilla chips
1-1/2 cups grated sharp Cheddar cheese

In large bowl of electric mixer, dissolve yeast and sugar in warm water. Let stand until foamy, 5 to 10 minutes. Add milk, oil, jalapeños, salt, cornmeal, and 2 to 2-1/2 cups flour. Beat at medium speed with electric mixer 4 minutes, or 400 vigorous strokes by hand. Stir in enough remaining flour to make a stiff batter. Cover with a slightly damp towel; set in a warm place free from drafts. Let rise until doubled in bulk, about 1 hour. Generously grease 2 (8" x 4") loaf pans. Sprinkle 2 tablespoons finely crushed tortilla chips over bottom and sides of each pan; set aside.

Stir down batter. Stir in 1 cup coarsely crushed tortilla chips and 1 cup cheese until evenly distributed. Divide batter evenly between prepared pans. Smooth tops, sprinkling each with 1/4 cup remaining cheese, then 2 tablespoons finely crushed tortilla chips. Cover with buttered waxed paper or plastic wrap. Let rise until doubled in bulk, about 45 minutes.

Preheat oven to 375F (190C). Bake 35 to 40 minutes, or until bread sounds hollow when tapped on the bottom. Remove from pans; cool on racks.

Makes 2 loaves.

Three-Pepper Fennel Bread

*T*he lively trio of Tabasco sauce, cayenne, and black pepper add a distinctive pizzazz to this bread. Though it's not necessary, toasting the fennel seeds (see Tip, page 262) brings out their flavor.

1 (1/4-oz.) package active dry yeast
2 tablespoons sugar
1/4 cup warm water (110F, 45C)
1 cup creamed cottage cheese
2 eggs
2 tablespoons olive oil
2 tablespoons chopped fresh chives
4 teaspoons fennel seeds
1 teaspoon salt
1/2 teaspoon Tabasco sauce
1/2 teaspoon freshly ground black pepper
1/4 teaspoon red (cayenne) pepper
1-3/4 to 2-1/4 cups bread or all-purpose flour
1 egg white mixed with 1 tablespoon water for glaze

In large bowl of electric mixer, dissolve yeast and a pinch of the sugar in warm water. Let stand until foamy, 5 to 10 minutes. Add remaining sugar, cottage cheese, eggs, oil, chives, 3-1/2 teaspoons fennel seeds, salt, Tabasco sauce, black pepper, cayenne, and 1 to 1-1/2 cups of the flour. Beat at medium speed with electric mixer 4 minutes, or 400 vigorous strokes by hand. Stir in enough remaining flour to make a stiff batter. Cover with a slightly damp towel; set in a warm place free from drafts. Let rise until doubled in bulk, about 1-1/2 hours. Grease and flour a 2-quart casserole dish or a 9" x 5" loaf pan; set aside.

Stir down batter. Turn into prepared pan, smoothing top. Brush with egg-white glaze; sprinkle with remaining 1/2 teaspoon fennel seeds. Cover with buttered waxed paper or plastic wrap. Let rise until doubled in bulk, 45 to 60 minutes.

Preheat oven to 350F (175C). Bake 30 to 40 minutes, or until bread sounds hollow when tapped on the top. Remove from pan; cool on rack.

Makes 1 loaf.

Peanut Butter–Bacon Bread

This is one of my favorite breads. It's great for bacon, lettuce, and tomato sandwiches and enticingly fragrant when toasted. The bacon fat adds a wonderful flavor to this bread, but if you're watching cholesterol, substitute the same amount of vegetable oil.

1/2 pound bacon
2 (1/4-oz.) packages active dry yeast
1/3 cup packed brown sugar
1/3 cup warm water (110F, 45C)
2 eggs
1/2 cup chunky peanut butter
3/4 cup milk
1 teaspoon salt
2-3/4 to 3-1/4 cups bread or all-purpose flour
Melted unsalted butter or margarine

Cook bacon until crisp; drain on paper towels. Crumble bacon when cool; set aside. Reserve about 2-1/2 tablespoons bacon drippings.

In large bowl of electric mixer, dissolve yeast and 1 teaspoon of the sugar in warm water. Let stand until foamy, 5 to 10 minutes. Add remaining sugar, eggs, peanut butter, milk, 2 tablespoons reserved bacon drippings, salt, and 1-1/2 to 2-1/4 cups of the flour. Beat at medium speed with electric mixer 4 minutes, or 400 vigorous strokes by hand. Stir in enough remaining flour to make a very stiff batter. Cover with a slightly damp towel; set in a warm place free from drafts. Let rise until doubled in bulk, about 1-1/2 hours. Generously grease a 9" x 5" loaf pan or 2-quart casserole dish; set aside.

Stir down batter. Add bacon; stir until evenly distributed. Turn into prepared pan. Smooth top and brush with 1 teaspoon bacon drippings. Cover with buttered waxed paper or plastic wrap; set in warm place free from drafts. Let rise until doubled in bulk, about 45 minutes.

Preheat oven to 375F (190C). Bake 35 to 40 minutes, or until bread sounds hollow when tapped on the bottom. Remove from pan; cool on rack.

Makes 1 loaf.

Triple-Corn Batter Bread

*F*resh corn kernels, corn puree, and cornmeal combine in this triple-treat, herb-scented bread. You can make it out of season with frozen, uncooked corn kernels, but the flavor won't be as rich.

1 (1/4-oz.) package active dry yeast
2 tablespoons sugar
1/4 cup warm water (110F, 45C)
2 cups fresh corn kernels
About 1-1/2 cups buttermilk
2 tablespoons vegetable oil
2 teaspoons salt
1-1/2 teaspoons minced fresh basil or 1/2 teaspoon dried basil
1-1/2 teaspoons minced fresh tarragon or 1/2 teaspoon dried tarragon
1/2 cup plus 2 tablespoons cornmeal
3-1/2 to 4 cups bread or all-purpose flour

In large bowl of electric mixer, dissolve yeast and 1 teaspoon of the sugar in warm water. Let stand until foamy, 5 to 10 minutes. In a blender, puree 1 cup corn with remaining sugar. Add enough buttermilk to corn puree to measure 2 cups. Add to yeast mixture along with oil, salt, basil, tarragon, 1/2 cup cornmeal, and 2 to 2-1/2 cups flour. Beat at medium speed with electric mixer 4 minutes, or 400 vigorous strokes by hand. Stir in remaining 1 cup corn kernels and enough remaining flour to make a stiff batter. Cover with a slightly damp towel; set in a warm place free from drafts. Let rise until doubled in bulk, 1 to 1-1/2 hours. Grease 2 (8" x 4") loaf pans or 1-1/2-quart casserole dishes. Sprinkle 1 tablespoon cornmeal over bottom and sides of each pan; set aside.

Stir down batter. Divide evenly between prepared pans, smoothing tops. Cover with buttered waxed paper or plastic wrap. Let rise until doubled in bulk, about 45 minutes.

Preheat oven to 375F (190C). Bake 35 to 40 minutes, or until bread sounds hollow when tapped on the bottom. Remove from pans; cool on racks.

Makes 2 loaves.

Italian Sausage Bread

*T*his is one of the most versatile recipes in this book. It makes a hearty partner for breakfast eggs, a meal with soups, and an ideal picnic food. Either mild or hot Italian sausage will work for this bread; I like to use half a pound of each. A low-fat chicken or turkey sausage can also be used, but probably won't render the 2 tablespoons fat necessary for this bread. If that's the case, simply substitute olive oil.

1 pound Italian sausage
2 (1/4-oz.) packages active dry yeast
3 tablespoons packed brown sugar
1/2 cup warm water (110F, 45C)
1-1/2 cups milk
1 egg
1 teaspoon salt
1/2 teaspoon freshly ground pepper
1-1/2 teaspoons minced fresh basil or 1/2 teaspoon dried basil
4-3/4 to 5-1/4 cups bread or all-purpose flour

Remove sausage from casings. In a large skillet over medium-high heat, cook sausage until crisp and brown, crumbling it into small pieces as it cooks. Remove from skillet with slotted spoon; drain well on paper towels. Set aside. Reserve 2 tablespoons sausage drippings.

In large bowl of electric mixer, dissolve yeast and 1 teaspoon of the sugar in warm water. Let stand until foamy, 5 to 10 minutes. Add remaining sugar, milk, egg, salt, pepper, basil, reserved sausage drippings, and 3 to 3-1/2 cups of the flour. Beat at medium speed with electric mixer 4 minutes, or 400 vigorous strokes by hand. Stir in crumbled sausage and enough remaining flour to make a stiff batter. Cover with a slightly damp towel; set in a warm place free from drafts. Let rise until doubled in bulk, about 1 hour. Grease 2 (9" x 5") loaf pans or 2-quart casserole dishes; set aside.

Stir down batter. Divide evenly between prepared pans, smoothing tops. Cover with buttered waxed paper or plastic wrap. Let rise until doubled in bulk, 30 to 45 minutes.

Preheat oven to 400F (205C). Bake 35 to 40 minutes, or until bread sounds hollow when tapped on the bottom. Remove from pans; cool on racks. Refrigerate leftovers.

Makes 2 loaves.

Gingered Hawaiian Bread

*F*resh gingerroot has a flavor completely different from that of powdered ginger. Use a paring knife to remove the thin brown skin before mincing the ginger. Cover chunks of leftover, peeled ginger with sherry and store in the refrigerator for up to three months.

2 (1/4-oz.) packages active dry yeast
1-1/2 cups warm pineapple juice (110F, 45C)
1/2 cup sugar
1 cup mashed potatoes
2 eggs
1/4 cup minced fresh gingerroot
1/4 cup plus 1 tablespoon unsalted butter, melted
1 teaspoon salt
1 teaspoon pure vanilla extract
1/4 teaspoon ground ginger
4-1/2 to 5 cups bread or all-purpose flour

In large bowl of electric mixer, dissolve yeast in pineapple juice. Let stand until foamy, 5 to 10 minutes. Add sugar, mashed potatoes, eggs, gingerroot, 1/4 cup butter, salt, vanilla, ground ginger, and 2 to 2-1/2 cups of the flour. Beat at medium speed with electric mixer 4 minutes, or 400 vigorous strokes by hand. Stir in enough remaining flour to make a stiff batter. Cover with a slightly damp towel; set in a warm place free from drafts. Let rise until doubled in bulk, about 1 hour. Grease 2 (9" x 5") loaf pans or 2-quart casserole dishes; set aside.

Stir down batter. Divide evenly between prepared pans, smoothing tops. Cover with buttered waxed paper or plastic wrap. Let rise until doubled in bulk, about 45 minutes.

Preheat oven to 375F (190C). Bake 30 to 40 minutes, or until bread sounds hollow when tapped on the bottom. For browner bottom crusts, remove bread from pans and place directly on oven rack during final 5 minutes of baking time. Brush tops with remaining tablespoon melted butter. Cool on racks.

Makes 2 loaves.

Little Yeast Breads

Don't think of little breads only as muffins and biscuits. There are dozens of little yeast creations that are so easy to make they'll soon be a regular part of your repertoire. They're the perfect answer for on-the-run breakfasts, lunch or dinner accompaniments, or quick and delicious snacks. In short, they're great for almost any occasion!

Bagels are little yeast breads the entire family can enjoy making. How do you make a bagel? Well, according to an old Yiddish recipe, "First you take a hole, then you put some dough around it." One of the many legends of the bagel's origin is that it was created by a Viennese baker in 1683 in honor of the Polish prince who liberated Vienna from Turkish invaders. The ring-shaped bread was supposedly shaped like the prince's stirrup, or *buegal*. Whatever its origin, there are few breads as satisfyingly chewy as the bagel. This chewiness is in part the result of simmering bagels in lightly sugared water before baking them. The water bath also reduces the bagel's starch content and produces their famous sheen and sturdy crust.

In sharp contrast to the earthy bagels are the elegant, buttery Danish pastries and croissants. These two flaky creations are the perfect way to begin your day in sensory splendor. The main difference between croissants and Danish pastry is that Danish pastry dough doesn't require the lengthy rising period of croissant dough. Both require keeping butter and dough chilled during the forming process. Don't be intimidated by the long recipes for croissants and Danish pastries; they're time consuming, but not really difficult. If you love pastries but haven't the time for croissants or Danish, try the Quick Cheese Pastries. They take only 1-1/2 hours from start to finish and taste like they took days!

This chapter offers a bevy of little yeast breads from which to choose, so get busy and have fun. And involve the whole family—little yeast breads are just the right size for little hands. Unlike quick breads, most of the doughs won't suffer from overhandling while serious little bakers get it just right.

Quick Cheese Pastries

These buttery pastries have a citrus-cheese filling and take only about 1-1/2 hours from start to finish.

>   1 (1/4-oz.) package active dry yeast
>   2 tablespoons sugar
>   1/4 cup warm water (110F, 45C)
>   2-1/4 cups all-purpose flour
>   1/4 teaspoon salt
>   1 cup cold unsalted butter, cut into 16 pieces
>   1 egg
>   1 teaspoon pure vanilla extract
>   Sweet Cheese Filling, see below
>   1 cup finely chopped walnuts or pecans
>   1 egg yolk mixed with 1 tablespoon cream for glaze
>   Powdered sugar

Sweet Cheese Filling:
>   2 (3-oz.) packages cream cheese, softened
>   3/4 cup sugar
>   1/2 teaspoon ground cinnamon
>   1-1/2 teaspoons freshly grated lemon zest
>   1-1/2 teaspoons freshly grated orange zest

In a small bowl, dissolve yeast and 1 teaspoon of the sugar in warm water. Let stand until foamy, 5 to 10 minutes. In a large bowl, combine remaining sugar, flour, and salt. Use a pastry cutter or 2 knives to cut butter into flour mixture until mixture resembles coarse crumbs; set aside. Stir egg and vanilla into yeast mixture. Stir into flour mixture until combined but still crumbly. Turn out onto a well-floured surface.

Knead 12 to 15 strokes, or only until dough holds together. Dough will be very moist and sticky. Use a pastry scraper or metal spatula to scrape dough off work surface. Divide dough in half. Wrap each half in plastic wrap; refrigerate. Lightly grease 2 large baking sheets; set aside. Prepare Sweet Cheese Filling; set aside.

Preheat oven to 375F (190C). Remove half of dough from refrigerator. On a well-floured surface, roll out dough into a 20" x 10" rectangle. Spread with half of Sweet Cheese Filling mixture; sprinkle with 1/2 cup chopped nuts. Loosen pastry from work surface with pastry scraper or metal spatula. Fold dough in half lengthwise. Cut into 20 (1-inch) strips. Holding each strip at both ends, twist in opposite directions twice, forming a spiral. Place 1-1/2 inches apart on prepared baking sheets, pressing ends down lightly to secure. Repeat with remaining dough. Pastries may be covered and refrigerated overnight at this point. If refrigerated, let sit 30 minutes at room temperature before baking. Brush pastries with egg-yolk glaze. Bake in preheated oven 15 to 25 minutes, or until golden brown. Transfer to racks; dust lightly with powdered sugar. Serve slightly warm or at room temperature.

Makes about 40 pastries.

Sweet Cheese Filling: In small bowl of electric mixer or a food processor fitted with a metal blade, beat all ingredients until light and creamy.

TIP: Using the food processor to cut butter or other fat into flour is quick, easy, and effortless. Use the metal blade to combine the flour with any other dry ingredients. With the machine off, add the cold butter. Using quick ON/OFF pulses, process until the mixture resembles coarse crumbs. The pulsing is an important technique. Letting the machine run could overprocess the mixture, thereby creating a baked good that's dense, rather than flaky.

Old-Fashioned Cinnamon Rolls

*S*hape and refrigerate these big, beautiful rolls the night before for hassle-free raves the next morning. Cinnamon in the glaze gives these rolls double-spice goodness. For a triple treat, serve them with Cinnamon Cream (page 263). Once the rolls are baked, separate by gently pulling them apart with two forks positioned back-to-back. If you like your rolls gooey-good, be sure to try the Maple-Nut Sticky Buns variation, opposite.

Basic Sweet Yeast Dough (page 82)
Cinnamon-Nut Filling, see below
3 tablespoons unsalted butter, softened
Cinnamon Glaze, see below

Cinnamon-Nut Filling:
3/4 cup packed brown sugar
2 teaspoons ground cinnamon
1 cup chopped toasted walnuts or pecans (Tip, page 262)

Cinnamon Glaze:
1 cup powdered sugar
1/4 teaspoon ground cinnamon
1/2 teaspoon pure vanilla extract
1 to 2 tablespoons half-and-half or milk

Prepare Basic Sweet Yeast Dough as directed through first rising.

Punch down dough; knead 30 seconds. Cover dough; let stand 10 minutes. Grease a 13" x 9" baking pan; set aside. Prepare Cinnamon-Nut Filling; set aside. On a lightly floured surface, roll out dough into a 24" x 12" rectangle. Spread with butter, leaving 1/2 inch unbuttered on 1 narrow end. Sprinkle buttered area evenly with Cinnamon-Nut Filling. Use your fingers or the back of a spoon to lightly press filling into surface of dough. Beginning on buttered short side, roll up tightly, jelly-roll fashion. Pinch seam to seal. Cut roll into 12 equal slices. Arrange cut side down and about 1/2 inch apart in prepared pan. Cover tightly with plastic wrap. (May be refrigerated overnight at this point.) Set in a warm place free from drafts. Let rise until doubled in bulk, about 1-1/2 hours (2 hours if dough has been refrigerated).

Preheat oven to 375F (190C). Bake 30 to 35 minutes, or until deep golden brown. Prepare Cinnamon Glaze. Transfer rolls to a rack set over waxed paper; drizzle with glaze.

Makes 12 large rolls.

Cinnamon-Nut Filling:

In a small bowl, stir together sugar, cinnamon, and nuts.

Cinnamon Glaze:

In a small bowl, stir together powdered sugar and cinnamon. Stir in vanilla and enough half-and-half to make a smooth and creamy glaze of drizzling consistency.

Variation

Maple-Nut Sticky Buns: Before arranging cut rolls in baking pan, combine 1/2 cup pure maple syrup, 1/4 cup packed brown sugar, 1/3 cup butter, and 1/4 teaspoon salt in a small saucepan. Cook over medium heat, stirring occasionally, just until sugar melts. Pour into baking pan; sprinkle evenly with 1 cup chopped nuts. Arrange rolls on top of syrup. Cover, let rise, and bake as directed above. Let rolls stand in pan 1 minute before inverting onto a serving platter. Spoon any topping remaining in pan over rolls. Let stand 5 minutes before serving.

TIP: To cut rolled dough into slices, wrap a long piece of thread around area to be cut; slowly pull thread ends together until it slices through cleanly. This technique also works for delicate breads.

Best-Ever Bagels

The earliest mention of bagels was in 1610 in Krakow, Poland, when the town council decreed that bagels were to be given only to women in childbirth and their attendants, perhaps as a symbol of the endless circle of life. If you like chewy bagels, you'll love these. Bagels made without fat are chewier than their counterparts, egg bagels. Potato water (water in which peeled potatoes have been cooked) adds starch, which also contributes to chewiness.

1 (1/4-oz.) package active dry yeast
About 4 tablespoons sugar
1-1/2 cups warm potato water or plain water (110F, 45C)
2 teaspoons salt
4 to 4-1/2 cups bread or all-purpose flour
3 quarts water
1 egg yolk mixed with 1 tablespoon water for glaze
Coarse salt, minced onion, sesame seeds, poppy seeds, or caraway seeds for topping
  (optional)

In large bowl of electric mixer, dissolve yeast and 1 teaspoon sugar in warm water. Let stand until foamy, 5 to 10 minutes. Add 2 tablespoons sugar, salt, and 2 to 2-1/2 cups of the flour. Beat at medium speed with electric mixer 2 minutes, or beat 200 vigorous strokes by hand. Stir in enough remaining flour to make a soft dough. Change to dough hook(s) if using mixer, or turn out dough onto a lightly floured surface.

Knead dough 8 to 10 minutes, or until smooth and elastic, adding only enough flour to prevent sticking. Clean and butter bowl. Place dough in bowl, turning to coat all surfaces. Cover with a slightly damp towel; set in a warm place free from drafts. Let rise until doubled in bulk, about 1 hour.

Punch down dough; knead 30 seconds. Divide dough into 14 pieces. Roll each piece into a cigar shape about 8 inches long. Hold one end of dough with thumb and index finger; wrap dough around hand to form a doughnut shape. Moisten ends slightly with water; pinch firmly to seal. Or, shape each piece of dough into a ball; flatten slightly. Press your thumb through center of ball, gently enlarging hole and smoothing edges. Place bagels on lightly floured surface. Cover with a dry towel; set in a warm place free from drafts 10 minutes. Grease 2 large baking sheets; set aside.

Preheat oven to 375F (190C). In a large pot or kettle, combine 2 tablespoons sugar and 3 quarts water; bring to a boil. Reduce heat so water boils gently. Using a slotted spoon, carefully lower bagels into water, one at a time. Cook 3 to 4 bagels at a time. Bagels will sink, then rise to surface almost immediately. Boil 30 seconds on each side, turning with slotted spoon. Remove from water with slotted spoon; blot on paper towels. Place boiled bagels on prepared baking sheets. Brush with egg-yolk glaze; sprinkle with desired topping. Bake 25 to 30 minutes, or until golden brown. Transfer to racks to cool.

Makes 14 bagels.

Variations

Egg Bagels: Reduce water to 1 cup; add 2 eggs.

Beer-Rye Bagels: Substitute a 12-ounce can or bottle of warm beer (110F, 45C) for 1-1/2 cups warm water. Substitute 1-1/2 cups rye flour for 1-1/2 cups bread flour. Add 1 tablespoon each caraway seeds and freshly grated orange zest. Sprinkle tops with caraway seeds.

Cheese Bagels: Reduce salt to 1-1/2 teaspoons; add 1 cup grated Cheddar, Swiss, Jack, Gouda, or other cheese. Knead in cheese during first kneading.

Almond-Raisin Bagels: Add 1/2 cup finely chopped, toasted almonds, 1 cup raisins, 1 teaspoon pure vanilla, 1 teaspoon grated lemon zest, and 1/2 teaspoon each ground cinnamon and ground nutmeg. Knead in raisins and nuts during first kneading.

Whole-Wheat Bagels: Substitute 2 cups whole-wheat flour for 2 cups bread flour, and 2 tablespoons honey for 2 tablespoons sugar.

Onion Bagels: Sauté 1/2 cup finely chopped onions in 1 tablespoon butter until soft. Add with second addition of flour.

Seed Bagels: Add 1 tablespoon poppy seeds, 1 tablespoon caraway seeds, or 2 tablespoons toasted sesame seeds with first addition of flour. Sprinkle same seeds over tops of boiled, glazed bagels.

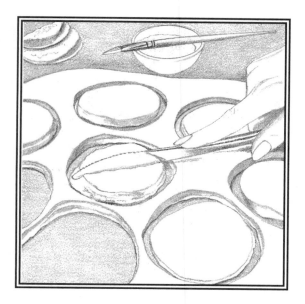 

Rolls & Buns

*U*se your favorite bread dough recipe and vary the shape according to your preference. The following yields are for the Basic White Bread dough—other recipes may yield more or less.

1 recipe Basic White Bread (page 32) or other bread dough
Melted butter, milk, or 1 egg white mixed with 2 teaspoons water for glaze

Prepare Basic White Bread dough or other bread dough through first rising. Punch down dough and shape as desired. Cover with buttered waxed paper and let rise until doubled in bulk, 30 to 45 minutes. Preheat oven to 375F (190C). Bake about 15 minutes, or until golden brown.

Parker House Rolls: Grease 2 large baking sheets; set aside. Roll out dough until 1/2 inch thick. With a floured 3- to 3-1/2-inch biscuit cutter or inverted drinking glass, cut out dough. With the back edge of a knife, make a crease barely off-center. Fold at crease, pressing down slightly. Place rolls 2 inches apart on prepared baking sheets. Let rise; brush with melted butter. Sprinkle with sesame or other seeds, if desired. Bake as directed.
Makes 20 to 25 rolls.

Cloverleaf Rolls: Grease 24 muffin cups; set aside. Divide dough into 24 pieces. Separate each piece into 3 portions; roll each into a smooth ball. Place 3 balls in each prepared muffin cup. Let rise; brush with melted butter or milk. Bake as directed.
Makes about 24 rolls.

Spiral Rolls: Grease 2 large baking sheets; set aside. Divide dough into 24 pieces. Shape each piece into a 12-inch rope. Shape each rope into a tight spiral, tucking end under and pinching to seal. Place 2 inches apart on prepared baking sheets; flatten slightly with your palm. Let rise. Brush with egg glaze; sprinkle with sesame or poppy seeds, if desired. Bake as directed.
Makes 24 rolls.

Knot-Shaped Rolls: Grease 2 large baking sheets; set aside. Divide dough into 24 pieces. Shape each piece into a 12-inch rope. Tie each rope into a loose knot. Place rolls 2 inches apart on prepared baking sheets. Let rise; brush with melted butter. Bake as directed.
Makes 24 rolls.

Oval or Round Rolls: Grease 2 large baking sheets; set aside. Divide dough into 24 pieces. For Oval Rolls: Shape each piece into a football-shape, slightly tapering ends. For Round Rolls: Form each piece into a smooth ball, pinching underside to seal. Place rolls 2 inches apart on prepared baking sheets. Let rise. With a razor blade, cut a 1/4-inch-deep slash lengthwise down center top of oval rolls; cut a cross in top of round rolls. Brush with egg-white glaze. Bake as directed.
Makes 24 rolls.

Pan Rolls: Grease a 13" x 9" baking pan; set aside. Divide dough into 24 smooth balls. Place balls in prepared pan in 6 rows of 4 each. Let rise; brush with melted butter or milk. Bake as directed. **Makes 24 rolls.**

Handprint Rolls: Grease 2 large baking sheets; set aside. Roll out dough to a 1/2-inch thickness. Place your hand, palm down and fingers spread, on surface of dough. Using a sharp knife, cut around hand. Place cutouts 2 inches apart on prepared baking sheets, curving fingers as desired. Let rise; brush with egg-white glaze. Bake as directed. **Makes about 8 to 12 rolls.**

Hamburger or Hot Dog Buns: Grease 2 large baking sheets; set aside. Divide dough into 18 pieces. For Hamburger Buns: Shape each piece into a smooth ball; flatten into a 5-inch circle. For Hot Dog Buns: Shape each piece into a 6-inch-long rope. Place buns 2 inches apart on prepared baking sheets. Let rise; brush with butter. Bake 20 to 25 minutes or until golden brown. **Makes 18 buns.**

Onion Buns: In a large skillet over medium heat, sauté 1-1/4 cups finely chopped onions in the 1/4 cup butter called for in Basic White Bread recipe until soft. Cool to room temperature. Reserve 3 tablespoons cooked onions for topping. Stir remaining onions into flour mixture. Complete bread through first rising. Grease 2 large baking sheets; set aside. Divide dough into 18 pieces; shape as for Hamburger Buns. Place 2 inches apart on prepared baking sheets. Press some of reserved cooked onions into surface of each bun. Let rise. Bake 20 to 25 minutes or until golden brown. **Makes 18 buns.**

Whole-Wheat Pita

*A*lso called pocket bread, this Middle Eastern flat bread is perfect for sandwiches. Simply cut in half crosswise and fill each half with meat, cheese, avocado, bacon, alfalfa sprouts, or chicken, tuna, or egg salad. Or, split pitas horizontally, cut into wedges, toast in the oven until crisp, and use for dips.

1 (1/4-oz.) package active dry yeast
1/2 teaspoon sugar
1-1/2 cups warm water (110F, 45C)
2 teaspoons salt
2 tablespoons vegetable oil
2-1/2 to 3 cups bread or all-purpose flour
2 cups whole-wheat flour
Sesame seeds (optional)
Cornmeal

In large bowl of electric mixer, dissolve yeast and sugar in warm water; let stand until foamy, 5 to 10 minutes. Add salt, oil, and 2 to 2-1/2 cups bread flour. Beat at medium speed with electric mixer 2 minutes, or beat 200 vigorous strokes by hand. Stir in whole-wheat flour and enough remaining bread flour to make a soft dough. Change to dough hook(s) if using mixer, or turn out dough onto a lightly floured surface.

Knead dough 8 to 10 minutes, or until smooth and elastic, adding only enough flour to prevent sticking. Roll dough into a 12-inch rope; cut into 12 equal pieces. Shape each piece into a smooth ball, pulling sides of dough to center bottom. Pinch dough at bottom to seal. Cover with a dry towel; let stand 10 minutes. On a lightly floured surface, roll each ball into a 6-inch round. If desired, sprinkle with sesame seeds; press lightly into surface. Place rounds about 1 inch apart on a lightly floured surface. Cover with dry towels; set in a warm place free from drafts. Let rise until almost doubled in bulk, about 30 minutes.

Arrange 1 oven shelf at lowest position possible; the second shelf at the center position. Preheat oven 15 minutes at 500F (260C). Lightly sprinkle 2 large baking sheets with cornmeal. Using a spatula, gently transfer 3 to 4 rounds to prepared baking sheets. Set 1 baking sheet aside; place the other baking sheet on lower shelf of preheated oven. Bake pita 3 to 4 minutes, or until puffed. Move baking sheet with puffed pita to upper oven shelf. Place second baking sheet on bottom shelf. Work quickly to avoid loss of oven heat. Bake pitas on top shelf 2 to 4 minutes longer, or until pale golden. Remove from oven. Continue baking pitas and rotating their placement in oven until all rounds are baked. Cool pitas on racks 3 minutes before stacking them together in a plastic bag. Seal bag; set aside for pitas to soften. Serve warm, or cool completely and store in plastic bags. Serve within 1 to 2 days or wrap airtight and freeze.

Makes 12 pitas.

Variations

Pumpernickel Pita: Add 1 tablespoon unsweetened cocoa and 1 teaspoon caraway seeds. Substitute 2 cups rye flour for 2 cups whole-wheat flour.

White Pita: Substitute 2 cups bread or all-purpose flour for whole-wheat flour.

Cinnamon Crispies

*T*hese big, thin, crispy spirals are perfect for Sunday brunch. They take a lot of room (only 6 rolls fit on an 11" x 17" baking sheet), but don't worry if you don't have 4 baking sheets. Simply let rolls rise on a greased sheet of parchment paper or foil. Transfer the rolls (on the parchment paper or foil) to a cooled baking sheet and bake. If you don't have flat baking sheets (necessary for final rolling out of Crispies), turn jelly-roll pans upside down and use the bottoms.

>   1 (1/4-oz.) package active dry yeast
>   1/4 cup sugar
>   1/4 cup warm water (110F, 45C)
>   3/4 cup milk
>   1/3 cup butter, melted
>   1 egg
>   1 egg yolk
>   1 teaspoon salt
>   1 teaspoon pure vanilla extract
>   3 to 3-1/2 cups all-purpose flour
>   Cinnamon-Sugar Filling, see below
>   Cinnamon-Nut Topping, see below
>   4 tablespoons butter, softened

Cinnamon-Sugar Filling:
>   1/2 cup packed brown sugar
>   1/2 cup granulated sugar
>   3/4 teaspoon ground cinnamon

Cinnamon-Nut Topping:
>   1 cup granulated sugar
>   3/4 cup finely chopped walnuts, almonds, or pecans
>   1 teaspoon ground cinnamon

In large bowl of electric mixer, dissolve yeast and a pinch of the sugar in warm water; let stand until foamy, 5 to 10 minutes. Add remaining sugar, milk, melted butter, egg, egg yolk, salt, vanilla, and 2 cups flour. Beat at medium speed with electric mixer 2 minutes, or beat 200 vigorous strokes by hand. Stir in enough remaining flour to make a soft dough. Change to dough hook(s) if using mixer, or turn out dough onto a lightly floured surface.

Knead dough 2 to 3 minutes, or until smooth and pliable, adding only enough flour to prevent sticking. Clean and butter bowl. Place dough in bowl, turning to coat all surfaces. Cover with a slightly damp towel; set in a warm place free from drafts. Let rise until doubled in bulk, 1-1/2 to 2 hours. Prepare Cinnamon-Sugar Filling and Cinnamon-Nut Topping; set aside. Grease 2 to 4 large baking sheets; set aside.

Punch down dough; knead 30 seconds. Divide dough in half. Roll out one half into a 12-inch square. Spread with 2 tablespoons softened butter; sprinkle with half the Cinnamon-Sugar Filling (about 3/4 cup). Roll up tightly, jelly-roll fashion. Pinch seam to seal. Repeat with remaining dough. Cut each roll into 12 equal slices. Place slices at least 3 inches apart on prepared baking sheets; flatten slightly with your fingers. Cover with buttered waxed paper and set in a warm place free from drafts. Let rise until doubled in bulk, about 30 minutes.

Preheat oven to 375F (190C). Leave buttered waxed paper on top of rolls. Use a rolling pin to flatten rolls to a 1/8-inch thickness. Remove waxed paper; evenly sprinkle each roll with about 1 heaping tablespoon Cinnamon-Nut Topping. Try not to get any sugar on baking sheets or bottoms of rolls will burn. Cover with unbuttered waxed paper. Use a rolling pin to press topping into pastry circles. Remove waxed paper. Bake 10 minutes, or until golden brown. Cool on racks. Rolls will crisp as they cool. Store in airtight container. Recrisp in preheated 300F (150C) oven, if necessary.

Makes 24 large pastries.

Cinnamon-Sugar Filling: In a small bowl, stir together all ingredients.

Cinnamon-Nut Topping: In a medium-size bowl, stir together all ingredients.

Wheat-Bran Buns

Cottage cheese and whole bran give these delicious, light rolls a nutritional bonus.

2 (1/4-oz.) packages active dry yeast
1/3 cup packed brown sugar
1/2 cup warm water (110F, 45C)
1 cup small curd cottage cheese
2 eggs
2 tablespoons vegetable oil
2 teaspoons salt
1-1/3 cups oat or wheat bran
3-1/4 to 3-3/4 cups bread or all-purpose flour
1 cup whole-wheat flour
1/4 cup unsalted butter or margarine, melted

In large bowl of electric mixer, dissolve yeast and 1 teaspoon of the brown sugar in warm water. Let stand until foamy, 5 to 10 minutes. Add remaining brown sugar, cottage cheese, eggs, oil, salt, 2/3 cup bran, and 1-1/2 to 2 cups bread flour. Beat at medium speed with electric mixer 2 minutes, or beat 200 vigorous strokes by hand. Stir in whole-wheat flour and enough remaining bread flour to make a soft dough. Change to dough hook(s) if using mixer, or turn out dough onto a lightly floured surface.

Knead dough 8 to 10 minutes, or until smooth and elastic, adding only enough flour to prevent sticking. Clean and butter bowl. Place dough in bowl, turning to coat all surfaces. Cover with a slightly damp towel; set in a warm place free from drafts. Let rise until doubled in bulk, about 1 hour. Grease a 13" x 9" baking pan; set aside.

Punch down dough; knead 30 seconds. Divide dough into 24 pieces. Form each piece into a smooth ball. Place melted butter in 1 small bowl and remaining 2/3 cup bran in another. Dip each ball in melted butter, then roll in bran. Arrange balls in prepared pan. Cover with a dry towel; let rise until doubled in bulk, about 45 minutes.

Preheat oven to 375F (190C). Bake 20 to 25 minutes, or until golden brown. Remove from pan and cool on racks 5 minutes before serving.

Makes 24 rolls.

Linzer Spirals

*I*nspired by Austria's famous linzertorte, these easy yeast rolls have raspberry-almond spirals. To quickly soften almond paste, pop it in a microwave oven at HIGH for 30 seconds.

Basic Sweet Yeast Dough (page 82)
2/3 cup seedless raspberry preserves
1/2 cup packed almond paste, softened
1 egg white
2 tablespoons butter, softened
1 teaspoon almond extract
Almond Crunch Topping, see below
Powdered sugar

Almond Crunch Topping:
1/3 cup finely chopped almonds
1/4 cup all-purpose flour
1/4 cup sugar
1/4 cup butter, softened
1/4 teaspoon ground cinnamon

Prepare Basic Sweet Yeast Dough through first rising. Liberally butter 24 muffin cups; set aside. Punch down dough; knead 30 seconds. Cover and let rest 10 minutes. In a medium-size bowl, stir together preserves, almond paste, egg white, butter, and almond extract until smooth; set aside. Prepare Almond Crunch Topping; set aside. On a lightly floured surface, roll out dough into a 24" x 12" rectangle. Using a rubber spatula, gently spread raspberry mixture over surface of dough to within 1/2 inch of edges. Beginning on 1 long side, roll up dough, jelly-roll fashion. Pinch ends and seam to seal. Using a floured knife, cut roll into 24 (1-inch) slices. Place slices, cut side up, in prepared muffin cups. Sprinkle tops of rolls with Almond Crunch Topping. Cover with waxed paper and set in a warm place free from drafts. Let rise until almost doubled, 1 to 1-1/2 hours.

Preheat oven to 350F (175C). Bake about 25 minutes, or until pale golden brown. Remove from muffin cups; cool on racks at least 10 minutes. Just before serving, dust lightly with powdered sugar.

Makes 24 rolls.

Almond Crunch Topping: In a medium-size bowl, combine all ingredients until mixture is crumbly.

Oatmeal Honor Rolls

*D*ried cherries or cranberries or toasted nuts can be substituted for the raisins in these versatile rolls. No matter what, you'll go to the top of the class with these oaty, orange-scented winners.

> 1 (1/4-oz.) package active dry yeast
> 1/4 cup honey
> 1/4 cup warm water (110F, 45C)
> 2 eggs
> 1 cup milk
> 1/4 cup vegetable oil
> 2 teaspoons freshly grated orange zest
> 1-1/2 teaspoons salt
> 1/4 teaspoon ground cinnamon
> 1-1/4 cups regular or quick-cooking rolled oats
> 3/4 cup golden raisins
> 3-1/2 to 4 cups bread or all-purpose flour
> 3 tablespoons unsalted butter or margarine, melted
> Additional rolled oats for garnish

In large bowl of electric mixer, dissolve yeast and 1 teaspoon of the honey in warm water. Let stand until foamy, 5 to 10 minutes. Add remaining honey, eggs, milk, oil, orange zest, salt, cinnamon, 1-1/4 cup oats, raisins, and 1 to 1-1/2 cups of the flour. Beat at medium speed with electric mixer 2 minutes, or beat 200 vigorous strokes by hand. Stir in enough remaining flour to make a soft dough. Change to dough hook(s) if using mixer, or turn out dough onto a lightly floured surface.

Knead dough 5 minutes, or until smooth, adding only enough flour to prevent sticking. Clean and butter bowl. Place dough in bowl, turning to coat all surfaces. Cover with a slightly damp towel; set in a warm place free from drafts. Let rise until doubled in bulk, about 1-1/2 hours.

Punch down dough; knead 30 seconds. Cover and let stand 10 minutes. Grease 2 large baking sheets; set aside. On a lightly floured surface, roll out dough into a 15" x 9" rectangle. Cut into 15 (3-inch) squares; brush with melted butter. With the back of a knife, score each square horizontally across center. Fold squares at crease. Place rolls 2 inches apart on prepared baking sheets. Cover with buttered waxed paper; set in a warm place free from drafts. Let rise until almost doubled in bulk, 30 to 45 minutes.

Preheat oven to 400F (205C). Brush rolls with melted butter; sprinkle with remaining oats. Bake 15 to 20 minutes, or until evenly browned. Remove from pans; cool on racks 5 minutes before serving.

Makes 15 large rolls.

Potato-Chive Rolls

*T*here's absolutely no kneading necessary for these fluffy sour cream and chive rolls. Low-fat sour cream can be substituted for the regular style, but your rolls won't be as tender if you use nonfat sour cream.

2 (1/4-oz.) packages active dry yeast
2 teaspoons sugar
3/4 cup warm water (110F, 45C)
1 cup sour cream
1 cup mashed potatoes
3 eggs
3 to 5 cloves Roasted Garlic (page 256)
1 tablespoon salt
4-1/2 to 5 cups bread or all-purpose flour
1-1/2 tablespoons finely chopped chives

In large bowl of electric mixer, dissolve yeast and sugar in warm water. Let stand until foamy, 5 to 10 minutes. Add sour cream, potatoes, eggs, garlic, salt, and 2 to 2-1/2 cups of the flour. Beat at medium speed with electric mixer 4 minutes or 400 vigorous strokes by hand. Stir in chives and enough remaining flour to make a stiff dough. Cover with a slightly damp towel; set in a warm place free from drafts. Let rise until doubled in bulk, about 1-1/2 hours. Grease a 13" x 9" baking pan; set aside.

Punch down dough. On a generously floured surface, toss dough until no longer sticky. Divide dough into 24 equal pieces. Shape each piece into a ball; place in prepared pan. Cover with buttered waxed paper and set in a warm place free from drafts. Let rise until doubled in bulk, about 45 minutes.

Preheat oven to 375F (190C). Bake 30 to 35 minutes, or until deep golden brown. Remove rolls from pan; place on rack. Dust rolls with flour. Let cool 5 minutes before serving.

Makes 24 rolls.

Heavenly Sesame Biscuits

Only one rise is necessary for these old-fashioned biscuits that use a combination of yeast, baking powder, and baking soda. They're wonderful with everything from breakfast to dinner.

> 1 (1/4-oz.) package active dry yeast
> 2 teaspoons sugar
> 1/4 cup warm water (110F, 45C)
> 2-1/2 cups all-purpose flour
> 1 teaspoon salt
> 1 teaspoon baking powder
> 1/2 teaspoon baking soda
> 1/3 cup cold unsalted butter
> 3/4 cup buttermilk
> 1/4 cup unsalted butter, melted
> About 1/2 cup sesame seeds

Grease 2 large baking sheets; set aside. In a small bowl, dissolve yeast and sugar in warm water. Let stand until foamy, 5 to 10 minutes. In a large bowl, stir together flour, salt, baking powder, and baking soda. Use a pastry blender or 2 knives to cut in butter until mixture resembles coarse crumbs. Add yeast mixture and buttermilk, stirring only until dry ingredients are moistened. Turn out dough onto a lightly floured surface. Place melted butter in 1 small bowl, sesame seeds in another; set aside.

Knead dough 2 to 3 minutes, or until pliable and smooth. Sprinkle work surface with more flour, if necessary. Roll out dough until 1/2 inch thick. Using a round 2- or 2-1/2-inch biscuit cutter, cut out dough. Dip biscuits first in melted butter, then in sesame seeds. Arrange biscuits 2 inches apart on prepared baking sheets. Gather leftover dough together; knead, roll, and cut as before. Cover biscuits with buttered waxed paper and set in a warm place free from drafts. Let rise until doubled in bulk, about 1 hour.

Preheat oven to 425F (220C). Bake 12 to 15 minutes, or until golden brown. Serve warm, or cool on racks.

Makes about 22 biscuits.

Easy Cheesy Beer Buns

I've used Cheddar cheese in the following recipe, but these one-rise buns are just as good with Gouda or Gruyere.

> **About 1/3 cup sesame seeds**
> **2 (1/4-oz.) packages active dry yeast**
> **2 teaspoons sugar**
> **1 cup warm beer (110F, 45C)**
> **1 egg**
> **2 tablespoons vegetable oil**
> **1 teaspoon salt**
> **2-1/4 to 2-3/4 cups bread or all-purpose flour**
> **1 cup grated sharp Cheddar cheese**
> **16 (1/2-inch) cubes sharp Cheddar cheese**
> **1 egg yolk mixed with 2 teaspoons water for glaze**

Generously grease 16 muffin cups. Sprinkle about 1/2 teaspoon sesame seeds over bottom and sides of each cup; set aside. In large bowl of electric mixer, dissolve yeast and sugar in warm beer. Let stand until foamy, 5 to 10 minutes. Add egg, oil, salt, and 1-1/2 cups flour. Beat at medium speed with electric mixer 4 minutes, or 400 vigorous strokes by hand. Stir in grated cheese and enough remaining flour to make a stiff batter.

Spoon 1 heaping tablespoon batter into each prepared muffin cup. Press a cheese cube lightly into center of batter; top with a heaping teaspoon of remaining batter. With your buttered fingers or the back of a spoon, press batter around cheese cubes to seal. Cover with buttered waxed paper and set in a warm place free from drafts. Let rise until batter reaches tops of muffin cups, about 45 minutes.

Preheat oven to 350F (175C). Brush tops of buns with egg-yolk glaze; sprinkle with remaining sesame seeds. Bake 25 to 30 minutes, or until golden brown. Remove buns from muffin cups and cool on racks 5 minutes before serving.

Makes 16 buns.

TIP: Twisting a biscuit cutter compresses the dough. For high-rising biscuits, cut out dough with a clean, sharp, downward motion.

Classic Croissants

*T*ime and patience are necessary for these tender, butter-layered classics, but they'll earn you raves. For a nice change of pace, try the chocolate and whole-wheat variations (page 145).

1 (1/4-oz.) package active dry yeast
1 tablespoon sugar
1/4 cup warm water (110F, 45C)
3/4 cup milk
1/2 teaspoon salt
2 tablespoons unsalted butter, melted
About 3 cups all-purpose flour
1 cup cold unsalted butter
2 egg yolks mixed with 2 teaspoons cream for glaze

In large bowl, dissolve yeast and a pinch of the sugar in warm water. Let stand until foamy, 5 to 10 minutes. Add remaining sugar, milk, salt, melted butter, and about 2-1/2 cups flour. Stir until dough forms a ball, adding more flour if necessary. Change to dough hook(s) if using mixer, or turn out dough onto a lightly floured surface. Cover and let stand 5 minutes. Clean and butter bowl; set aside.

Knead dough about 1 minute, or until smooth but not elastic, adding more flour if dough is very sticky. A pastry scraper will help in working with this soft, moist dough. Handle dough gently to prevent overdeveloping gluten. Place dough in buttered bowl, turning to coat all sides. Cover with plastic wrap; set in a warm place free from drafts. Let rise until tripled in bulk, about 1-1/2 hours. Gently punch down dough. Cover; let rise again until doubled in bulk, about 1 hour. Punch down dough; cover tightly and refrigerate 30 minutes or overnight.

To prepare butter: Sprinkle 2 tablespoons flour over work surface; place cold butter on top. Lightly pound butter with floured rolling pin until softened. With heel of your hand or a pastry scraper, combine butter and flour until of spreading consistency yet still cold. If butter begins to melt, refrigerate immediately until firm. Butter should be as close as possible to consistency of croissant dough. Set butter aside at room temperature while rolling out dough.

To combine butter and dough: On a lightly floured surface, roll out dough into a 16" x 12" rectangle; brush excess flour from dough. Using a rubber spatula, spread butter over two-thirds of dough, leaving a 1/2-inch margin around outside edges. Fold unbuttered third over center third; fold remaining third over top, as if folding a letter. Press edges together to seal. This is called turn one. Lightly flour work area and surface of dough. Working rapidly and using a firm, even pressure, roll out dough again into a 16" x 12" rectangle. Roll from center of dough to within 1 inch of sides to avoid pushing butter through seams. Fold again in thirds for turn two. Dust surface of dough lightly with flour. Wrap in plastic wrap; refrigerate 1 hour.

Lightly flour work surface and cold dough. Roll out and fold dough again for turn three; repeat for turn four. Dust surface of dough lightly with flour. Wrap in plastic wrap; refrigerate 1-1/2 hours or overnight. If refrigerated overnight, place a small cutting board or baking sheet and a 5-pound weight on top of dough to prevent rising.

To cut out dough and shape croissants: On a lightly floured surface, roll out dough into a 24" x 16" rectangle, about 1/8 inch thick. Cut rectangle in half lengthwise, making 2 (24" x 8") strips. Lightly dust 1 strip with flour. Fold in thirds, wrap in plastic wrap and refrigerate. Score remaining strip on 1 long side at 6-inch intervals. On opposite long side, starting 3 inches from 1 end, score at 6-inch intervals. Begin cutting strip from the 3-inch mark, making 2 diagonal cuts to opposite 6-inch marks, forming a triangle. Each triangle will have a 6-inch base and 8-1/2-inch sides. Press center edges of 2 end pieces together to form a triangle. Brush excess flour from triangle surfaces. Beginning at 6-inch base and stretching ends slightly, roll triangle toward point. If necessary, dampen tip of triangle with a drop of cold water so it will stick to roll. Curve ends slightly to form a crescent. Lightly spray cold water on a large, ungreased baking sheet. Arrange croissants 1-1/2 to 2 inches apart on damp baking sheet. Point of croissant should just rest on baking sheet; do not tuck under. Repeat with remaining dough. Cover lightly with buttered waxed paper. Set in a warm place (not over 75F, 25C) free from drafts. Let rise until doubled in bulk, about 1-1/2 hours.

Preheat oven to 400F (205C). Brush croissants with egg-yolk glaze. Bake 15 to 20 minutes, or until nicely browned.

Makes about 16 croissants.

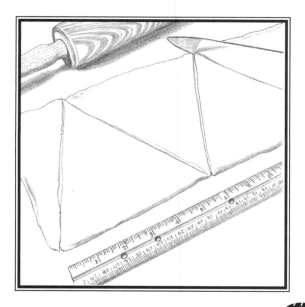

Quick Croissants

*T*hese buttery taste-alikes are a little easier and a lot quicker to make. They'll also fool most croissant lovers.

5 cups all-purpose flour
2 cups cold unsalted butter
2 (1/4-oz.) packages active dry yeast
3 tablespoons sugar
1-3/4 cups warm milk (110F, 45C)
2 teaspoons salt
1/4 cup unsalted butter, melted
Additional butter, softened (optional)
2 egg yolks mixed with 2 teaspoons cream for glaze

In large bowl of electric mixer or food processor fitted with the metal blade, combine 3 cups flour and 2 cups cold butter. Mix at low speed (ON/OFF pulses with food processor) until butter particles are the size of small lima beans. Cover and refrigerate. In a large bowl, dissolve yeast and a pinch of the sugar in warm milk. Stir in remaining sugar and 2 cups flour; beat until batter is smooth. Cover tightly with plastic wrap; set in a warm place free from drafts. Let rise until doubled in bulk, about 20 to 30 minutes.

Stir down batter. Add salt and 1/4 cup melted butter; stir to blend. Add refrigerated butter-flour mixture, folding only until flour is moistened. Mixture should be quite crumbly and butter should remain in large pieces. Turn out crumbly dough onto a lightly floured work surface. Handling dough as little as possible with your hands, gently roll out into a large rectangle 1/2 inch thick. Brush excess flour from surface. Dough will be sticky.

Using a pastry scraper or metal spatula, fold top third of dough over middle third; fold opposite end over top, as if folding a letter. This is called turn one. Repeat rolling out and folding dough 3 more times, sprinkling flour over work surface and top of dough between each turn. If butter begins to soften and break through dough, place dough in plastic bag. Refrigerate or freeze 10 to 20 minutes to refirm. After 4 turns, wrap dough airtight in plastic wrap. Refrigerate 1-1/2 to 2 hours.

To roll out dough and form croissants: Place refrigerated dough on lightly floured work surface. Deflate dough by rapping firmly with rolling pin. Divide dough into 4 equal pieces; cover and refrigerate 3 pieces. Roll remaining dough into a 14-inch circle. If a more buttery flavor is desired, thinly spread dough with softened butter to within 1/4 inch of edges. Cut circle into 8 triangles. Beginning at outer edge of each triangle and stretching ends slightly, roll up dough toward point. If necessary, dampen tip of triangle with a drop of water so it will stick to roll. Curve ends slightly to form a crescent.

Arrange 1-1/2 inches apart on buttered baking sheets. Point of crescent should just rest on baking sheet; do not tuck under. Repeat with remaining dough, removing 1 piece at a time from refrigerator. Cover loosely with plastic wrap and set in a warm place (not over 75F, 25C) free from drafts. Let rise until almost doubled in bulk, about 1 hour.

Preheat oven to 400F (205C). Brush croissants with egg-yolk glaze. Bake 12 to 18 minutes, or until croissants are nicely browned. Cool on racks.

Makes 32 croissants.

Croissant Variations

Petits Pains au Chocolat (Chocolate-Filled Croissants): For Classic Croissants, you'll need about 8 ounces semisweet chocolate pieces; 16 ounces for Quick Croissants. Roll out dough until 1/8 inch thick; cut into 4-inch squares. Sprinkle about 1 tablespoon chocolate in a row along 1 side of square, about 1/2 inch from edge. Beginning on chocolate side, roll up, jelly-roll fashion. Arrange 1-1/2 inches apart on buttered baking sheets. Let rise and bake as directed.

Whole-Wheat Croissants: Substitute whole-wheat pastry flour for half the all-purpose flour. Add 1/4 cup toasted wheat germ to Classic Croissants recipe; 1/2 cup to Quick Croissants recipe. After brushing with egg-yolk glaze, sprinkle with wheat germ.

Danish Pastries

*Y*ou can form these butter-rich pastries in a variety of shapes (pages 151–152), and fill them with your favorite filling (pages 148–149). What a perfectly delicious way to start the day!

2 (1/4-oz.) packages active dry yeast
1/2 cup sugar
1/2 cup warm water (110F, 45C)
1/2 cup milk
2 eggs
1 teaspoon salt
1 teaspoon pure vanilla extract
1/4 teaspoon ground cardamom
3 tablespoons unsalted butter, softened
About 4-1/2 cups all-purpose flour
2 cups cold, unsalted butter
Choice of filling (pages 148–149)
1 egg mixed with 2 teaspoons cream for glaze
Coarse decorator's sugar or granulated sugar

In large mixing bowl, dissolve yeast and a pinch of the sugar in warm water. Let stand until foamy, 5 to 10 minutes. Add remaining sugar, milk, eggs, salt, vanilla, cardamom, 3 tablespoons softened butter, and 4 cups of the flour. Stir until dry ingredients have absorbed liquid. Turn out dough onto a lightly floured surface.

Knead dough 2 to 3 minutes, or just until smooth, adding only enough flour to prevent sticking. Dust surface of dough lightly with flour; place in plastic bag. Refrigerate 1 to 1-1/2 hours.

To prepare butter: Sprinkle 3 tablespoons flour over work surface. Place 2 cups cold butter on floured surface. Lightly pound butter with floured rolling pin until softened. With heel of your hand or a pastry scraper, combine butter and flour until of spreading consistency yet still cold. If butter begins to melt, refrigerate immediately until firm. Butter should be as close as possible to consistency of pastry dough. Set butter aside at room temperature while rolling out dough.

To combine butter and dough: On a lightly floured surface, roll out dough into an 18" x 12" rectangle; brush excess flour from dough. Using a rubber spatula, spread butter over two-thirds of dough, leaving a 1/2-inch margin around outside edges. Fold unbuttered third over center third; fold remaining third over top, as if folding a letter. Press edges together to seal. This is called turn one. Lightly flour work area and surface of dough. Working rapidly and using a firm, even pressure, roll out dough again into an 18" x 12" rectangle. Roll from center of dough to within 1 inch of sides to avoid pushing butter through seams. Fold again in thirds for turn two. Repeat rolling and folding of dough a third time. Dust surface of dough lightly with flour. Wrap in plastic wrap; refrigerate 45 minutes.

Lightly flour work surface and cold dough. Repeat rolling and folding 3 more times. If butter begins to soften, refrigerate dough 15 minutes between turns. After final turn, dust surface of dough lightly with flour. Wrap in plastic wrap; refrigerate at least 2 hours or overnight. If refrigerated overnight, place a small cutting board or baking sheet and a 5-pound weight on top of dough to prevent rising.

To shape pastries: Choose desired filling (pages 148–149) and shape (pages 151–152). For variety, make 2 or 3 different shapes and fillings. Deflate dough by rapping firmly with a rolling pin. Shape half of dough at a time, keep remaining dough refrigerated. After shaping, place pastries 2 inches apart on lightly buttered baking sheets. Cover with plastic wrap; refrigerate at least 30 minutes.

Preheat oven to 400F (205C). Brush pastries with egg-yolk glaze. If desired, sprinkle lightly with sugar. Bake 5 minutes. Reduce heat to 350F (175C). Bake about 10 minutes longer, or until golden brown. Cool on racks.

Makes about 48 pastries.

Variation

Quick Danish Pastry: Prepare Quick Croissants dough (page 144), reducing salt to 1 teaspoon and adding 1/3 cup sugar, 1/4 teaspoon ground cardamom, and 1 teaspoon pure vanilla extract. Roll and fold as directed above, to first (45-minute) refrigeration. Remove dough from refrigerator; roll and fold only two more times. Refrigerate 1-1/2 hours before shaping and filling as desired.

TIP: Unsalted butter allows you to control the amount of salt added to your bread. It's a must for delicate pastries like croissants and Danish pastry. Since salt acts as a preservative, unsalted butter is more perishable than regular butter and should be refrigerated for no more than 2 weeks. It can be wrapped airtight and frozen for up to 6 months.

Croissant & Danish Pastry Fillings

For croissants, spread 1 heaping teaspoonful at base of each dough triangle; roll from base to point. Let rise and bake as directed. For Danish Pastry, fill as directed in Danish Pastry Shapes (pages 151–152).

Sweet Cheese Filling:

1 (8-oz.) package cream cheese, softened
1/4 cup sugar
1 tablespoon all-purpose flour
1 egg yolk
1 tablespoon rum or brandy (optional)
1 teaspoon grated lemon or orange zest
1 teaspoon pure vanilla extract
Pinch of salt
2 tablespoons currants (optional)

In small bowl of electric mixer or food processor with metal blade, process all ingredients (except currants) until creamy. Stir in currants, if desired.

Spiced Apple Filling:

1 cup finely chopped peeled apple
2 tablespoons packed brown sugar
1/4 teaspoon ground cinnamon
1/8 teaspoon ground allspice
1/8 teaspoon ground nutmeg
1/4 cup currants or raisins (optional)

In a medium-size bowl, combine all ingredients.

Crunchy Almond Filling:

1 egg white
2/3 cup almond paste, softened
1/4 cup unsalted butter, softened
Pinch of salt
1/2 cup toasted finely chopped almonds

In small bowl of electric mixer or food processor with metal blade, process egg white, almond paste, butter, and salt until smooth. Add almonds; stir to combine.

Cherry-Cheese Filling:

2 (3-oz.) packages cream cheese, softened
2 tablespoons sugar
1/2 teaspoon almond extract
2/3 cup cherry preserves

In small bowl of electric mixer or food processor with metal blade, process cream cheese, sugar, and almond extract until smooth. Add preserves; stir to combine.

Brandied Apricot or Prune Filling:

1 cup dried apricots or pitted prunes
1/2 cup apricot nectar or prune juice
1/2 cup brandy
1/2 cup sugar
2 tablespoons unsalted butter, softened
Pinch of salt

In a medium-size saucepan, combine dried fruit, nectar, and brandy. Cover and simmer 20 to 25 minutes, or until fruit is tender. Turn mixture into a blender or food processor with a metal blade. Add sugar, butter, and salt; process until mixture is smooth. Cool to room temperature.

Ground Nut Filling:

1 egg, lightly beaten
1/2 cup packed brown sugar
3/4 cup ground hazelnuts, walnuts, or pecans
1/2 teaspoon ground cinnamon
Pinch of salt

In a medium-size bowl, combine all ingredients.

Rum Cream Filling:

3 tablespoons sugar
2 tablespoons cornstarch
1/4 teaspoon salt
3/4 cup half-and-half
1/4 cup light rum
2 egg yolks, lightly beaten
1 teaspoon pure vanilla extract

In top of a double boiler, combine sugar, cornstarch, and salt. Slowly stir in half-and-half, rum, and egg yolks. Stirring constantly, cook over simmering water until mixture becomes very thick, about 15 minutes. Cool to room temperature; stir in vanilla.

※

Hints for Perfect Croissants & Danish Pastries

Try to choose a cool day to make croissants or Danish pastry. If kitchen is hot, the butter may begin to melt, causing the dough to soften.

It's best to allow two days to make Classic Croissants, which take a minimum of 12 hours from start to finish. Prepare the dough one day, then roll, shape, and bake it the next.

All-purpose flour should be used for croissants and Danish pastry because it contains less gluten. High-gluten bread flour will produce pastries that are chewy instead of tender.

Butter produces soft, fine-grained croissants and Danish pastry with an unbeatable flavor. On the other hand, pastries made with margarine are usually flakier. For the best of both worlds, use half butter and half margarine.

Gentle handling of croissant and Danish pastry dough is necessary to avoid overdeveloping the gluten, which will toughen the pastries. The dough is sufficiently kneaded when it's smooth.

Using a pastry scraper or metal spatula makes it easier to handle the soft, buttery dough in its early stages.

If dough becomes too soft to handle, refrigerate it briefly until the butter becomes firm again.

When rolling butter into the dough, work rapidly and use a firm and even pressure. Roll to within 1 inch of edges to avoid pushing butter through seams or weak spots in the dough.

If butter does begin to break through dough, lightly dust the butter spot with flour. Place the dough in freezer about 5 minutes to firm.

Refrigerate dough between turns (the process by which the layers of butter and dough are increased) to keep the rising action at a minimum.

Only work with part of the dough while cutting and shaping it. Tightly wrap and refrigerate the dough you're not working on.

When cutting dough, use a knife with a sharp, thin blade. Cut down cleanly through the dough, rather than drawing the knife through it.

Croissants and Danish pastries may be frozen before baking. Place the pastries 1/2 inch apart on a baking sheet lined with plastic wrap. Freeze pastries until solid, then seal airtight in freezerproof plastic bags or heavy-duty foil. Freeze up to 6 months.

To bake frozen unbaked croissants, place 2 inches apart on unbuttered baking sheets. Let rise at room temperature until doubled in bulk, 2 to 2-1/2 hours. Bake in preheated 400F (205C) oven 15 to 20 minutes, or until nicely browned.

To bake frozen unbaked Danish pastries, place 2 inches apart on lightly buttered baking sheets. Place frozen pastries in a preheated 425F (220C) oven. Bake 10 to 15 minutes, or until golden brown.

To freeze baked croissants and Danish pastries, cool, then wrap airtight in a freezer-proof plastic bag or in heavy-duty foil. Freeze for up to 4 months.

To reheat frozen baked croissants or Danish pastries, place 1-1/2 inches apart on unbuttered baking sheets. Heat croissants in a preheated 400F (205C) oven 5 to 8 minutes. Heat Danish pastries in a preheated 350F (150C) oven 5 to 10 minutes.

Danish Pastry Shapes

Danish pastry can be formed in myriad shapes—here are just a few to spark your imagination.

Cockscombs

Dust work surface with granulated sugar. Roll dough into a strip 9 inches wide and 1/8 inch thick. Spread a thin layer of filling lengthwise over half of dough, to within 1/4 inch of edges. Fold dough lengthwise over top of filling, making a strip 4-1/2 inches wide. Gently pinch edges to seal. Cut crosswise into 2-1/2-inch strips. Make 4 cuts along 1 side of each strip to within 1/2 inch of opposite edge. Place pastry strips 2 inches apart on buttered baking sheets, curving slightly to separate fingers of dough and form cockscomb. Brush with egg-yolk glaze. Suggested fillings: Sweet Cheese, Ground Nut, or Apricot.

Danish Twists

Dust work surface with granulated sugar. Roll out dough 10 inches wide and 1/8 inch thick. Cut dough in half crosswise. Spread a thin layer of filling over 1 piece of dough to within 1/4 inch of edges. Place second piece of dough over filling; press together lightly. Cut filled dough in half lengthwise to make 2 (5-inch-wide) strips. Cut strips crosswise into 1/2-inch pieces. Lift pieces and carefully twist 3 or 4 times. Place 2 inches apart on buttered baking sheets. Suggested fillings: Crunchy Almond or Ground Nut. After brushing pastries with egg glaze, sprinkle with finely chopped almonds, or nuts used in Ground Nut Filling.

Rum Cream Packages

Dust work surface with granulated sugar. Roll out dough into an 18" x 12" rectangle, about 1/8 inch thick. Cut into 24 (3-inch) squares. Place 1 teaspoon Rum Cream Filling in center of each square. Bring all four corners to center; pinch slightly to seal. Brush with egg-yolk glaze. Corners will open during baking.

Snails, Fans, Baskets, and Spectacles

Dust work surface with granulated sugar. Roll out dough 10 inches wide and 1/8 inch thick. Spread a thin layer of Apricot or Prune Filling, Ground Nut Filling, or raspberry jam to within 1/4 inch of edges. Beginning on 1 long side, roll tightly, jelly-roll fashion. Cover; refrigerate 20 to 30 minutes to make slicing easier.

To make snails: Cut dough crosswise into 1/2-inch-thick slices. Lay slices, cut side down, on buttered baking sheet.

To make fans: Cut dough crosswise in 1-1/2-inch slices. Cutting from top of slice, use a sharp knife or scissors to make 2 cuts, 1/2 inch apart and to within 1/4-inch of bottom. Lay flat on buttered baking sheet, spreading slices apart into a fan shape.

To make baskets: Cut as for Fans. On buttered baking sheet, lay 2 outside slices flat; leave center slice upright for handle.

To make spectacles: With a sharp knife, cut roll almost through 1/2 inch from end. Move knife over 1/2 inch and cut all the way through. Repeat until all dough is cut. On a buttered baking sheet, pull joined sections apart so they lay flat, like spectacles with a strip of dough forming the bridge.

Breadsticks Basilico

The oil in these breadsticks is what gives them their pronounced crunch. Fill pretty glasses with these crispy sticks for edible table decorations for an Italian dinner. Try the variation for Southwest Breadsticks the next time you serve chili.

1 (1/4-oz.) package active dry yeast
1 teaspoon sugar
1-1/2 cups warm beer or water (110F, 45C)
3/4 cup olive oil or vegetable oil
1/3 cup finely chopped fresh basil or 2 tablespoons dried basil
2 teaspoons freshly grated lemon zest
1-1/2 teaspoons salt
1 teaspoon freshly ground pepper
4-3/4 to 5-1/4 cups bread or all-purpose flour
1 egg mixed with 1 tablespoon water for glaze
About 1/2 cup grated Parmesan cheese

In large bowl of electric mixer, dissolve yeast and sugar in warm beer or water. Let stand until foamy, 5 to 10 minutes. Add oil, basil, lemon zest, salt, pepper, and 2-1/2 to 3 cups of the flour. Beat at medium speed with electric mixer 2 minutes, or beat 200 vigorous strokes by hand. Stir in enough remaining flour to make a soft dough. Change to dough hook(s) if using mixer, or turn out dough onto a lightly floured surface.

Knead dough 6 to 8 minutes, or until smooth and elastic. Clean and butter bowl. Place dough in buttered bowl, turning to coat all surfaces. Cover with a slightly damp towel; set in a warm place free from drafts. Let rise until doubled in bulk, about 1 hour. Grease 2 to 4 large baking sheets; set aside.

Punch down dough; knead 30 seconds. Divide dough in half. Cover 1 piece and set aside. Roll or pat remaining dough into a 20" x 6" rectangle. Cut crosswise into 40 (1/2-inch) strips. Brush with egg glaze; sprinkle lightly with Parmesan. Arrange on prepared baking sheets, stretching strips to 8 inches. Make sure strips are of a uniform thickness. Repeat with second half of dough. Let rise 20 minutes, uncovered, in a warm place free from drafts.

Preheat oven to 350F (175C). Bake about 20 minutes, or until golden brown. Remove from baking sheets; cool on racks.

Makes about 80 breadsticks.

Variations

Southwest Breadsticks: Omit basil; add 2 to 3 tablespoons finely chopped cilantro, 2 teaspoons chili powder, and 1/2 teaspoon red (cayenne) pepper. Brush with egg glaze; sprinkle with chili powder.

Little Quick Breads

The basic rules for making little quick breads are the same as for loaf-style quick breads—work fast and with a light touch. The batter should only be stirred until the dry ingredients are moistened.

For tender, flaky biscuits, the butter or other fat should be very cold. Cut it into the dry ingredients only until the mixture resembles coarse (about 1/4-inch) crumbs. A food processor fitted with a metal blade makes quick work of this process—use ON/OFF pulses for maximum control. Don't overhandle the dough or you'll wind up with tough, dense biscuits. Once the dough is rolled out, cut as many biscuits as possible from the first rolling. Rerolling toughens the dough. Cutting out square biscuits eliminates the need for rerolling. Dip a biscuit cutter into flour to keep it from sticking to the dough. If you don't like the way drop biscuits spread, drop the batter into greased muffin cups.

Nonstick cooking spray makes greasing muffin cups a breeze. For perfectly rounded muffin tops, only grease the muffin-cup bottoms and halfway up the sides. Don't grease muffin cups that won't be used; the grease will burn and make a mess of your pan. Overmixing muffin batter produces coarse-textured muffins with pointy tops. Any muffin can be made lighter by separating the eggs, beating the whites, and folding them in after the rest of the ingredients are combined.

Fill muffin cups one-half to three-quarters full—more than three-quarters full, and you're liable to get muffins with flying-saucer tops. To remove muffins from their cups, run a knife around the edges, then under the bottom to lift them out of the pan. Turn baked muffins on their sides in the muffin pans for a couple of minutes so they don't get soggy from trapped steam.

Leftover little quick breads can be split and toasted, or loosely wrapped in foil and reheated in a 350F (175C) oven for 5 to 10 minutes. Or, wrap in waxed paper and microwave at HIGH for 10 to 30 seconds, depending on the amount. Don't overheat in the microwave oven or you'll turn your baked goods into stones.

Wild Rice–Apple Muffins

*S*ave leftover wild rice to make these enticing muffins the next day. If preferred, substitute an equal amount of brown rice for the wild rice. Leaving the peel on apples adds color.

1-1/2 cups all-purpose flour
2 teaspoons baking powder
1/2 teaspoon baking soda
3/4 teaspoon salt
1/4 teaspoon ground nutmeg
1/4 teaspoon ground cinnamon
1-1/4 cups cooked wild rice
3 eggs
3/4 cup milk
1/3 cup vegetable oil
1/4 cup pure maple syrup
1 cup chopped unpeeled apple

Grease 12 muffin cups or line with paper liners. Preheat oven to 400F (205C). In a medium-size bowl, combine flour, baking powder, baking soda, salt, nutmeg, cinnamon, and 1 cup rice; set aside. In a medium-size bowl, lightly beat eggs. Stir in milk, oil, maple syrup, and apple. Add to flour mixture, stirring only until dry ingredients are moistened. Spoon batter into greased muffin cups until about two-thirds full. Sprinkle 1 teaspoon of remaining wild rice over top of each muffin. Bake 12 to 18 minutes, or until a wooden pick inserted in center comes out clean. Serve hot.

Makes 12 muffins.

Baked Hush Puppies

*A*ccording to legend, Southern cooks used to toss scraps of fried cornmeal batter to placate begging dogs with the admonition, "Hush, puppy!" Not only is this nonfried version lower in calories, but it's a lot less messy to prepare. The tops of baked hush puppies are crinkled and funny looking, the result of dropping the batter into hot, oiled muffin cups.

> **About 1/3 cup vegetable oil**
> **1-3/4 cups yellow cornmeal**
> **3/4 cup all-purpose flour**
> **1 tablespoon baking powder**
> **1 teaspoon baking soda**
> **1 teaspoon salt**
> **1/8 to 1/4 teaspoon red (cayenne) pepper**
> **1 egg**
> **1-1/2 cups buttermilk**
> **1/2 cup chopped green onions, green part only**

Preheat oven to 425F (220C). Place 1 teaspoon oil in each of 12 muffin cups. Turn pan to coat sides of cups; place in oven to preheat 10 minutes. In a medium-size bowl, combine cornmeal, flour, baking powder, baking soda, salt, and cayenne; set aside. In a medium-size bowl, lightly beat egg. Stir in buttermilk and green onions. Add to flour mixture, stirring only until dry ingredients are moistened. Remove muffin pan from oven. Working quickly, spoon batter into greased muffin cups until about two-thirds full. Batter will bubble in the hot oil. Bake 12 to 15 minutes, or until golden brown. Serve hot.

Makes 12 muffins.

Variation

Hush Puppy Crisps: Use a serrated knife to cut leftover hush puppies into 1/4-inch slices. Arrange slices on large, ungreased baking sheet. Bake in a 350F (175C) oven 5 minutes, or until golden brown. Remove from oven; turn over slices. Bake an additional 5 minutes, or until nicely browned. Cool 5 minutes.

Hominy Honeys

Hominy is one of the first food gifts the Native Americans gave the colonists. Serve these old-fashioned, honey-dipped corn muffins with Honey Butter (page 260).

  2 cups all-purpose flour
  2 teaspoons baking powder
  1/2 teaspoon baking soda
  1 teaspoon salt
  1 (15-oz.) can golden hominy
  Milk, if needed
  2 eggs
  1/4 cup vegetable oil
  3/4 cup honey
  2 tablespoons unsalted butter, melted

Grease 12 muffin cups or line with paper liners. Preheat oven to 400F (205C). In a medium-size bowl, combine flour, baking powder, baking soda, and salt; set aside. Drain hominy, reserving 1/2 cup of the liquid. If necessary, add milk to make 1/2 cup. Reserve 12 large hominy kernels for garnish. In a blender or food processor with a metal blade, process 1 cup hominy until finely ground but not pureed. In a medium-size bowl, lightly beat eggs. Stir in reserved hominy liquid, ground hominy, oil, and 1/4 cup honey. Add to flour mixture, stirring only until dry ingredients are moistened.

Spoon batter into greased muffin cups until about two-thirds full. Place 1 hominy kernel in center of each unbaked muffin. Bake 15 to 20 minutes, or until a wooden pick inserted in center comes out clean. While muffins are baking, combine melted butter and remaining 1/2 cup honey in a small bowl, stirring until smooth. Remove baked muffins from muffin cups; dip tops in honey-butter mixture. Let topping set 3 to 4 minutes before serving. Serve remaining honey-butter mixture with muffins. Serve warm.

Makes 12 muffins.

Peanutty Branana Muffins

My favorite childhood sandwich was peanut butter and banana, which is probably why I created this taste-alike muffin. The muffins, however, have the nutritional bonus of bran. Whether you use chunky or smooth peanut butter is strictly up to you.

    1-1/4 cups all-purpose flour
    1 cup oat or wheat bran
    2-1/2 teaspoons baking powder
    1/2 teaspoon baking soda
    3/4 teaspoon cinnamon
    1/2 teaspoon salt
    2 eggs
    1 cup pureed ripe banana
    1/2 cup peanut butter
    1/3 cup pure maple syrup
    1 tablespoon vegetable oil

Grease 12 muffin cups or line with paper liners. Preheat oven to 400F (205C). In a medium-size bowl, combine flour, bran, baking powder, baking soda, cinnamon, and salt; set aside. In a medium-size bowl, lightly beat eggs. Stir in banana, peanut butter, maple syrup, and oil. Add to flour mixture, stirring only until dry ingredients are moistened. Spoon batter into greased muffin cups until about two-thirds full. Bake 13 to 18 minutes, or until a wooden pick inserted in center comes out clean. Serve hot.

Makes 12 muffins.

Coconuty Carrot Muffins

*K*ids of all ages will love these muffins—in the morning, at lunch, for a snack—any time at all. They're great spread with Orange Cream (page 263).

    2 cups all-purpose flour
    2 teaspoons baking powder
    1/2 teaspoon baking soda
    3/4 teaspoon salt
    1 cup shredded carrots
    3/4 cup shredded coconut
    2 eggs
    1 (8-oz.) carton orange or vanilla yogurt
    1/4 cup packed brown sugar
    3 tablespoons vegetable oil
    1 tablespoon freshly grated orange zest

Grease 12 muffin cups or line with paper liners. Preheat oven to 400F (205C). In a medium-size bowl, combine flour, baking powder, baking soda, salt, carrots, and 1/2 cup coconut; set aside. In a medium-size bowl, lightly beat eggs. Stir in yogurt, sugar, oil, and orange zest. Add to flour mixture, stirring only until dry ingredients are moistened. Spoon batter into greased muffin cups until about two-thirds full. Sprinkle top of each muffin with a little of the remaining 1/4 cup coconut. Bake 20 to 25 minutes, or until a wooden pick inserted in center comes out clean. Serve hot.

Makes 12 muffins.

Marmalade Muffins

*F*resh orange juice and freshly grated orange zest give these muffins a rise-and-shine flavor. For a lively change of pace, substitute lemonade for the orange juice, lemon zest for the orange zest, and use lemon marmalade.

> 2 cups all-purpose flour
> 2 teaspoons baking powder
> 1/2 teaspoon baking soda
> 1/2 teaspoon salt
> 2 eggs
> 3/4 cup orange juice
> 1/2 cup sugar
> 1/3 cup unsalted butter, melted
> Finely grated zest of 1 medium-size orange
> 1/4 cup orange, ginger, or other marmalade

Grease 12 muffin cups or line with paper liners. Preheat oven to 400F (205C). In a medium-size bowl, combine flour, baking powder, baking soda, and salt; set aside. In a medium-size bowl, lightly beat eggs. Stir in orange juice, sugar, butter, and orange zest. Add to flour mixture, stirring only until dry ingredients are moistened. Spoon batter into greased muffin cups until about two-thirds full. Spoon about 1 teaspoon orange marmalade onto center of each muffin, slightly pressing into batter. Bake about 20 minutes, or until a wooden pick inserted in center comes out clean. Serve hot.

Makes 12 muffins.

Praline Rum Rolls

A rich praline spiral flavors these rum-glazed treats that are elegant enough for special company. If you don't keep rum around the house, use 1/4 teaspoon rum extract plus 1-3/4 teaspoons milk for the glaze.

> Easy Cream Biscuits dough (page 165), made with 1/2 teaspoon salt
> 1/4 cup unsalted butter or margarine, softened
> 2/3 cup packed brown sugar
> 1/3 cup finely chopped pecans
> 1 teaspoon ground cinnamon
> 12 pecan halves
> Rum Glaze, see below

Rum Glaze:
> 1 cup powdered sugar
> 2 teaspoons rum
> 2 to 4 teaspoons milk

Grease 12 muffin cups (don't use paper liners). Preheat oven to 425F (220C). Prepare Easy Cream Biscuits dough. Turn out dough onto a lightly floured surface; knead gently 10 to 12 strokes. Roll out dough into an 18" x 12" rectangle. Spread with butter. In a small bowl, combine brown sugar, pecans, and cinnamon; reserve 1/4 cup for topping. Sprinkle remaining mixture evenly over dough. Beginning on 1 long side, roll tightly, jelly-roll fashion. Pinch seam to seal. Cut roll into 24 (3/4-inch) slices. Stand 2 slices side by side and on edge in each muffin cup. Gently spread slices apart. Spoon 1 teaspoon reserved brown sugar mixture in center of each roll. Top each with pecan half, pressing down lightly. Bake 15 to 20 minutes, or until golden brown. While rolls are baking, prepare Rum Glaze. Remove rolls from muffin cups; place on a rack over waxed paper. Drizzle with Rum Glaze. Let glaze set 5 minutes before serving.

Makes 12 rolls.

Rum Glaze: In a small bowl, combine powdered sugar, rum, and enough milk to make a smooth and creamy glaze of drizzling consistency.

Parmesan-Prosciutto Popovers

*P*opovers are leavened by eggs and steam. They're super easy to prepare and make impressive company fare. Special popover pans are available in kitchenware shops, but custard cups or a muffin pan work just as well. Popovers have naturally moist interiors. For a drier popover, remove the baked puffs from the oven and prick in several places with the tip of a pointed knife. Return to turned-off oven with door ajar and let stand 10 minutes. Serve these savory puffs piping hot with plenty of butter.

1 cup milk
2 large eggs
1 tablespoon vegetable oil
1 cup all-purpose flour
2 teaspoons granulated sugar
1/4 teaspoon salt
1/4 teaspoon freshly ground pepper
1/2 cup finely grated Parmesan cheese
1/2 cup finely chopped prosciutto

Generously butter 8 (5- to 6-ounce) custard cups, 10 muffin cups, or 12 popover cups. Place custard cups on a heavy baking sheet. Place muffin cups, popover cups, or baking sheet with custard cups on center rack of oven. Preheat to 450F (230C). Combine all ingredients except prosciutto in a blender or food processor fitted with metal blade. Process until batter is smooth, scraping sides of container as necessary. Add prosciutto; process until coarsely pulverized; large specks of prosciutto should still be discernible.

Remove hot baking cups from oven. Working quickly, fill each cup two-thirds full with batter. Immediately return filled cups to oven. Bake 20 minutes. Reduce heat to 350F (175C). Bake 20 to 25 minutes longer, or until nicely browned. IMPORTANT: Keep oven door closed during first 30 minutes of baking; a draft will collapse popovers. Run a knife around edge of baking cups to loosen popovers. Serve immediately.

Makes 8 to 12 popovers.

Ginger-Berry Drops

I've used everything from raspberries to blueberries to cranberries in these quick, easy biscuits. Choose a berry that's small enough to be used whole. Strawberries, for instance, require cutting and release too much of their moisture during baking. Dried cranberries, blueberries, or cherries also work well.

1-3/4 cups all-purpose flour
1 tablespoon baking powder
1/2 teaspoon salt
1/4 teaspoon ground ginger
3 tablespoons packed brown sugar
1/3 cup cold unsalted butter, cut in 5 pieces
1 cup orange juice
1 tablespoon minced gingerroot
1 cup blueberries, cranberries, or raspberries

Grease 2 large baking sheets. Preheat oven to 450F (230C). In a food processor fitted with metal blade or a medium-size bowl, combine flour, baking powder, salt, ground ginger, and sugar. Add butter; process in quick ON/OFF pulses just until mixture resembles coarse crumbs. Or use a pastry cutter or 2 knives to cut butter into flour mixture. Add juice and ginger; process or stir only until dry ingredients are moistened. Drop heaping tablespoons of batter, 2 inches apart, on prepared baking sheets. Bake 12 to 15 minutes, or until golden brown.

Makes about 18 biscuits.

Easy Cream Biscuits

My Granddaddy Buck taught me how to make these biscuits when I was eight years old, so you know they must be super-easy. The secret is the whipping cream: The heavier the cream, the more tender the biscuits. In lieu of the traditional round shape, this dough's cut into squares (big, for grandpa-size appetites!), which also means you don't have to reroll dough scraps.

2 cups all-purpose flour
4 teaspoons baking powder
1 tablespoon sugar
1 teaspoon salt
3/4 to 1 cup whipping cream
1/3 cup butter, melted (optional)

Preheat oven to 425F (220C). In a medium-size bowl, combine flour, baking powder, sugar, and salt. Stir in enough of the cream to make a soft dough. Turn out onto a lightly floured surface. Gently knead 12 to 15 strokes, or only until dough holds together. Pat or roll out dough into a square 1/2 inch thick. Cut into 2- to 3-inch squares. If desired, dip in melted butter. Arrange biscuits 2 inches apart on ungreased baking sheets. Bake 15 to 18 minutes, or until golden brown. Serve hot.

Makes about 12 biscuits.

Variations

Whole-Wheat Biscuits: Substitute 1 cup whole-wheat flour for 1 cup all-purpose flour; add 2 tablespoons wheat germ.

Jam Biscuits: After placing unbaked biscuits on baking sheet, place 1 teaspoon jam on center of each biscuit, slightly pressing into dough with tip of spoon.

Raisin-Nut Biscuits: Increase sugar to 3 tablespoons; add 1/2 teaspoon cinnamon and 1/3 cup each raisins and chopped nuts. Add the raisins and nuts with cream.

Herbed Cheese Biscuits: Add 1/2 teaspoon each crumbled oregano and basil, and 3/4 cup grated Cheddar cheese.

Seed Biscuits: Add 1/3 cup toasted, hulled sunflower kernels, 2 tablespoons toasted sesame seeds (Tip, page 262), or 1 tablespoon poppy seeds.

Sherried Tea Biscuits

These buttery little biscuits are scented with sherry and perfect with afternoon tea—or anytime at all.

1-1/2 cups all-purpose flour
1 tablespoon baking powder
1/2 teaspoon salt
1 tablespoon sugar
1/2 cup cold butter, cut in 8 pieces
About 1/3 cup dry sherry
1/3 cup currants
1 tablespoon melted butter mixed with 1 teaspoon each sherry and sugar for glaze

Preheat oven to 400F (205C). In a food processor fitted with metal blade or medium-size bowl, combine flour, baking powder, salt, and sugar. Add butter; process in quick ON/OFF pulses just until mixture resembles coarse crumbs. Or use a pastry cutter or 2 knives to cut butter into flour mixture. Add 1/3 cup sherry and currants; process or stir only until dry ingredients are moistened. If necessary, add additional sherry, a teaspoon at a time, until dough clings together. Turn out dough onto a lightly floured surface. Gently knead 12 to 15 strokes. Pat or roll out dough until 1/2 inch thick. Using a round 1-1/2- or 2-inch cutter, cut out dough. Place biscuits 1-1/2 inches apart on ungreased baking sheets. Brush with butter-sherry glaze. Bake 6 to 8 minutes, or until golden.

Makes about 26 biscuits.

Chocolate-Hazelnut Scones

*P*ronounced "skons" by the British, these biscuits are tender, fragrant, and buttery-good. The nice surprise about these particular scones is that they make marvelous shortcakes. Split them horizontally, then layer with fresh berries and Frangelico-scented whipped cream. To die for!

2 cups all-purpose flour
1/4 cup granulated sugar
2-1/2 teaspoons baking powder
1/2 teaspoon baking soda
1/2 teaspoon salt
1/2 cup cold butter, cut in 8 pieces
3/4 cup chocolate pieces
1/2 cup coarsely chopped hazelnuts
2 eggs
1/2 cup whipping cream
1/2 teaspoon pure vanilla extract
Finely grated zest of 1 large orange
Cream or milk (optional)

Grease 2 large baking sheets; set aside. Preheat oven to 425F (220C). In a medium-size bowl, combine flour, sugar, baking powder, baking soda, and salt. Use a pastry cutter or 2 knives to cut in butter until mixture resembles coarse crumbs. Stir in chocolate and nuts. In a small bowl, lightly beat eggs. Stir in cream, vanilla, and orange zest. Add to flour mixture, stirring only until dry ingredients are moistened. Turn out dough onto a generously floured surface; gently press dough until it holds together (dough will be very soft). Divide dough in half. Flour your hands and pat each half into a circle about 1/2 inch thick. With a floured knife, cut each circle into 6 pie-shaped pieces. Brush excess flour off tops of scones. Use a metal spatula to place scones, 2 inches apart, on prepared baking sheets. If desired, brush tops of scones with a little cream or milk; sprinkle with sugar. Bake 12 to 15 minutes, or until golden brown.

Makes 12 scones.

Italian Cheese Crescents

Don't tell anyone how easy these crispy-rich pastries are—just enjoy the raves.

2-1/2 cups all-purpose flour
2 teaspoons baking powder
1/2 teaspoon salt
1/3 cup granulated sugar
1 (8-oz.) carton ricotta cheese (1 cup)
1 cup unsalted butter or margarine, softened
1 teaspoon freshly grated lemon zest
1/2 teaspoon almond extract
3/4 cup packed brown sugar
3/4 cup finely chopped toasted almonds
1/2 teaspoon ground cinnamon
1/4 cup butter or margarine, melted
1 egg mixed with 1 tablespoon sugar for glaze

Grease 2 or 3 large baking sheets; set aside. In a medium-size bowl, combine flour, baking powder, salt, and granulated sugar; set aside. In large bowl of electric mixer, beat ricotta, 1 cup softened butter, lemon zest, and almond extract until smooth and creamy. Fold in flour mixture, a third at a time, blending only until dry ingredients are moistened. Turn out onto a lightly floured surface. Using a pastry scraper or metal spatula (dough will be very moist), gently knead dough 10 to 12 strokes. Divide dough into 3 pieces. Place on a large plate; cover and refrigerate 20 minutes.

Preheat oven to 400F (205C). In a small bowl, combine brown sugar, almonds, and cinnamon; set aside. Remove 1 piece of dough from refrigerator. On a lightly floured surface, roll or pat dough into a 13-inch circle, about 1/8 inch thick. Brush with melted butter; sprinkle with 1/3 nut mixture, pressing it lightly into surface. Cut circle into 16 pie-shaped pieces. Roll each piece tightly from outer edge to point. Place on prepared baking sheets, points down, curving ends slightly to form crescents. Brush with egg glaze. Repeat with remaining refrigerated dough. Bake 15 to 20 minutes, or until golden brown.

Makes 48 rolls.

Seeded Cheese Pinwheels

*S*erve these crisp Cheddar crackers with aperitifs, or soups or salads, or simply to eat as a snack. Store leftovers airtight so they'll retain their crispness.

2 cups all-purpose flour
1 teaspoon baking powder
1/2 teaspoon baking soda
1/2 teaspoon salt
1/2 cup cold butter, cut in 8 pieces
1 cup grated Cheddar cheese
1 cup sour cream
2 tablespoons butter, melted
1/4 cup poppy seeds
1/4 cup sesame seeds
1 egg white mixed with 1 tablespoon water for glaze

Lightly grease 2 baking sheets; set aside. Preheat oven to 425F (220C). In a food processor fitted with metal blade or medium-size bowl, combine flour, baking powder, baking soda, and salt. Add butter; process in quick ON/OFF pulses just until mixture resembles coarse crumbs. Or use a pastry cutter or 2 knives to cut butter into flour mixture. Add cheese and sour cream; process or stir only until dry ingredients are moistened. Turn out dough onto a lightly floured surface. Gently knead 10 to 12 strokes. Pat or roll out dough into a 15" x 12" rectangle; brush with melted butter. Evenly sprinkle poppy seeds and sesame seeds over dough. Beginning on 1 long side, roll up tightly, jelly-roll fashion. Pinch seam to seal. Cut into 30 (1/2-inch) slices. Place slices 2 inches apart on prepared baking sheets. With a metal spatula, slightly flatten each piece until about 1/4 inch thick. Brush with egg-white glaze. Bake 15 to 18 minutes, or until golden brown.

Makes 30 crackers.

Orange-Pecan Spirals

The appearance of these showy pastries belies the ease with which they're made. Let it be your secret.

    2 cups all-purpose flour
    1 tablespoon baking powder
    1/2 teaspoon salt
    1/4 cup sugar
    1/2 cup cold unsalted butter, cut into 8 pieces
    1 egg
    1/2 cup whipping cream
    1/3 cup orange marmalade
    1/3 cup finely chopped pecans
    Cinnamon-Orange Glaze, see below

Cinnamon-Orange Glaze:
    1 cup powdered sugar
    1/2 teaspoon ground cinnamon
    2 to 4 tablespoons orange juice

Lightly grease 2 baking sheets; set aside. Preheat oven to 450F (230C). In a food processor fitted with metal blade or medium-size bowl, combine flour, baking powder, salt, and sugar. Add butter; process in quick ON/OFF pulses just until mixture resembles coarse crumbs. Or use a pastry cutter or 2 knives to cut butter into flour mixture. In a small bowl, beat egg and cream until combined. Add to flour mixture; process or stir only until dry ingredients are moistened.

Turn out dough onto a lightly floured surface; knead gently 10 to 12 strokes. Roll out dough into a 15" x 8" rectangle. Spread with marmalade; sprinkle with pecans. Fold dough in half lengthwise to make a 15" x 4" rectangle. Cut crosswise into 15 (1-inch) strips. Holding each strip at both ends, twist in opposite directions twice, forming a spiral. Arrange spirals 2 inches apart on prepared baking sheets; press ends onto baking sheets to secure. Bake 10 to 12 minutes, or until golden brown. Transfer twists to racks set over waxed paper. Prepare Cinnamon-Orange Glaze. Drizzle warm spirals with Cinnamon-Orange Glaze. Let glaze set 3 to 4 minutes before serving. Spirals become crisp as they cool.

Makes 15 pastries.

Cinnamon-Orange Glaze: In a small bowl, combine powdered sugar and cinnamon. Stir in enough orange juice to make a smooth and creamy glaze of drizzling consistency.

Polenta-Cheese Crisps

*P*olenta (coarsely ground cornmeal) can be found in Italian markets and most supermarkets. If you can't find it, simply substitute regular yellow cornmeal.

1-1/3 cups polenta or regular cornmeal
1/2 teaspoon salt
1/8 teaspoon red (cayenne) pepper
1 1/3 cups boiling water
2 1/2 tablespoons olive oil or vegetable oil
1 cup grated fontina, Cheddar, Swiss, or Monterey Jack cheese
1 tablespoon minced fresh herbs, such as oregano, basil, or chervil, or 1 teaspoon dried herbs

Lightly oil a 15" x 10" jelly-roll pan; set aside. Position oven rack in middle of oven; preheat oven to 325F (165C). In a medium-size bowl, stir together cornmeal, salt, and cayenne. Gradually add boiling water and oil, stirring until well combined. Stir in cheese and herbs. Use your fingers, a rubber spatula, or the back of a spoon to press mixture evenly over bottom of the prepared pan. Use a pointed knife to score polenta into 24 squares, cutting 6 strips crosswise, 4 lengthwise. Bake 60 to 70 minutes, or until deep golden brown. The edges will brown faster than the center. Remove from oven and immediately cut through scoring to separate crackers. Cool to room temperature before serving.

Makes 2 dozen crackers.

Savory Quick Breads

*Q*uick breads are hands-down favorites with beginning bakers. Discovering that they can actually create delicious homemade bread in about an hour from start to finish is immensely satisfying and bolsters their confidence to move on to higher-rising aspirations. As for quick breads and experienced bakers . . . well, we just love them because they're so easy and delicious.

Quick breads are so named because, unlike yeast breads, they don't require kneading or a waiting period for rising. Baking powder and baking soda are the seemingly magic leaveners that, when combined with a liquid, release carbon dioxide and produce an almost-instant rising power. Oven heat gives double-acting baking powder a second burst of energy. Because of this quick-rising action, the pans should be greased and the oven preheated before the batter is mixed. Room-temperature ingredients promote a more natural gas expansion, which ensures light and tender breads.

The key to success with quick breads is gentle but speedy handling. Once the ingredients are combined, mix only until the dry ingredients are moistened. Overmixing will stretch the flour's gluten and dissipate the carbon dioxide gas, thereby producing a dense, heavy loaf. Bake quick breads on the middle rack of an oven. In general, the bread is done when a wooden pick inserted in the middle comes out clean. It's natural for most quick breads to have a cracked top, the result of leavening gases expanding during baking. Letting the bread stand in the pan 10 minutes before removing to a rack to cool allows it to set, making it easier to handle.

If wrapped airtight, quick breads can be stored at room temperature about three days, in the refrigerator up to a week, or in the freezer for up to six months. Quick breads with fruits and nuts usually develop a fuller flavor by the second day.

Savory quick breads past their prime can be thinly sliced and brushed with melted butter, then placed on a baking sheet and toasted under an oven broiler until golden brown on both sides. These thin, crispy toasts are perfect accompaniments for soups or salads.

Pull-Apart Cheese Ring

❦⚊✕⚊❦

*G*uests can pull off their own helpings of this fragrant wine-and-cheese bread.

2 tablespoons cheese cracker crumbs or dry bread crumbs
2 cups all-purpose flour
1 tablespoon baking powder
1 teaspoon salt
1/2 teaspoon dry mustard
1/8 teaspoon red (cayenne) pepper
1 cup grated Cheddar cheese (4 oz.)
1/3 cup dry white wine
1/3 cup olive or vegetable oil
1/3 cup milk
6 tablespoons unsalted butter or margarine, melted
1 cup grated Parmesan cheese (3 oz.)

Generously grease an 8-inch tube pan or ring mold. Sprinkle crumbs over bottom and sides of pan; set aside. Preheat oven to 400F (205C). In a large bowl, combine flour, baking powder, salt, mustard, cayenne, and Cheddar cheese; set aside. In a small bowl, combine wine, oil, and milk. Add to dry ingredients, stirring only until mixture no longer sticks to bowl. Shape dough into 26 (1-inch) balls. Dip balls in melted butter; roll in Parmesan cheese. Arrange in 2 layers in prepared pan. Drizzle with any remaining butter; sprinkle with any remaining Parmesan. Bake 25 to 30 minutes, or until a wooden pick inserted in center comes out clean. Let stand in pan 10 minutes. Turn out onto a serving dish. Serve warm.

Makes 1 loaf.

TIP: Your bread will only be as good as the ingredients that go into it. When a wine or beer is called for, be sure to use one that's full-flavored. Never substitute a so-called cooking wine or light beer.

Pepita-Oat Bread

*P*epitas (puh-PEE-tahs) are pumpkin seeds and can be found in natural food stores, Mexican markets, and many supermarkets. If you can't find the dry-roasted style, substitute raw hulled pumpkin seeds. Before using raw seeds, toast them in a large, ungreased skillet over medium heat until they turn golden brown and make popping sounds.

1-1/2 cups regular or quick-cooking rolled oats
1-1/2 cups milk
2 cups all-purpose flour
1 tablespoon baking powder
1 teaspoon salt
1/4 cup sugar
1 egg, lightly beaten
3 tablespoons vegetable oil
1 cup plus 2 tablespoons dry-roasted pumpkin seeds

Generously grease a 9" x 5" loaf pan; set aside. Preheat oven to 350F (175C). In a medium-size bowl, combine 1 cup oats and milk; set aside to soak 10 minutes. In a blender, process remaining 1/2 cup oats until the consistency of flour. In a large bowl, combine oat flour, all-purpose flour, baking powder, salt, and sugar; set aside. To milk-oat mixture, add egg and oil. Add to flour mixture, stirring only until dry ingredients are moistened. Stir in pumpkin seeds. Turn into prepared pan; smooth top. Sprinkle with remaining 2 tablespoons pumpkin seeds. Bake 50 to 60 minutes, or until a wooden pick inserted in center comes out clean. Let stand in pan 10 minutes. Turn out onto a rack to cool.

Makes 1 loaf.

Peanutty Pumpernickel

The coffee in this loaf adds rich color and flavor. Whether you use smooth or chunky peanut butter is entirely up to you.

2 teaspoons cornmeal
1-1/4 cups all-purpose flour
3/4 cup rye flour
1 tablespoon baking powder
1 teaspoon salt
1-1/2 teaspoons caraway seeds
2 eggs
1/2 cup peanut butter
1 tablespoon vegetable oil
1 tablespoon molasses
1-1/4 cups coffee

Grease a 1-1/2-quart casserole dish or 8" x 4" loaf pan. Sprinkle cornmeal over bottom and sides of pan; set aside. Preheat oven to 350F (175C). In a medium-size bowl, combine all-purpose flour, rye flour, baking powder, salt, and 1 teaspoon of the caraway seeds; set aside. In a medium-size bowl, lightly beat eggs. Stir in peanut butter, oil, molasses, and coffee. Add to flour mixture, stirring only until dry ingredients are moistened. Turn into prepared pan. Smooth top and sprinkle with remaining 1/2 teaspoon caraway seeds. Bake 50 to 55 minutes, or until a wooden pick inserted in center comes out clean. Let stand in pan 10 minutes. Turn out onto a rack to cool.

Makes 1 loaf.

Poppy-Parmesan Bread

I love this bread for grilled cheese sandwiches. If you're grating the Parmesan in a food processor, use the metal blade, have the cheese at room temperature, and cut it into 1- to 1-1/2-inch chunks. With the machine running, drop the cheese through the feed tube, a piece at a time, processing until the Parmesan is finely grated.

> 2 cups all-purpose flour
> 2 teaspoons baking powder
> 1/2 teaspoon baking soda
> 3/4 teaspoon salt
> 1 cup grated Parmesan cheese (3 oz.)
> About 1-1/2 tablespoons poppy seeds
> 1 egg
> 1 tablespoon vegetable oil
> 1 cup buttermilk
> 1 small garlic clove, minced

Grease and flour an 8" x 4" loaf pan or 1-1/2-quart casserole dish; set aside. Preheat oven to 350F (175C). In a medium-size bowl, combine flour, baking powder, baking soda, salt, cheese, and 1-1/2 tablespoons poppy seeds; set aside. In a medium-size bowl, lightly beat egg. Stir in oil, buttermilk, and garlic. Add to flour mixture, stirring only until dry ingredients are moistened. Turn into prepared pan. Smooth top and sprinkle with about 1 teaspoon poppy seeds. Bake 45 to 50 minutes, or until a wooden pick inserted in center comes out clean. Let stand in pan 10 minutes. Turn out onto a rack to cool.

Makes 1 loaf.

Variation

Poppy-Cheddar Bread: Substitute 1 cup grated Cheddar (4 oz.) for Parmesan cheese.

Jack-Be-Nimble Quick Brown Bread

This wholesome loaf is my quick version of the classic steamed brown bread, which takes hours. Spread it with Orange Cream (page 263) and serve for snacks or breakfast.

1 cup all-purpose flour
1/2 cup whole-wheat flour
1/2 cup medium rye flour
1/2 cup yellow cornmeal
1/2 cup oat or wheat bran
2 teaspoons baking powder
1 teaspoon baking soda
1 teaspoon salt
1/2 teaspoon ground nutmeg
1 cup orange juice
1/3 cup molasses
3 tablespoons vegetable oil
1 teaspoon grated orange zest
1 cup raisins (optional)

Grease an 8" x 4" loaf pan; set aside. Preheat oven to 350F (175C). In a medium-size bowl, combine all-purpose flour, whole-wheat flour, rye flour, cornmeal, bran, baking powder, baking soda, salt, and nutmeg; set aside. In a medium-size bowl, combine orange juice, molasses, oil, and orange zest. Add to flour mixture, stirring only until dry ingredients are moistened. Stir in raisins, if desired. Turn into prepared pan; smooth top. Bake 55 to 65 minutes, or until a wooden pick inserted in center comes out clean. Let stand in pan 10 minutes. Turn out onto a rack to cool.

Makes 1 loaf.

TIP: Breads made with honey and molasses brown more quickly than breads made with other sugars.

Irish Soda Bread

My Irish grandmother, Elizabeth Mary Masterson, loved this bread from her native Eire. I've Sharonized it with the nontraditional touches of Irish whiskey, honey, and orange zest. If you don't have Irish whiskey, Scotch can be used. For a nonalcoholic loaf, substitute buttermilk.

4 cups all-purpose flour
1 tablespoon baking powder
1 teaspoon baking soda
1 teaspoon salt
1 cup currants
2 teaspoons caraway seeds (optional)
1-1/2 cups buttermilk
1/4 cup honey
1/4 cup unsalted butter or margarine, melted
1/4 cup Irish whiskey
2 teaspoons freshly grated orange zest

Generously grease 2 round 8-inch cake or pie pans; set aside. Preheat oven to 350F (175C). In a large bowl, combine flour, baking powder, baking soda, salt, currants, and caraway seeds, if desired; set aside. In a medium-size bowl, combine buttermilk, honey, butter, whiskey, and orange zest. Add to flour mixture, stirring only until dry ingredients are moistened.

Turn out dough (which will be sticky) onto a generously floured surface; knead 1 minute. Cut dough in half. Shape each piece into a round loaf; place in prepared pans. Dip a sharp knife or razor blade into flour; cut a 1/2-inch-deep cross in top of each loaf. Brush loaves with a little whiskey or milk. Let loaves stand 10 minutes. Bake 35 to 40 minutes, or until bread sounds hollow when tapped on the bottom. For a lighter texture, invert deep, round cake pans over the loaves during the first 20 minutes of baking, then remove pans. Cool on racks. Slice thinly or cut into wedges.

Makes 2 loaves.

Variation

Whole-Wheat Irish Soda Bread: Substitute 2 cups whole-wheat flour for 2 cups all-purpose flour; add 1/4 cup wheat germ.

Lemon-Cream Loaf

*T*he only thing sweet about this sprightly loaf is its sugar-crystal topping. It's wonderful spread with Lemon Cream (page 263). Since there's no other fat in this recipe, the whipping cream is necessary for tenderness.

2 cups all-purpose flour
2 teaspoons baking powder
1 teaspoon baking soda
1 teaspoon salt
4 eggs
1/2 cup sugar
1 cup whipping cream
Freshly grated zest from 2 large lemons
1/2 cup finely chopped almonds, walnuts, or pecans
3 tablespoons lemon juice

Grease and flour a 1-1/2-quart casserole dish or 8" x 4" loaf pan; set aside. Preheat oven to 325F (165C). In a medium-size bowl, combine flour, baking powder, baking soda, and salt; set aside. In a medium-size bowl, lightly beat eggs. Stir in 1/4 cup of the sugar, cream, and lemon zest. Add to flour mixture, stirring only until dry ingredients are moistened. Stir in nuts. Turn into prepared pan; smooth top. Bake 55 to 65 minutes, or until a wooden pick inserted in center comes out clean. Let stand in pan 10 minutes. In a small bowl, combine remaining 1/4 cup sugar and lemon juice (sugar will not dissolve). Turn bread out onto a rack set over waxed paper. Spoon or brush glaze over hot bread, allowing excess to drizzle down sides. Cool to room temperature.

Makes 1 loaf.

Olive-Cheese Bread

A surprise layer of pimiento-stuffed olives hides inside this cheese-flecked loaf. To add extra piquancy, substitute 1/4 cup olive brine for 1/4 cup of the buttermilk and omit the salt. If you like things spicy-hot, substitute jalapeño-stuffed olives, which are available in gourmet markets and some supermarkets.

2 cups all-purpose flour
2 teaspoons baking powder
1/2 teaspoon baking soda
1/4 teaspoon salt
1 tablespoon sugar
1 cup grated Cheddar cheese (4 oz.)
2 eggs
About 1/4 cup olive oil
3/4 cup buttermilk
34 pimiento-stuffed green olives

Grease an 8" x 4" loaf pan; set aside. Preheat oven to 350F (175C). In a medium-size bowl, combine flour, baking powder, baking soda, salt, sugar, and cheese; set aside. In a medium-size bowl, lightly beat eggs. Stir in 1/4 cup oil and buttermilk. Add to flour mixture, stirring only until dry ingredients are moistened. Spoon half of batter into prepared pan. Arrange 28 olives, on their sides and evenly spaced, on top of batter, making 4 rows of 7 olives each. Cover with remaining batter; smooth top. Place 6 olives, pimiento end up, evenly spaced down center of batter. Lightly brush top with olive oil. Bake 35 to 45 minutes, or until a wooden pick inserted in center comes out clean. Let stand in pan 10 minutes. Turn out onto a rack to cool.

Makes 1 loaf.

Corny Tex-Mex Cornbread

*A*ccompany this moist, spicy, and colorful bread with Cheddar Butter (page 257) and serve it with chili. Diced jalapeño chiles are available canned. Caution is the byword if using fresh jalapeños (see page 116). If you don't like the heat of jalapeños, substitute a 4-ounce can of diced green chiles, well drained.

1-1/2 cups all-purpose flour
1 cup yellow cornmeal
1 tablespoon baking powder
1 tablespoon sugar
1 teaspoon salt
1/2 teaspoon ground cumin
1/4 teaspoon red (cayenne) pepper
2 cups grated Cheddar cheese (8 oz.)
3 eggs
1 cup milk
1/4 cup vegetable oil
1/3 cup finely chopped green onions with green tops
2 to 3 tablespoons diced jalapeño chiles
1 (4-oz.) jar diced pimientos, well drained
2 teaspoons minced cilantro
1-1/2 teaspoons minced fresh oregano or 1/2 teaspoon dried oregano leaves
1-1/2 cups fresh or frozen, unthawed corn kernels

Grease a 9-inch springform pan with center tube or an 8- to 10-cup ring mold; set aside. Preheat oven to 400F (205C). In a medium-size bowl, combine flour, cornmeal, baking powder, sugar, salt, cumin, cayenne, and 1-2/3 cups cheese; set aside. In a medium-size bowl, lightly beat eggs. Stir in milk, oil, green onions, chiles, pimientos, cilantro, and oregano. Add to flour mixture, stirring only until dry ingredients are moistened. Stir in corn. Turn into prepared pan; smooth top.

Bake 25 minutes; sprinkle top with remaining 1/3 cup cheese. Bake 10 to 20 minutes longer, or until a wooden pick inserted in center comes out clean. Baked bread will be moist, but no particles will cling to pick. Let stand in pan 15 minutes. Carefully turn out onto a rack, then right side up onto a serving plate to cool. Handle gently to avoid breaking.

Makes 1 loaf.

Branapple Bread

*D*on't make the mistake of using bran-flake cereal in this recipe or the bread won't turn out right.

About 1-2/3 cups Kellogg's whole-bran cold cereal
1-3/4 cups all-purpose flour
2 teaspoons baking powder
1/2 teaspoon baking soda
1/2 teaspoon salt
2 eggs
1/3 cup vegetable oil
2 tablespoons honey
1 cup apple juice

Generously grease an 8" x 4" loaf pan. Sprinkle 2 tablespoons bran cereal over bottom and sides; set aside. Preheat oven to 350F (175C). In a medium-size bowl, combine 1-1/2 cups bran cereal, flour, baking powder, baking soda, and salt; set aside. In a medium-size bowl, lightly beat eggs. Stir in oil, honey, and orange juice. Add to flour mixture, stirring only until dry ingredients are moistened. Turn into prepared pan. Smooth top and sprinkle with 1 tablespoon whole-bran cereal. Bake 45 to 50 minutes, or until a wooden pick inserted in center comes out clean. Let stand in pan 10 minutes. Turn out onto a rack to cool.

Makes 1 loaf.

Peanut-Sausage Cornbread

*P*reheating the oiled baking pan gives this cornbread a crisper crust. Sausage drippings will give your cornbread more flavor, but the oil has less cholesterol.

1/4 cup olive oil or sausage drippings
1-1/2 cups cornmeal
1/2 cup all-purpose flour
2 teaspoons baking powder
1/2 teaspoon baking soda
1 teaspoon salt
2 tablespoons sugar
2 eggs
1/4 cup smooth or chunky peanut butter
1 cup buttermilk
1/2 to 1 teaspoon hot pepper sauce
1/2 pound cooked, crumbled sausage

Pour 1-1/2 tablespoons of the oil or drippings into an 8- or 9-inch square baking pan. Place pan in oven; preheat oven to 400F (205C). In a medium-size bowl, combine cornmeal, flour, baking powder, baking soda, salt, and sugar; set aside. In a medium-size bowl, beat eggs and peanut butter until blended. Stir in buttermilk, hot sauce, and remaining 2-1/2 tablespoons oil or drippings. Add to flour mixture, stirring only until dry ingredients are moistened. Stir in cooked sausage. Remove baking pan from oven; tilt to coat bottom and sides with oil. Immediately turn batter into preheated pan. Bake 20 to 30 minutes, or until a wooden pick inserted in center comes out clean. Let stand in pan 10 minutes. Cut into 9 to 12 squares; serve warm.

Makes 9 to 12 servings.

Sunflower Wheat Loaf

*S*unflower kernels are rich in iron, and this bread is rich in flavor. If dry-roasted kernels are unavailable, substitute raw hulled sunflower kernels that you've toasted until golden brown.

1-3/4 cups dry-roasted hulled sunflower kernels
1 cup all-purpose flour
1 cup whole-wheat flour
1/3 cup wheat germ
1 tablespoon baking powder
1 teaspoon salt
1 egg
2 tablespoons vegetable oil
2 tablespoons honey
1 cup milk

Grease an 8" x 4" loaf pan. Sprinkle 1 tablespoon of the sunflower kernels over bottom and sides of pan; set aside. Preheat oven to 350F (175C). In a blender or food processor fitted with the metal blade, process 1/2 cup of the sunflower kernels until finely ground. In a medium-size bowl, combine ground sunflower kernels, all-purpose flour, whole-wheat flour, wheat germ, baking powder, and salt; set aside. In a medium-size bowl, lightly beat egg. Stir in oil, honey, and milk. Add to flour mixture, stirring only until dry ingredients are moistened. Stir in 1 cup sunflower kernels. Turn into prepared pan. Smooth top and sprinkle with about 1 tablespoon sunflower seeds. Bake 60 to 70 minutes, or until a wooden pick inserted in center comes out clean. Let stand in pan 10 minutes. Turn out onto a rack to cool.

Makes 1 loaf.

TIP: Before measuring syrupy sweeteners such as honey or molasses, lightly coat a measuring spoon or cup with vegetable oil. Every drop of the syrup will slip out easily. If a recipe calls for both honey and oil, measure the oil first, then use the same, unwashed container for the honey.

Watercress-Herb Bread

Watercress and fresh herbs give this bread a sprightly flavor. Though you can substitute other fresh herbs of your choice, I don't suggest using dried herbs; their flavor will give you a lackluster loaf.

2-1/2 cups all-purpose flour
1 tablespoon sugar
2 teaspoons baking powder
1/2 teaspoon baking soda
1 teaspoon salt
2 eggs
1 cup buttermilk
2 tablespoons vegetable oil
1/4 cup chopped fresh watercress
3 tablespoons chopped fresh parsley
1 tablespoon chopped fresh basil
1 teaspoon chopped fresh oregano
2 teaspoons freshly grated lemon zest

Grease an 8" x 4" loaf pan; set aside. Preheat oven to 350F (175C). In a medium-size bowl, combine flour, sugar, baking powder, baking soda, and salt; set aside. In another medium-size bowl, lightly beat eggs. Stir in buttermilk, oil, watercress, parsley, basil, oregano, and lemon zest. Add to flour mixture, stirring only until dry ingredients are moistened. Turn into prepared pan; smooth top. Bake 40 to 50 minutes, or until a wooden pick inserted in center comes out clean. Let stand in pan 10 minutes. Turn out onto a rack to cool.

Makes 1 loaf.

Pepperoni Pizza Bread

Tomato sauce in the bread—rather than on top—gives this pizza-style loaf its distinctive flavor.

1 tablespoon cornmeal
1 cup shredded provolone cheese (4 oz.)
3/4 cup grated mozzarella cheese (3 oz.)
2 cups all-purpose flour
2 teaspoons baking powder
1/2 teaspoon baking soda
2 eggs
1 (8-oz.) can tomato sauce
2 tablespoons olive oil
1 medium-size garlic clove, minced
1-1/2 teaspoons chopped fresh basil
1 teaspoon chopped fresh oregano
1 cup finely chopped pepperoni (4 oz.)
9 slices pepperoni, 1/8 inch thick

Generously grease an 8- or 9-inch square baking pan. Sprinkle bottom with 1 tablespoon cornmeal; set aside. Preheat oven to 375F (190C). In a small bowl, combine provolone and mozzarella cheeses. Set aside 1 cup for topping. In a medium-size bowl, combine remaining 3/4 cup cheese, flour, baking powder, and baking soda; set aside. In a medium-size bowl, lightly beat eggs. Stir in tomato sauce, oil, garlic, basil, and oregano. Add to flour mixture, stirring only until dry ingredients are moistened. Stir in chopped pepperoni. Turn into prepared pan. Smooth top; sprinkle with reserved cheese. Arrange pepperoni slices in 3 rows over top of batter. Bake 35 to 40 minutes, or until a wooden pick inserted in center comes out clean. Let stand in pan 15 minutes. Cut and serve hot. Or turn out onto a rack to cool.

Makes 9 to 12 servings.

Sweet Quick Breads & Coffeecakes

The discovery of baking powder in 1855 was a boon to home bakers everywhere. Previously, the most widely used source of carbon dioxide gas was *saleratus* (baking soda). Because saleratus was alkaline and needed an acidic ingredient to neutralize its bitter undertaste, truly sweet quick breads were not always possible. But when it was discovered that three ingredients—baking soda, an acid agent such as cream of tartar, and a moisture-absorber such as cornstarch—could be combined in one powder, bakers everywhere rejoiced. Soon there was a renaissance in cake and quick breadmaking the likes of which hasn't been seen in the baking world since.

Fruits and nuts are natural enrichments for sweet quick breads. When working with fresh fruit, be sure it's ripe but firm. Cut away any bruised portions from large fruit, and discard bruised or soft berries. Frozen berries can be used, but won't retain either their color or flavor as well as fresh ones. Don't thaw frozen berries before adding them to the batter. Toss chopped dried apricots, dates, or other fruits with a little of the flour called for in the recipe to keep the pieces separate. For maximum flavor, always toast nuts to be used in quick breads (Tip, page 262). Coating nuts with flour will help keep them suspended in a quick-bread batter.

Don't throw out that dried leftover sweet quick bread—it has myriad uses. You can rehydrate it by using a skewer or fork to poke holes in it at 1/2-inch intervals, brushing with fruit juice or liqueur, then wrapping airtight and refrigerating for 24 hours. Or, make a triflelike dessert by cutting the bread into 1-inch chunks, drizzling with liqueur or fruit juice, and layering with berries and pudding or whipped cream. An easy bread pudding can be created by coarsely crumbling the bread, folding it into pudding, and refrigerating at least 4 hours before serving. Or, finely crumble the bread, spread the crumbs in a single layer on a baking sheet, and bake at 350F (175C) until crisp and golden brown. Use these crunchy crumbs as a topping for cobblers, ice cream, or puddings.

Cappuccino Coffeecake

A bittersweet chocolate swirl adds the perfect counterpoint to this coffee-flavored breakfast treat. It's so good you can serve it for dessert!

About 1/3 cup powdered sugar
3 tablespoons unsweetened cocoa powder
3 cups all-purpose flour
1-1/4 cups granulated sugar
1 tablespoon baking powder
1/2 teaspoon baking soda
1 teaspoon salt
1/3 cup instant coffee or 1/4 cup instant espresso
1-1/2 cups milk
4 eggs, lightly beaten
2/3 cup unsalted butter, melted
2 teaspoons pure vanilla extract

Generously grease and flour a 10-cup tube or Bundt pan; set aside. Preheat oven to 350F (175C). In a small bowl, combine 1/3 cup powdered sugar and cocoa; set aside. In a large bowl, combine flour, granulated sugar, baking powder, baking soda, and salt; set aside. In a 2-cup glass measuring cup, combine instant coffee and 1/4 cup of the milk. Microwave on HIGH 30 seconds. Remove from oven; stir until coffee dissolves. Or, combine instant coffee and milk in a small saucepan; stir over low heat until coffee dissolves. In a medium-size bowl, combine coffee liquid, remaining 1-1/4 cups milk, eggs, butter, and vanilla. Add to flour mixture, stirring only until dry ingredients are moistened. Turn half the batter into prepared pan; smooth surface. Using the back of a dinner teaspoon, make an indentation 1/2 inch deep in the batter, circling around the batter halfway between edge of pan and center tube. Spoon cocoa–powdered sugar mixture into the depression. Carefully spoon remaining batter over top of cocoa mixture. Using the broad side of a dinner knife, cut down through the batter to the bottom of the pan, moving the knife in a wide zig-zag pattern to create a marbled effect. Smooth surface of batter. Bake 45 to 50 minutes, or until a wooden pick inserted in center comes out clean. Turn out immediately onto a rack to cool. When completely cool, dust lightly with powdered sugar.

Makes 1 coffeecake.

Very Cranberry Bread

A crystallized sugar glaze adorns this double cranberry bread. Dried cranberries have an intense, fruity flavor, and aren't as tart as their fresh counterparts. You can find them in specialty markets and the gourmet section of many supermarkets.

2 cups all-purpose flour
3/4 cup sugar
1 tablespoon baking powder
1/2 teaspoon baking soda
1/2 teaspoon salt
1/4 teaspoon ground cinnamon
1 teaspoon freshly grated orange zest
1 teaspoon minced gingerroot
2 eggs
1/4 cup vegetable oil
1/2 cup plus 1-1/2 tablespoons cranberry or raspberry-cranberry juice
1-1/2 cups dried cranberries

Grease an 8" x 4" loaf pan; set aside. Preheat oven to 350F (175C). In a large bowl, combine flour, 1/2 cup of the sugar, baking powder, baking soda, salt, cinnamon, orange zest, and gingerroot. In a medium-size bowl, lightly beat eggs. Stir in oil, 1/2 cup cranberry juice, and cranberries. Add to flour mixture, stirring only until dry ingredients are moistened. Turn into prepared pan; smooth top. Bake 45 to 55 minutes, or until a wooden pick inserted in center comes out clean. Let stand in pan 10 minutes. Turn out onto a rack.

In a small bowl, combine remaining 1/4 cup sugar and 1-1/2 tablespoons cranberry juice (sugar will not dissolve). Spoon over hot bread, allowing excess to drizzle down sides. Cool completely.

Makes 1 loaf.

TIP: Measure flour and other dry ingredients by stirring, then spooning into measuring cup. Level off with the flat edge of a knife.

Tea Brach

My Irish ancestors served this on chilly afternoons with steaming pots of tea. Canadian whiskey, bourbon, or Scotch can be substituted for the Irish whiskey. For an alcohol-free loaf, substitute 1/3 cup additional tea. Cut Tea Brach into thin slices and spread with sweet butter or whipped cream cheese.

1 cup golden raisins
1/2 cup currants
1-1/4 cups strong, full-flavored tea
1/3 cup Irish whiskey
1 cup packed brown sugar
Finely grated zest from 1 medium-size orange
2 cups all-purpose flour
1-1/2 teaspoons baking powder
3/4 teaspoon salt
1/2 teaspoon ground cinnamon
1/2 teaspoon ground allspice
1/4 teaspoon ground nutmeg
1 egg, slightly beaten
2 tablespoons vegetable oil
1/2 cup toasted chopped walnuts

In a medium-size bowl, combine raisins, currants, tea, whiskey, sugar, and orange zest. Cover tightly with plastic wrap; set aside overnight to soak. Or, heat mixture in a microwave oven at HIGH 60 to 90 seconds; let stand 20 minutes. Generously grease a 9" x 5" loaf pan; set aside. Preheat oven to 325F (165C). In a large bowl, combine flour, baking powder, salt, cinnamon, allspice, and nutmeg; set aside. Stir egg and oil into raisin mixture. Add to flour mixture, stirring only until dry ingredients are moistened. Stir in nuts. Turn into prepared pan; smooth top. Bake about 1-1/2 hours, or until a wooden pick inserted in center comes out clean. Let stand in pan 10 minutes. Turn out onto a rack to cool. Wrap tightly in plastic wrap or plastic bag; store 1 day before serving.

Makes 1 loaf.

Strawberries Romanoff Bread

This orange-scented strawberry bread is patterned after the classic dessert of the same name. Spread slices of it with Strawberry Devonshire Cream (page 264) for a heavenly treat with morning coffee or afternoon tea.

1-3/4 cups all-purpose flour
1/2 teaspoon baking powder
1/4 teaspoon baking soda
1/2 teaspoon salt
1/4 teaspoon ground cinnamon
1/2 cup unsalted butter, softened
3/4 cup sugar
2 eggs
1/2 cup sour cream
1 teaspoon pure vanilla extract
1 teaspoon freshly grated orange zest
1 cup coarsely chopped fresh strawberries

Grease an 8" x 4" loaf pan; set aside. Preheat oven to 350F (175C). In a large bowl, combine flour, baking powder, baking soda, salt, and cinnamon; set aside. In small bowl of electric mixer, cream butter. Gradually add sugar; beat until light and fluffy. Beat in eggs, one at a time, then sour cream, vanilla, and orange zest. Add to flour mixture, stirring only until dry ingredients are moistened. Fold in strawberries. Turn into prepared pan; smooth top. Bake 60 to 65 minutes, or until a wooden pick inserted in center comes out clean. Let stand in pan 10 minutes. Turn out onto a rack to cool.

Makes 1 loaf.

Nut 'n' Honey Graham Loaf

❊⟛❊

*G*raham crackers, a favorite childhood memory for many of us, were invented by Dr. Sylvester Graham as a health food in the nineteenth century. Honey Butter (page 260) is the perfect complement for this honey-almond-graham cracker bread.

1 cup toasted finely chopped almonds
1-1/4 cups graham cracker crumbs
1-1/4 cups all-purpose flour
1/4 cup toasted wheat germ
2 teaspoons baking powder
1/2 teaspoon baking soda
1/2 teaspoon salt
1/4 teaspoon ground cinnamon
1 egg
1 cup milk
1/3 cup plus 1 tablespoon honey
3 tablespoons vegetable oil
1 teaspoon pure vanilla extract

Generously grease an 8" x 4" loaf pan or 1-1/2-quart casserole dish. Sprinkle 1-1/2 tablespoons almonds over bottom and sides of pan; set aside. Preheat oven to 350F (175C). In a large bowl, combine graham cracker crumbs, flour, wheat germ, baking powder, baking soda, salt, and cinnamon; set aside. In a medium-size bowl, lightly beat egg. Stir in milk, 1/3 cup honey, oil, and vanilla. Add to flour mixture, stirring only until dry ingredients are moistened. Reserve 1-1/2 tablespoons almonds; stir remaining almonds into batter. Turn into prepared pan. Smooth top; sprinkle with reserved almonds. Bake 35 to 40 minutes, or until a wooden pick inserted in center comes out clean. Let stand in pan 10 minutes. Turn out onto a rack to cool.

Makes 1 loaf.

Raspberry Ripple Coffeecake

A swirl of red raspberry preserves flavors this raspberry-yogurt–enriched coffeecake. If you can't find seedless preserves or jam, put regular-style preserves in a fine strainer and use the back of a spoon to press the fruit through. Straining isn't necessary if you don't mind the seeds.

> 2 cups all-purpose flour
> 1 cup sugar
> 1/2 teaspoon baking powder
> 1 teaspoon baking soda
> 1/2 teaspoon salt
> 1 egg
> 1/2 cup unsalted butter, melted
> 1 (8-oz.) carton raspberry yogurt
> 1 teaspoon pure vanilla extract
> 2/3 cup seedless red raspberry preserves
> About 25 fresh raspberries or whole blanched almonds for garnish

Grease a 9-inch springform pan; set aside. Preheat oven to 350F (175C). In a large bowl, combine flour, sugar, baking powder, baking soda, and salt; set aside. In a medium-size bowl, lightly beat egg. Stir in butter, yogurt, and vanilla. Add to flour mixture, stirring only until dry ingredients are moistened. Turn two-thirds of batter into prepared pan; smooth top. Drop 1/3 cup preserves, by teaspoonfuls, randomly over top of batter. Spoon remaining batter evenly over surface. Using the broad side of a dinner knife, cut down through the batter to the bottom of the pan, moving the knife in a wide zig-zag pattern to create a marbled effect. Bake 40 to 45 minutes, or until a wooden pick inserted in center comes out clean. Let stand in pan 10 minutes.

Remove side of pan. Use 2 large spatulas to remove coffeecake from pan bottom. Place top side up on a serving plate. In a small saucepan over low heat, melt remaining 1/3 cup raspberry preserves. Or, place preserves in a 1-cup measuring cup; heat at HIGH in a microwave oven about 45 seconds. Stir until preserves are smooth. Spoon over top of coffeecake. Let cool at least 10 minutes before garnishing with fresh raspberries or almonds. Serve warm or at room temperature.

Makes 1 coffeecake.

Mango-Macadamia Bread

The mango you use for the chopped fruit should be fairly firm, whereas the one to be pureed can be softer. A mango is ripe when the skin is yellow and blushed with red. Underripe mangoes can be placed in a paper bag with an apple and set at room temperature for a few days.

2 cups all-purpose flour
3/4 cup finely chopped mango
2 teaspoons baking powder
1 teaspoon baking soda
3/4 teaspoon salt
1/2 teaspoon ground nutmeg
2 eggs
1 cup pureed mango
2/3 cup sugar
1/2 cup milk
1/3 cup vegetable oil
1 tablespoon fresh lime juice
1 cup toasted chopped macadamias (Tip, page 262)

Grease a 9" x 5" loaf pan; set aside. Preheat oven to 350F (175C). In a large bowl, toss flour and chopped mango together until fruit is coated. Add baking powder, baking soda, salt, and nutmeg; set aside. In a medium-size bowl, lightly beat eggs. Stir in mango puree, sugar, milk, oil, and lime juice. Add to flour mixture, stirring only until dry ingredients are moistened. Stir in 3/4 cup macadamias. Turn into prepared pan. Smooth top and sprinkle with remaining 1/4 cup nuts. Use the back of a spoon to press nuts lightly into surface of batter. Bake about 70 minutes, or until a wooden pick inserted in center comes out clean. If bread begins to overbrown after about 40 minutes, lightly tent top with foil. Let stand in pan 10 minutes. Turn out onto a rack to cool.

Makes 1 loaf.

Red, White, & Blueberry Coffeecake

*Y*ou don't have to wait until the Fourth of July to serve this rich sour-cream coffeecake studded with raspberries, blueberries, and chunks of cream cheese. Freezing the cream cheese for 20 minutes will make it easier to cube.

Cinnamon-Nut Topping, see below
3 cups all-purpose flour
1 tablespoon baking powder
1/2 teaspoon baking soda
1 teaspoon salt
1 cup sugar
1 teaspoon freshly grated lemon zest
1 (8-oz.) package cold cream cheese, cut into 1/2-inch cubes
3/4 cup fresh blueberries
3/4 cup fresh raspberries
3 eggs
1/2 cup sour cream
1/2 cup unsalted butter, melted
2/3 cup milk

Cinnamon-Nut Topping:
1/4 cup all-purpose flour
1/3 cup packed brown sugar
1 teaspoon ground cinnamon
1/4 cup cold unsalted butter
1/2 cup chopped walnuts or pecans

Grease a 13" x 9" baking pan; set aside. Preheat oven to 350F (175C). Prepare Cinnamon-Nut Topping; set aside. In a large bowl, combine flour, baking powder, baking soda, salt, sugar, and lemon zest. Add cream cheese and berries, tossing to coat thoroughly with flour mixture; set aside. In a medium-size bowl, lightly beat eggs. Stir in sour cream, butter, and milk. Add to flour mixture, stirring only until dry ingredients are moistened. Turn into prepared pan. Smooth top; sprinkle evenly with Cinnamon-Nut Topping. Bake 55 to 60 minutes, or until a wooden pick inserted in center comes out clean. Let stand in pan 15 minutes before cutting. Serve warm or at room temperature.

Makes 12 to 18 servings.

Cinnamon-Nut Topping: In a medium-size bowl, combine flour, brown sugar, and cinnamon. Cut in butter until mixture resembles coarse crumbs. Stir in nuts.

Caramel Apple Twist

The technique for this uniquely shaped coffeecake is really quite simple. Gather and measure all the ingredients the night before for quick assembly the next morning.

Caramel-Apple Filling, see below
2 cups all-purpose flour
2 teaspoons baking powder
3/4 teaspoon salt
1/4 cup packed brown sugar
1/4 cup cold unsalted butter, cut into 4 pieces
1 egg
1/2 cup milk
1 teaspoon pure vanilla extract
Apple Glaze, see below

Caramel-Apple Filling:
2/3 cup packed brown sugar
1/2 teaspoon ground cinnamon
Pinch of salt
1 cup finely chopped peeled tart apple
1/2 cup finely chopped walnuts or pecans
1/3 cup raisins or currants (optional)

Apple Glaze:
2 tablespoons unsalted butter
2 tablespoons apple juice
1/4 cup packed brown sugar

Grease a large baking sheet; set aside. Preheat oven to 350F (175C). Prepare Caramel-Apple Filling; set aside. In a large bowl, combine flour, baking powder, salt, and sugar. Use a pastry cutter or 2 knives to cut in butter until mixture resembles coarse crumbs; set aside. In a medium-size bowl, lightly beat egg. Stir in milk and vanilla. Add to flour mixture, stirring only until dry ingredients are moistened. Turn dough out onto a well-floured surface. Knead gently only until dough holds together, about 12 to 15 strokes. Roll out dough into a 13-inch square. Spread Caramel-Apple Filling over dough to within 1 inch of edges. Roll up tightly, jelly-roll fashion. Pinch seam and ends to seal. Place seam side down on prepared baking sheet. Using a sharp knife, cut roll into 1-inch slices, leaving 1/2 inch at the bottom uncut and still attached to roll. Gently lift and turn every other piece of dough to opposite side of roll, turning each piece cut side up. Bake 20 to 30 minutes, or until golden brown.

Using 2 large metal spatulas, carefully remove coffeecake from baking sheet. Place on rack over waxed paper. Prepare Apple Glaze and brush or spoon hot Apple Glaze over top of coffeecake. Let stand 5 minutes before transferring to serving plate. Serve warm.

Makes 1 coffeecake.

Caramel-Apple Filling: In a medium-size bowl, combine brown sugar, cinnamon, salt, apples, nuts, and raisins, if desired.

Apple Glaze: In a small saucepan, combine all ingredients. Stirring constantly, bring to a boil over medium-high heat. Boil 3 minutes without stirring.

TIP: If breads are browning too fast, cover them lightly with a tent of foil.

Piña Colada Bread

*L*ike the popular Caribbean drink, this bread is heady with pineapple, rum, and coconut. It keeps beautifully and makes a great gift.

    2-3/4 cups all-purpose flour
    2 teaspoons baking powder
    1/2 teaspoon baking soda
    1 teaspoon salt
    3/4 cup sugar
    1-1/2 cups shredded coconut
    1 egg
    1 cup unsweetened pineapple juice
    1/2 cup light rum
    2 tablespoons vegetable oil
    1 teaspoon pure vanilla extract

Generously grease a 9" x 5" loaf pan; set aside. Preheat oven to 350F (175C). In a large bowl, combine flour, baking powder, baking soda, salt, sugar, and all but 1/4 cup coconut; set aside. In a medium-size bowl, lightly beat egg. Stir in pineapple juice, rum, oil, and vanilla. Add to flour mixture, stirring only until dry ingredients are moistened. Turn into prepared pan; smooth top. Sprinkle with remaining 1/4 cup coconut. Bake 55 to 60 minutes, or until a wooden pick inserted in center comes out clean. Let stand in pan 10 minutes. Turn out onto a rack to cool.

Makes 1 loaf.

Banana Daiquiri Bread

Rum and fresh lime juice add a tropical touch to this winsome loaf. The riper the banana, the more flavorful the bread will be. Light rum can be substituted for dark, though the flavor won't be as intense.

>   2 cups all-purpose flour
>   1 teaspoon baking powder
>   1/4 teaspoon baking soda
>   1/2 teaspoon salt
>   1/2 cup unsalted butter, softened
>   3/4 cup sugar
>   1/2 cup pureed banana (about 1 medium)
>   2 eggs
>   1/3 cup dark rum
>   2 tablespoons fresh lime juice
>   1/2 cup toasted chopped almonds (optional) (Tip, page 262)

Grease an 8" x 4" or 9" x 5" loaf pan; set aside. Preheat oven to 350F (175C). In a large bowl, combine flour, baking powder, baking soda, and salt; set aside. In small bowl of electric mixer, cream butter. Gradually add sugar; beat until light and airy. Add banana, eggs, rum, and lime juice; beat to combine. Add to flour mixture, stirring only until dry ingredients are moistened. Stir in nuts, if desired. Turn into prepared pan; smooth top. Bake 55 to 60 minutes, or until a wooden pick inserted in center comes out clean. Let stand in pan 10 minutes. Turn out onto a rack to cool.

Makes 1 loaf.

Ginger-Peachy Bread

*C*rystallized ginger is available in most supermarkets, often in the Asian or gourmet section. Chop an entire jar of crystallized ginger slices by putting them into a food processor fitted with the metal blade. Process until finely chopped, adding a little sugar if the ginger begins to stick together. Return the minced ginger to its original jar—it'll be ready and waiting whenever you need it.

Ginger Streusel, see below
2 cups all-purpose flour
3/4 cup sugar
1 teaspoon baking powder
3/4 teaspoon baking soda
3/4 teaspoon salt
1/4 teaspoon ground ginger
1/4 teaspoon ground nutmeg
2 eggs
1 (8-oz.) carton peach-flavored yogurt
1/3 cup unsalted butter, melted
2 teaspoons minced crystallized ginger
1 teaspoon pure vanilla extract
2 small peeled peaches, finely chopped

Ginger Streusel:
1/4 cup all-purpose flour
1/4 cup sugar
1 teaspoon minced crystallized ginger
1/4 teaspoon ground ginger
2 tablespoons cold unsalted butter

Grease an 8" x 4" loaf pan, or 1-1/2-quart casserole dish; set aside. Preheat oven to 350F (175C). Prepare Ginger Streusel; set aside. In a large bowl, combine flour, sugar, baking powder, baking soda, salt, ginger, and nutmeg; set aside. In a medium-size bowl, lightly beat eggs. Stir in yogurt, butter, ginger, vanilla, and peaches. Add to flour mixture, stirring only until dry ingredients are moistened. Turn into prepared pan. Smooth top; sprinkle with Ginger Streusel. Bake about 60 minutes, or until a wooden pick inserted in center comes out clean. Let stand in pan 10 minutes. Turn out onto a rack to cool. **Makes 1 loaf.**

Ginger Streusel: In a small bowl, combine flour, sugar, crystallized ginger, and ground ginger. Use a pastry cutter or 2 knives to cut in butter until mixture resembles coarse crumbs. Or, place all ingredients in a food processor fitted with a metal blade. Using ON/OFF pulses, process until mixture resembles coarse crumbs.

Tomato Chutney Bread

*T*omato chutney is available in many supermarkets and most specialty food shops. Another fruit chutney, such as mango, may be substituted, but most won't have the piquancy of tomato chutney. For an incredibly intense flavor, look for dried tomato chutney.

> 2-1/2 cups all-purpose flour
> 1/2 cup sugar
> 2 teaspoons baking powder
> 1/2 teaspoon baking soda
> 3/4 teaspoon salt
> 1 cup tomato chutney, pureed
> 1-1/4 cups milk
> 1/4 cup vegetable oil
> 1 cup chopped toasted walnuts

Grease a 9" x 5" loaf pan; set aside. Preheat oven to 375F (190C). In a medium-size bowl, combine flour, sugar, baking powder, baking soda, and salt; set aside. In a medium-size bowl, combine pureed chutney, milk, and oil. Add to flour mixture, stirring only until dry ingredients are moistened. Stir in all but 2 tablespoons nuts. Turn into prepared pan. Smooth top; sprinkle with remaining 2 tablespoons nuts. Bake 50 to 60 minutes, or until a wooden pick inserted in center comes out clean. If top of bread begins to overbrown, cover lightly with foil. Let stand in pan 10 minutes. Turn out onto a rack to cool.

Makes 1 loaf.

Dutch Apple Streusel Bread

*C*rispy streusel tops this tender bread made with fresh apples, apple juice, and walnuts.

Cinnamon Streusel Topping, see below
2 cups all-purpose flour
2 teaspoons baking powder
1 teaspoon baking soda
1 teaspoon salt
1/2 teaspoon ground cinnamon
1/2 cup unsalted butter, softened
1 cup packed brown sugar
2 eggs
1/3 cup apple juice
1 teaspoon pure vanilla extract
1 cup finely chopped peeled or unpeeled tart apple
1 cup finely chopped toasted walnuts

Cinnamon Streusel Topping:
3 tablespoons all-purpose flour
1/4 cup packed brown sugar
1/2 teaspoon ground cinnamon
2 tablespoons cold unsalted butter

Generously grease an 8" x 4" or 9" x 5" loaf pan; set aside. Preheat oven to 350F (175C). Prepare Cinnamon Streusel Topping; set aside. In a large bowl, combine flour, baking powder, baking soda, salt, and cinnamon; set aside. In small bowl of electric mixer, beat butter and sugar until light. Add eggs, apple juice, and vanilla; beat until blended. Stir in apple and nuts. Fold into flour mixture only until dry ingredients are moistened. Turn into prepared pan. Smooth top; sprinkle with Cinnamon Streusel. Bake 50 to 60 minutes, or until a wooden pick inserted in center comes out clean. Let stand in pan 10 minutes. Turn out onto a rack to cool.

Makes 1 loaf.

Streusel Topping: In a small bowl, combine flour, sugar, and cinnamon. Use a pastry cutter or 2 knives to cut in butter until mixture resembles coarse crumbs. Or, place all ingredients in a food processor fitted with a metal blade. Using ON/OFF pulses, process until mixture resembles coarse crumbs.

Brown Rice Pudding Bread

*T*he flavors of mom's old-fashioned rice pudding combine in this moist, chewy loaf. Regular brown rice takes about 50 minutes to cook. However, you can use quick brown rice, which cooks in a mere 15 to 20 minutes. Thoroughly drain the cooked rice and blot it on paper towels before adding it to the recipe.

> 1-3/4 cups all-purpose flour
> 1 cup cooked brown rice, unsalted
> 1 tablespoon baking powder
> 1 teaspoon salt
> 1/4 teaspoon ground cinnamon
> 1/4 teaspoon ground allspice
> 1/4 teaspoon ground nutmeg
> 1 teaspoon freshly grated orange zest
> 2 eggs
> 3/4 cup milk
> 1/4 cup unsalted butter, melted
> 2 teaspoons pure vanilla extract
> 1/3 cup raisins
> 2/3 cup packed brown sugar

Generously grease an 8" x 4" loaf pan; set aside. Preheat oven to 350F (175C). In a large bowl, toss flour and rice together until rice is well coated and separated. Stir in baking powder, salt, cinnamon, allspice, nutmeg, and orange zest; set aside. In a medium-size bowl, lightly beat eggs. Stir in milk, butter, vanilla, raisins, and all but 2 tablespoons of the sugar. Add to flour mixture, stirring only until dry ingredients are moistened. Turn into prepared pan. Smooth top and sprinkle with remaining 2 tablespoons sugar. Bake 55 to 60 minutes, or until a wooden pick inserted in center comes out clean. Let stand in pan 10 minutes. Turn out onto a rack to cool.

Makes 1 loaf.

Apricot Nectar Bread

*E*ven better the second day, this tartly sweet bread combines dried apricots with apricot nectar. If your apricots are particularly dry and hard, cover them with boiling water. Let stand 15 minutes, then drain well and blot up excess moisture with paper towels.

2-1/2 cups all-purpose flour
2 teaspoons baking powder
1/2 teaspoon baking soda
1 teaspoon salt
1/2 cup sugar
3/4 cup finely chopped dried apricots
1 egg
1-1/2 cups apricot nectar
2 tablespoons vegetable oil
1/2 teaspoon pure vanilla extract
3/4 cup toasted chopped walnuts

Grease an 8" x 4" or 9" x 5" loaf pan; set aside. Preheat oven to 350F (175C). In a large bowl, combine flour, baking powder, baking soda, salt, sugar, and apricots; set aside. In a medium-size bowl, lightly beat egg. Stir in apricot nectar, oil, and vanilla. Add to flour mixture, stirring only until dry ingredients are moistened. Stir in all but 2 tablespoons of the nuts. Turn into prepared pan. Smooth top; sprinkle with reserved 2 tablespoons nuts. Bake 60 to 65 minutes, or until a wooden pick inserted in center comes out clean. Let stand in pan 10 minutes. Turn out onto a rack to cool.

Makes 1 loaf.

Variations

Apricot-Orange Bread: Add 2 teaspoons freshly grated orange zest. Substitute 1-1/2 cups orange juice for apricot nectar.

Apricot-Raisin Bread: Add 1/2 teaspoon ground cinnamon. Substitute 1/2 cup raisins for 1/2 cup chopped nuts.

Apricot–Chocolate Chip Bread: Substitute 3/4 cup semisweet chocolate pieces for 1/2 cup chopped nuts.

Hot Buttered Rum Loaf

꧁꧂

Rum's heady flavor and fragrance is especially pronounced when this bread is warm. Whether served warm or at room temperature, the perfect spread is Rum Butter (see Spiked Butter, page 261).

> 2-1/2 cups all-purpose flour
> 2 teaspoons baking powder
> 1/2 teaspoon baking soda
> 1 teaspoon salt
> 1/2 teaspoon ground nutmeg
> 2 eggs
> 1 cup packed brown sugar
> 3/4 cup plus 1-1/2 tablespoons dark rum
> 3/4 cup milk
> 1/2 cup unsalted butter, melted
> 1 teaspoon pure vanilla extract
> 3/4 cup chopped toasted pecans
> 1/4 cup granulated sugar

Grease an 8" x 4" loaf pan; set aside. Preheat oven to 350F (175C). In a large bowl, combine flour, baking powder, baking soda, salt, and nutmeg; set aside. In a medium-size bowl, lightly beat eggs. Stir in brown sugar, 3/4 cup rum, milk, butter, and vanilla. Add to flour mixture, stirring only until dry ingredients are moistened. Stir in nuts. Turn into prepared pan; smooth top. Bake 65 to 75 minutes, or until a wooden pick inserted in center comes out clean. Let stand in pan 10 minutes. In a small bowl, combine granulated sugar and remaining 1-1/2 tablespoons rum (sugar will not dissolve). Turn bread out onto a rack set over waxed paper. Spoon or brush sugar glaze over hot bread, allowing excess to drizzle down sides. Serve warm or at room temperature.

Makes 1 loaf.

Twice Gingerbread

*C*rystallized ginger adds new magic to this old favorite. Serve it warm with Whipped Ginger Cream (page 265).

3 cups all-purpose flour
1-1/2 teaspoons baking powder
1 teaspoon baking soda
1 teaspoon salt
1-1/2 teaspoons ground ginger
1/2 teaspoon ground allspice
1/2 teaspoon ground cinnamon
1/4 to 1/3 cup minced crystallized ginger
2 eggs
1/2 cup unsalted butter, melted
3/4 cup dark molasses
1/2 cup packed brown sugar
1 (5.33-oz.) can evaporated milk
1 cup chopped walnuts (optional)

Grease a 9" x 5" loaf pan or an 8- or 9-inch square baking pan; set aside. Preheat oven to 350F (175C). In a large bowl, combine flour, baking powder, baking soda, salt, ground ginger, allspice, cinnamon, and crystallized ginger; set aside. In a medium-size bowl, lightly beat eggs. Stir in butter, molasses, brown sugar, and milk. Add to flour mixture, stirring only until dry ingredients are moistened. Stir in nuts, if desired. Turn into prepared pan; smooth top. Bake 60 to 70 minutes for the loaf pan, 50 to 60 minutes for the square pan, or until a wooden pick inserted in center comes out clean. If bread begins to brown too fast, cover with a foil tent. Let bread baked in loaf pan stand in pan 10 minutes. Turn out onto a rack to cool. Do not turn out bread baked in square pan. Serve warm or at room temperature.
Makes 1 loaf.

Variations

Orange Gingerbread: Substitute 3/4 cup orange juice for evaporated milk. Add 3 tablespoons freshly grated orange zest.

Banana Gingerbread: Reduce ground ginger to 1 teaspoon. Substitute 1 cup pureed ripe banana for evaporated milk.

Berry Gingerbread: Add 1 cup dried cranberries or cherries.

Ginger-Date Bread: Reduce crystallized ginger to 1 tablespoon. Add 1-3/4 cups chopped dates and 1 tablespoon freshly grated orange zest. Omit nuts.

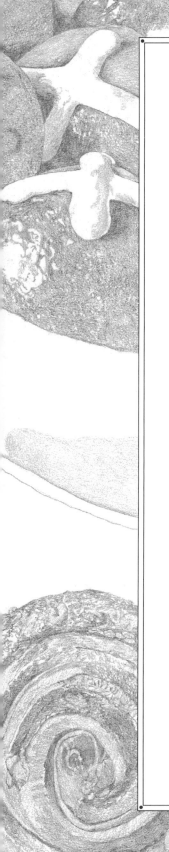

Festive & Holiday Breads

For centuries, bread has played an integral role in festive celebrations and religious holidays. The Christmas holiday tradition of exchanging homemade loaves, generously endowed with fruits and nuts, often imbued with spirits, has long been a demonstration of love and joy.

When I was a little girl, I remember the anticipation as we toasted the nuts, gathered the candied fruits, and prepared the pans for our annual holiday bake-fest. To this day, I still feel that same excitement every year.

Many festive breads have European roots dating back hundreds of years. One example is Italian Easter Bread, featuring gaily colored Easter eggs nestled in a twisted bread wreath. The Greeks have a similar bread called *tsoureki* or *lambropsomo*. Children love to help dye the eggs for this festive bread.

Two European Christmas breads handed down through the years are Germany's *stollen* and the delicately perfumed Italian *panettone*. The *stollen*, rum-spiked and laden with fruit, is an elegant folded loaf from Dresden that resembles a giant Parkerhouse roll. It's been said that the shape of the bread represents the Christ child wrapped in swaddling clothes. Italians serve the wonderfully fragrant *panettone* not only at Christmas but at special occasions throughout the year. This cylindrical, cakelike bread features raisins, citron, and pine nuts, and is delicately scented with anise and orange peel.

Don't think of festive breads only for Christmas and Easter holidays. Any celebration can be made special with the addition of personalized, homemade breads depicting a special event. For example, Sweetheart Bread is just as appropriate for an anniversary as it is for Valentine's Day. Cranberry Streusel Coffeecake is festive enough for dozens of fall and winter celebrations from birthdays and anniversaries to Thanksgiving and Christmas. Almost any bread dough can be shaped to spell out someone's name, or to form a jack-o-lantern for Halloween, or a football for Superbowl Sunday. Always remember when you're making free-form breads that they require a firm dough. Otherwise, they might flatten out too much during baking and distort or ruin your design.

Cherry Cordial Loaf

*G*ive this chocolate-cherry loaf to your true love on Valentine's Day and win his or her heart forever. Dried cherries are available at specialty gourmet markets and many supermarkets. If you can't find them, use canned cherries, thoroughly drained and blotted dry on paper towels. Coarsely chop canned cherries before adding to the batter.

> 1 to 1-1/2 cups dried sweet or sour cherries
> 3 cups all-purpose flour
> 1/2 cup plus 2 teaspoons sugar
> 1 tablespoon baking powder
> 1/2 teaspoon salt
> 1 egg
> 1 cup milk
> 1/4 cup brandy
> 2 tablespoons vegetable oil
> 2 teaspoons pure vanilla extract
> 1 cup semisweet chocolate chips

In a small bowl, cover cherries with very hot water. Let stand 20 minutes. Generously grease a 9" x 5" loaf pan; set aside. Preheat oven to 350F (175C). In a medium-size bowl, stir together flour, the 1/2 cup sugar, baking powder, and salt; set aside. Drain cherries; blot on paper towel. In a medium-size bowl, lightly beat egg. Add cherries, milk, brandy, oil, and vanilla. Add to flour mixture, stirring only until dry ingredients are moistened. Stir in chocolate chips. Turn into prepared pan; smooth top. Sprinkle with remaining 2 teaspoons sugar. Bake 65 to 70 minutes, or until a wooden pick inserted in the center comes out clean. Let stand in pan 10 minutes before turning out onto a rack to cool.

Makes 1 loaf.

Sweetheart Bread

Show your love on Valentine's day with this cherry-filled heart.

> 1 recipe Basic Sweet Yeast Dough (page 82)
> 1 (21-oz.) can cherry pie filling
> 3/4 cup toasted chopped almonds
> 1/2 cup packed brown sugar
> 1/3 cup all-purpose flour
> 1/2 teaspoon ground nutmeg
> 1/4 teaspoon almond extract
> 1 egg white mixed with 1 teaspoon water for glaze
> Cherry Glaze, see below

Cherry Glaze:
> 1-1/2 cups sifted powdered sugar
> 1/4 teaspoon almond extract
> 1 teaspoon pure vanilla extract

Prepare Basic Sweet Yeast Dough through first rising. Grease a large baking sheet; set aside. Using a coarse sieve, strain as much sauce as possible from cherries, being careful not to crush cherries. Set sauce aside. In a medium-size bowl, combine cherries, almonds, brown sugar, flour, 2 tablespoons of the reserved cherry pie sauce, nutmeg, and almond extract; set aside.

Punch dough down; knead 30 seconds. Divide dough in half. Cover one half; set aside. Roll out remaining dough into a 14" x 8" rectangle. Spread half the cherry mixture in an even layer to within 1 inch of edges. Beginning on a long side, roll up carefully, jelly-roll fashion. When almost to opposite edge, stop rolling; bring dough up to meet roll. Tightly pinch seam and ends to seal. Place lengthwise on prepared baking sheet, seam side down, curving to form half a heart. Repeat with second half of dough, forming second half of heart. Pinch rolls together at seams to seal. Cover with a dry towel; let rise until doubled in bulk, about 1-1/2 hours. If seams of heart pull apart, gently pinch back together.

Preheat oven to 350F (175C). Brush top of bread with egg-white glaze. Bake 30 to 40 minutes, or until bread sounds hollow when tapped on the top. Transfer to a rack to cool. Prepare Cherry Glaze. Drizzle over cooled coffeecake.

Makes 1 coffeecake.

Cherry Glaze: In a small bowl, combine powdered sugar, almond extract, and vanilla extract. Stir in enough reserved cherry pie sauce to make a smooth and creamy glaze of drizzling consistency.

TIP: If your powdered sugar is lumpy, put it in a food processor fitted with a metal blade; process a few seconds until smooth.

Special-Occasion Breads

Let your imagination lead the way in creating personalized breads for special occasions. Here are just a few ideas:

Handprint Rolls (page 131) are perfect for children's birthday parties. Let the children cut out their own handprints in dough and watch them bake into edible party favors.

Use your favorite yeast bread recipe to create unique holiday breads. After the first rising, simply roll the dough into long ropes. Use the bread ropes to form a special shape or message, and let rise again. For example, outline a big shamrock for St. Patrick's Day; or divide dough into 3 pieces, roll into ropes, and shape the letters M O M or D A D for Mother's Day or Father's Day; or shape a big number four for the Fourth of July; or write a person's name for a special birthday.

There are dozens of ways to create special-occasion breads. Surprise and delight your family and friends with your creativity!

Challah

*B*raiding this rich, lightly textured Jewish bread makes it beautiful enough for the most festive occasions.

> 2 (1/4-oz.) packages active dry yeast
> 3 tablespoons sugar
> 1 cup warm water (110F, 45C)
> 1-1/2 teaspoons salt
> 1/3 cup vegetable oil
> 3 eggs
> 1 egg yolk
> 5 to 5-1/2 cups bread or all-purpose flour
> 3/4 cup golden raisins (optional)
> 1 egg yolk mixed with 2 teaspoons cream for glaze
> Cornmeal
> Sesame or poppy seeds (optional)

In large bowl of electric mixer, dissolve yeast and 1 tablespoon of the sugar in warm water. Let stand until foamy, 5 to 10 minutes. Add remaining 2 tablespoons sugar, salt, oil, eggs, egg yolk, and 2 to 2-1/2 cups of the flour. Beat at medium speed with electric mixer 2 minutes, or beat 200 vigorous strokes by hand. Stir in raisins, if desired, and enough remaining flour to make a soft dough. Turn dough out onto a lightly floured surface. Change to dough hook(s) if using mixer, or turn out dough onto a lightly floured work surface.

Knead dough 8 to 10 minutes, or until smooth and elastic, adding only enough flour to prevent sticking. Clean and butter bowl. Place dough in bowl, turning to coat all surfaces. Cover with a slightly damp towel; set in a warm place free from drafts. Let rise until doubled in bulk, about 1 hour. Grease 1 large baking sheet for 6-strand braid, 2 large baking sheets for smaller braids. Sprinkle lightly with cornmeal.

Punch dough down; knead 30 seconds. Braid as desired (page 104). Place formed braid(s) on prepared baking sheet(s). Cover with a dry towel. Let rise until doubled in bulk, about 1 hour.

Preheat oven to 325F (165C). Brush egg-yolk glaze over tops of loaves. Bake 25 minutes. Brush again with glaze; sprinkle with sesame or poppy seeds, if desired. Bake 10 to 20 minutes longer, or until bread is deep golden brown and sounds hollow when tapped on bottom. Transfer to racks to cool.

Makes 1 large or 2 small braids.

Italian Easter Bread

꙳꙳꙳꙳꙳꙳

*C*olorful Easter eggs nestle in the folds of this beautiful bread wreath. Careful handling is necessary when positioning the raw eggs in the dough twist. The eggs cook while the bread is baking. Be sure to dye the eggs ahead of time so they're ready when you need them.

    1 (1/4-oz.) package active dry yeast
    1/4 cup sugar
    1/4 cup warm water (110F, 45C)
    1/3 cup milk
    1/4 cup unsalted butter or margarine, melted
    2 eggs
    1/2 teaspoon anise seeds
    3/4 teaspoon salt
    2 teaspoons grated lemon zest
    1 teaspoon pure vanilla extract
    3-1/2 to 4 cups bread or all-purpose flour
    1/2 cup golden raisins, or chopped candied fruit
    1/3 cup toasted chopped almonds
    5 raw eggs in shell, each dyed a different color
    1 egg white mixed with 2 teaspoons water for glaze
    Frosting, see below
    Jelly beans or colored sprinkles (optional)
    Coconut Grass (page 217) (optional)

Frosting:
    1 cup powdered sugar
    1/4 teaspoon almond extract
    1 to 2 tablespoons milk

In large bowl of electric mixer, dissolve yeast and 1 teaspoon sugar in warm water. Let stand until foamy, 5 to 10 minutes. Add remaining sugar, milk, butter, 2 eggs, anise seeds, salt, lemon zest, vanilla, and 2 to 2-1/2 cups of the flour. Beat at medium speed with electric mixer 2 minutes, or beat 200 vigorous strokes by hand. Stir in raisins, almonds, and enough remaining flour to make a soft dough. Change to dough hook(s) if using mixer, or turn out dough onto a lightly floured work surface.

    Knead dough 6 to 8 minutes, or until smooth and elastic, adding only enough flour to prevent sticking. Clean and butter bowl. Place dough in bowl, turning to coat all surfaces. Cover with a slightly damp towel; set in a warm place free from drafts. Let rise until doubled in bulk, 1 to 1-1/2 hours.

Grease a large baking sheet and the outside of a custard cup. Invert custard cup onto center of baking sheet; set aside.

Punch down dough; knead 30 seconds. Divide dough in half. Roll each half into a 24-inch rope. Loosely twist ropes together; pinch ends to seal. On prepared baking sheet, shape twisted dough into a ring around inverted custard cup. Overlap ends; pinch lightly at sides to seal. Carefully place raw colored eggs at 5 equidistant points around ring, gently separating ropes and tucking eggs securely into dough. Eggs will touch bottom of baking sheet. Cover ring with a dry towel. Let rise until doubled in bulk, about 1 hour.

Preheat oven to 350F (175C). Brush top of bread with egg-white glaze. Do not get glaze on eggs. Bake 30 to 35 minutes, or until a skewer inserted in center comes out clean. Carefully transfer to a rack to cool. Prepare frosting; spoon over bread, between eggs. If desired, sprinkle jelly beans or colored sprinkles over frosting. If desired, create a nest in center of bread with green-tinted coconut (see page 217) and additional jelly beans.

Makes 1 ring-shaped loaf.

Frosting: In a small bowl, combine powdered sugar and almond extract. Stir in enough of milk to make a smooth and creamy glaze.

TIP: Use unsalted butter or vegetable shortening to grease baking pans and sheets. Salted butter causes some breads to stick to pans and may induce overbrowning at temperatures over 400F (205C).

Hot Cross Buns

Said to have originated in early Britain, Hot Cross Buns were traditionally baked on Good Friday and thought to have great magical powers. Today these fat, fruit-filled buns, decorated with an icing cross, are more often served on Easter Sunday.

2 (1/4-oz.) packages active dry yeast
1/3 cup sugar
1/3 cup warm water (110F, 45C)
1-1/4 cups milk
3 eggs
1/2 cup unsalted butter or margarine, melted
2 teaspoons grated orange zest
1 teaspoon ground nutmeg
1/2 teaspoon ground cinnamon
1/4 teaspoon ground cloves
1-1/2 teaspoons salt
6-3/4 to 7-1/4 cups bread or all-purpose flour
1 cup currants
1/2 cup finely chopped candied orange zest, lemon zest, or citron
1 egg yolk mixed with 2 teaspoons water for glaze
Lemon Frosting, see below

Lemon Frosting:
1-1/2 cups powdered sugar
3 teaspoons lemon juice
3 to 5 teaspoons milk

In large bowl of electric mixer, dissolve yeast and 1 teaspoon sugar in warm water. Let stand until foamy, 5 to 10 minutes. Add remaining sugar, milk, eggs, butter, orange zest, nutmeg, cinnamon, cloves, salt, and 2-1/2 to 3 cups of the flour. Beat at medium speed with electric mixer 2 minutes, or beat 200 vigorous strokes by hand. Stir in currants, candied fruit, and enough remaining flour to make a soft dough. Change to dough hook(s) if using mixer, or turn out dough onto a lightly floured work surface.

Knead dough 10 to 12 minutes, or until smooth and elastic, adding only enough flour to prevent sticking. Clean and butter bowl. Place dough in bowl, turning to coat all surfaces. Cover with a slightly damp towel; set in a warm place free from drafts. Let rise until doubled in bulk, about 1 hour. Grease 2 large baking sheets; set aside.

Punch down dough; knead 30 seconds. Divide dough into fourths. Divide each fourth into 8 equal pieces, making a total of 32 pieces. Shape each piece into a smooth ball. Place balls about 1-1/2 inches apart on prepared baking sheets. Cover with a dry towel. Let rise until doubled in bulk, 45 to 60 minutes.

Preheat oven to 375F (190C). With a razor blade, cut a shallow cross in the top of each bun. Brush egg-yolk glaze over tops of buns. Bake 20 to 25 minutes, or until deep golden brown. Remove from pans; cool on racks 10 minutes. Prepare Lemon Frosting. With a dinnerware teaspoon, spoon frosting into slashes. Let frosting set 5 minutes before serving.

Makes 32 buns.

Lemon Frosting: In a small bowl, combine powdered sugar and lemon juice. Stir in enough milk to make a thick frosting of drizzling consistency.

Coconut Grass

Place 2 to 3 cups shredded coconut in a large jar or a glass bowl with a lid. Add 2 to 4 drops green food coloring. Cover and shake until coconut reaches desired shade, adding more food coloring if necessary. Turn out coconut onto paper towels. Let stand 20 minutes for color to set. If desired, make two batches of coconut, one light green and one dark green. Let colors set before tossing together for realistic-looking coconut grass.

Easter Basket Bread

$\bowtie$

Fill this edible Easter basket with Hot Cross Buns (page 216) for a showstopping Easter brunch. The basket is formed around a soufflé dish; the deeper the dish, the taller the basket. I used a 2-1/2-quart soufflé dish, 7 inches in diameter and 4 inches high.

1 recipe Basic White Bread dough (page 32)
1 egg white mixed with 2 teaspoons water for glaze
Colored sprinkles (optional)
Coconut Grass (page 217) (optional)

Prepare Basic White Bread dough through first rising. Generously grease 2 large baking sheets and the outside of a 2- or 2-1/2-quart soufflé dish; set aside. Punch down dough; knead 30 seconds.

To make basket handle: Pinch off a piece of dough the size of a small orange. Cover remaining dough. Divide small piece into thirds. On a lightly floured surface, roll each third into a 16-inch rope. Braid ropes together (see page 104), pinching ends to seal. Cover braid; set aside. Divide remaining dough into 11 equal pieces. Cover 9 pieces of dough; set aside. Roll remaining 2 pieces into 28-inch ropes.

To make basket base: On center of 1 prepared baking sheet, loosely coil 1 (28-inch) rope into a spiral. Continue spiral with remaining rope, pinching ends tightly to seal. Tuck outside end under spiral; pinch to seal. Use the palm of your hand to flatten spiral so diameter is 1 inch larger than diameter of soufflé dish. Place prepared soufflé dish, open end up, on center of dough spiral, leaving a 1/2-inch extension on all sides; set aside.

To make basket side: Roll remaining pieces of dough into 26-inch ropes. Braid 3 ropes; pinching ends to seal. Repeat with remaining 6 ropes, making 2 more braids. Lightly brush water on edge of dough spiral that extends beyond soufflé dish. Arrange 1 of the 3 long braids around dish on edge of dough spiral. Stretch braid, if necessary, so ends touch. Tightly pinch ends to seal. Press braid tightly against dish. Lightly brush top of braid with water. Place another long braid on top of first braid. Pinch ends to seal; press against dish. Lightly brush top with water. Repeat with remaining long braid.

To shape handle: Measure diameter of dough basket. On second prepared baking sheet, shape reserved small braid into a U-shaped handle with space between ends equal to basket's diameter. Cover handle and basket with dry towel. Let rise until bulk has increased by half, 30 to 45 minutes. If any seams pull apart, lightly pinch back together.

Preheat oven to 350F (175C). Brush egg-white glaze over raised basket and handle. Place handle on upper oven rack and basket on middle or lower rack. Bake 20 minutes. Remove basket and handle from oven. Brush handle with egg-white glaze; decorate with colored sprinkles, if desired. Return to oven; bake 5 minutes longer, or until golden brown. Carefully remove handle from baking sheet; cool on rack. Gently loosen bread from soufflé dish by running a knife between bread and dish.

Remove dish. Brush inside of bread basket with egg-white glaze. Return basket to top oven rack. Bake 20 to 30 minutes longer, or until outside is golden brown and inside is pale golden. Remove basket from baking sheet; cool on rack.

To assemble basket: When basket and handle are completely cooled, insert a 4-inch wooden skewer halfway into the center of each handle end. Attach handle to basket by inserting protruding skewer into basket rim. If necessary, use toothpicks to secure handle in an upright position. If desired, line basket with Coconut Grass. Fill with Hot Cross Buns or your favorite rolls.

Makes 1 large bread basket.

Kulich

*T*his regal Russian Easter bread (pronounced KOO-lihch) is classically crowned with a rose. Candied fruit or colored sprinkles are often used to write XV (meaning "Christ is risen") on the top of this bread. Serve it with Pashka (page 222), a rich cheese mold.

    1/2 teaspoon packed saffron threads, crumbled
    2 (1/4-oz.) packages active dry yeast
    2/3 cup sugar
    1/3 cup warm water (110F, 45C)
    1 cup whipping cream
    1/2 cup unsalted butter or margarine, melted
    2 eggs
    2 teaspoons pure vanilla extract
    1/2 teaspoon almond extract
    1-1/2 teaspoons salt
    1-1/2 teaspoons grated fresh orange zest
    1-1/2 teaspoons grated fresh lemon zest
    6 to 6-1/2 cups bread or all-purpose flour
    1/2 cup toasted chopped almonds
    1/2 cup raisins
    1/2 cup chopped mixed candied fruit
    Frosting, see below
    2 small fresh roses or frosting roses
    Colored sprinkles (optional)

Frosting:
    1 egg white
    Pinch of salt
    2 cups powdered sugar
    1 teaspoon almond extract
    1 tablespoon lemon juice

One hour before beginning bread, combine saffron and 1 tablespoon water in a small bowl. Cover; set aside to soak. In large bowl of electric mixer, dissolve yeast and 1 teaspoon sugar in warm water. Let stand until foamy, 5 to 10 minutes. Add remaining sugar, cream, butter, eggs, vanilla, almond extract, salt, orange and lemon zest, saffron mixture, and 2-1/2 to 3 cups of the flour. Beat at medium speed with electric mixer 3 minutes or 300 vigorous strokes by hand. Stir in almonds, raisins, candied fruit, and enough remaining flour to make a soft dough. Turn dough out onto a lightly floured surface. Change to dough hook(s) if using mixer, or turn out dough onto a lightly floured work surface.

Knead dough 10 to 12 minutes, or until smooth and elastic, adding only enough flour to prevent sticking. Dough will feel buttery. Clean and butter bowl. Place dough in bowl, turning to coat all surfaces. Cover with a slightly damp towel; set in a warm place free from drafts. Let rise until doubled in bulk, about 1-1/2 hours. Generously grease 2 (2-lb.) coffee cans or 2 (3-lb.) shortening cans. Cut and oil circles of waxed paper to fit bottoms of cans.

Punch down dough; knead 30 seconds. Divide dough in half; shape into round balls. Place balls, smooth side up, in prepared cans. Cover with a dry towel; let rise until doubled in bulk, about 1-1/2 hours.

Preheat oven to 375F (190C). Position oven rack in lower third of oven to give bread room to rise. Bake 20 minutes. Reduce oven temperature to 325F (165C). Bake 35 to 45 minutes longer, or until a skewer inserted in the center comes out clean. If top begins to overbrown, cover lightly with tin foil. Let bread stand in cans 10 minutes. Turn out onto a rack to cool. Prepare Frosting; drizzle over cooled loaves, letting it drip down sides. Place roses in center of bread, or decorate with colored sprinkles. Cut loaves horizontally, saving top slices as covers to keep bread from drying.

Makes 2 loaves.

Frosting: In small bowl of electric mixer, beat egg white and salt together until firm peaks form. Gradually beat in sugar, almond extract, and lemon juice.

Pashka

*M*ake sure the flowers you use to garnish this creamy mold (pronounced PAHS-kuh) are nonpoisonous and pesticide-free. Edible flowers can be found at specialty produce markets and many supermarkets.

  4 (8-oz.) packages cream cheese, softened
  1/4 cup orange-flavored liqueur
  1/4 cup whipping cream
  1/2 teaspoon almond extract
  1 teaspoon pure vanilla extract
  1 tablespoon freshly grated orange zest
  1/4 teaspoon salt
  1 cup powdered sugar
  Colored sprinkles (optional)
  Fresh flowers for garnish (optional)

Lightly oil 2 (1-quart) bowls with slanted sides. Line with 2 layers of cheesecloth, allowing ends to hang over rims of containers; set aside. In large bowl of electric mixer, beat cream cheese until smooth and creamy. Add orange liqueur, cream, almond and vanilla extracts, orange zest, and salt; beat to combine. Gradually add sugar, beating until well blended. Divide mixture evenly between prepared containers. Run a knife through cheese mixture to expel any air bubbles. Cover tightly with foil; refrigerate overnight. To remove each Pashka from container, grab ends of cheesecloth and gently but firmly pull it out. Peel off cheesecloth. If desired, remove cheesecloth pattern from cheese by lightly rubbing with the back of a spoon that's been dipped in cold water. Place each Pashka on a serving plate. If desired, garnish top with colored sprinkles. Decorate plate with fresh rosebuds or other fresh flowers.

Makes 2 cheese molds.

Spicy Chocolate Cinnabuns

*T*hese chocolatey, no-knead cinnamon buns are the inspiration of my friend Donna. They're perfect for festive occasions like Mother's Day, Father's Day, or birthdays.

1 (1/4-oz.) package active dry yeast
About 2/3 cup packed brown sugar
3/4 cup warm water (110F, 45C)
1 egg
1/4 cup plus 2 tablespoons butter, melted
1/2 teaspoon salt
1-1/2 teaspoons ground cinnamon
1/3 cup unsweetened cocoa powder
2 to 2-1/2 cups bread or all-purpose flour
3/4 cup chocolate chips
1/2 cup finely chopped toasted walnuts (Tip, page 262)
Spicy Glaze (page 247) (optional)

In large bowl of electric mixer, dissolve yeast and a pinch of sugar in warm water. Let stand until foamy, 5 to 10 minutes. Add 1/3 cup brown sugar, egg, 1/4 cup of the butter, salt, 1/2 teaspoon of the cinnamon, cocoa, and 1 to 1-1/2 cups of the flour. Beat at medium speed with electric mixer 4 minutes, or 400 vigorous strokes by hand. Stir in enough remaining flour to make a soft dough. Cover bowl with a slightly damp towel; set in a warm place free from drafts. Let rise until doubled in bulk, 1 to 1-1/2 hours. Generously grease a round 9-inch baking pan; set aside.

Punch down dough. On a lightly floured surface, roll or pat out dough into a 15" x 10" rectangle. Brush with remaining 2 tablespoons melted butter, leaving 1/2 inch unbuttered on 1 long side. In a small bowl, combine remaining 1/3 cup brown sugar, chocolate chips, nuts, and remaining 1 teaspoon cinnamon. Sprinkle evenly over buttered area of dough. Beginning on buttered long side, roll up tightly, jelly-roll fashion. Pinch seam to seal. Cut roll into 10 (1-1/2-inch) slices. Arrange, cut side down, in prepared pan. Cover with a dry towel. Let rise until almost doubled in bulk, about 30 minutes.

Preheat oven to 375F (190C). Bake 20 to 25 minutes, or until lightly browned. If desired, prepare Spicy Glaze while buns are baking. Let buns cool 10 minutes before drizzling with glaze. Serve warm.

Makes 10 buns.

Pumpkin Praline Rolls

No need to knead these easy pumpkin rolls. They're perfect for fall and winter holidays, from Halloween to Thanksgiving to Christmas. Serve with Orange Cream (page 263) and watch the smiles.

1/2 cup raisins
2 tablespoons rum
2 (1/4-oz.) packages active dry yeast
1/3 cup packed brown sugar
1/3 cup warm water (110F, 45C)
2 eggs
2 tablespoons vegetable oil
3/4 cup canned pumpkin
1-1/2 teaspoons salt
1-1/2 teaspoons ground cinnamon
3/4 teaspoon ground nutmeg
1/4 teaspoon ground ginger
2-3/4 to 3-1/4 cups bread or all-purpose flour
1/2 cup chopped toasted pecans
Praline Topping, see below
24 pecan halves

Praline Topping:
1/2 cup packed brown sugar
1/2 teaspoon ground cinnamon
2 tablespoons cold unsalted butter or margarine
1/2 cup finely chopped pecans

In a small bowl, combine raisins and rum. Cover; set aside overnight or 3 to 4 hours to soak. Or, microwave on HIGH for 30 to 60 seconds; let stand 5 minutes. In large bowl of electric mixer, dissolve yeast and a pinch of the sugar in warm water. Let stand until foamy, 5 to 10 minutes. Add remaining brown sugar, eggs, oil, pumpkin, salt, cinnamon, nutmeg, ginger, and 1-1/2 to 2 cups flour. Beat at medium speed with electric mixer 4 minutes or 400 vigorous strokes by hand. Stir in pecans, raisins and rum, and enough remaining flour to make a stiff batter. Cover bowl with a slightly damp towel; set in a warm place free from drafts. Let rise until doubled in bulk, about 1 hour. Grease 24 muffin cups; set aside. Prepare Praline Topping; set aside.

Stir batter down. Spoon into prepared muffin cups, filling about half full. Smooth tops; sprinkle a heaping teaspoon Praline Topping into each muffin cup. Press lightly into batter with the back of a spoon. Press a pecan half into top of each roll. Cover lightly with buttered waxed paper. Let rise until almost doubled in bulk, about 30 minutes.

Preheat oven to 375F (190C). Bake 15 to 20 minutes, or until golden brown. Transfer from pans to a rack. Cool 5 minutes before serving.

Makes 24 rolls.

Praline Topping: In a medium-size bowl, combine brown sugar and cinnamon. Use a pastry cutter or 2 knives to cut in butter until mixture resembles coarse crumbs. Stir in pecans.

TIP: Rehydrate raisins or other dried fruit in seconds by combining them with a little liquid in a bowl. Cover and microwave at HIGH for 30 to 60 seconds (depending on the amount of fruit). Let stand 5 minutes.

Crispy Croutons

*T*hese oven-crisped croutons are a great base for stuffings, especially when made with Savory Stuffing Bread (page 226). They're also wonderful in salads and soups.

> **1/2 pound leftover bread such as French or Sourdough**
> **1/4 cup butter, softened**
> **Salt and freshly ground pepper to taste**

Preheat oven to 300F (150C). Remove crusts from bread, if desired. Cut bread into 1/2-inch slices. Lightly butter both sides of bread. Stack slices and cut into 1/2-inch cubes. Spread cubes in a single layer on 1 to 2 large baking sheets. Stirring occasionally, bake 20 to 30 minutes, or until crisp and golden brown. If desired, season with salt and pepper while warm. Cool to room temperature. Store in airtight container.

Makes about 4 cups.

Variation

Garlic-Cheese Croutons: To softened butter, add 1/3 cup grated Parmesan cheese, and 1 small clove garlic, crushed. Spread on bread as directed.

Savory Stuffing Bread

⋯⋯✕⋯⋯

*T*his savory bread will remind you of stuffing. It's great for turkey sandwiches. If you don't have poultry seasoning on hand, substitute 1/2 teaspoon each ground thyme, sage, and rosemary.

> 1/2 cup finely chopped onions
> 4 tablespoons olive oil
> 2 (1/4-oz.) packages active dry yeast
> 2 tablespoons packed brown sugar
> 1 (10-1/2-oz.) can condensed chicken broth, warmed to 110F, 45C
> 2 eggs
> 1-1/2 teaspoons poultry seasoning
> 1/2 teaspoon celery seeds
> 1/2 teaspoon freshly ground pepper
> 1-1/2 teaspoons salt
> 5 to 5-1/2 cups bread or all-purpose flour
> 1 egg white mixed with 1 tablespoon water for glaze

In a medium-size skillet over medium heat, sauté onions in 2 tablespoons of the oil until soft; set aside to cool. In large bowl of electric mixer, dissolve yeast and a pinch of the sugar in warm chicken broth. Let stand until foamy, 5 to 10 minutes. Add remaining 2 tablespoons oil, remaining sugar, eggs, poultry seasoning, celery seeds, pepper, salt, cooled onion mixture, and 2 to 2-1/2 cups of the flour. Beat at medium speed 2 minutes. Stir in enough remaining flour to make a soft dough. Change to dough hook(s) if using mixer, or turn out dough onto a lightly floured work surface.

Knead dough 6 to 8 minutes, or until smooth and elastic, adding only enough flour to prevent sticking. Clean and butter bowl. Place dough in bowl, turning to coat all surfaces. Cover with a slightly damp towel; set in a warm place free from drafts. Let rise until doubled in bulk, 45 to 60 minutes. Grease 2 (9" x 5") loaf pans or 2-quart casserole dishes; set aside.

Punch down dough; knead 30 seconds. Divide dough in half. Shape into loaves; place in prepared pans. Cover with a dry towel. Let rise until doubled in bulk, 30 to 45 minutes. Preheat oven to 375F. Slash tops of loaves as desired; brush with egg-white glaze. Bake 30 to 35 minutes, or until bread sounds hollow when tapped on the bottom. Remove from pans; cool on racks.

Makes 2 loaves.

Variation

Braided Stuffing Bread: After first rising, divide dough in half. Divide each half into 3 equal pieces. Roll each piece into a 15-inch rope. Form into 2 (3-rope) braids (see page 104).

Spicy Pumpkin Cornbread

This spicy cornbread makes a wonderful, homey gift. Omit the sugar and use it for stuffing or dressing—delicious!

1 tablespoon plus 1/2 cup cornmeal
1 cup all-purpose flour
1 teaspoon baking powder
1/2 teaspoon baking soda
1/2 teaspoon salt
1/4 teaspoon ground cinnamon
1/4 teaspoon ground nutmeg
1/4 teaspoon ground allspice
2 eggs
1 cup canned pumpkin
1/2 cup milk
1/4 cup vegetable oil
1/4 cup packed brown sugar
3 tablespoons molasses
1 tablespoon freshly grated orange zest
1/2 cup plus 1 tablespoon chopped walnuts

Grease an 8-inch square baking pan. Sprinkle bottom and sides with 1 tablespoon cornmeal; set aside. Preheat oven to 375F (190C). In a medium-size bowl, combine the remaining 1/2 cup cornmeal, flour, baking powder, baking soda, salt, cinnamon, nutmeg, and allspice; set aside. In a medium-size bowl, lightly beat eggs. Stir in pumpkin, milk, oil, brown sugar, molasses, and orange zest. Add to flour mixture, stirring only until dry ingredients are moistened. Stir in 1/2 cup nuts. Turn into prepared pan. Smooth top and sprinkle with remaining 1 tablespoon nuts. Bake 30 to 35 minutes, or until a wooden pick inserted in center comes out clean. Let stand in pan 10 minutes before cutting.

Makes 16 (2-inch) squares.

Cranberry Streusel Coffeecake

A festive, sweet-tart bread that's wonderful for holiday brunches and great for gift giving. For a change of pace, use cranberry-raspberry juice instead of cranberry juice.

Cranberry Streusel, see below
3 cups all-purpose flour
2 teaspoons baking powder
1 teaspoon baking soda
1 teaspoon salt
1-1/2 cups coarsely chopped cranberries (about 1-1/2 heaping cups whole cranberries)
2 eggs
3/4 cup sugar
1-1/4 cups cranberry juice
1/4 cup butter, melted
1 cup chopped toasted walnuts (Tip, page 262)
12 whole cranberries for garnish

Cranberry Streusel:
1/4 cup finely chopped cranberries (about 1/3 cup whole)
1/4 cup all-purpose flour
1/4 cup packed brown sugar
2 tablespoons finely chopped walnuts
1 tablespoon cold butter

Grease a 9-inch springform pan; set aside. Preheat oven to 350F (175C). Prepare Cranberry Streusel; set aside. In a large bowl, stir together flour, baking powder, baking soda, salt, and cranberries; set aside. In a medium-size bowl, lightly beat eggs. Stir in sugar, cranberry juice, and butter. Add to flour mixture, stirring only until dry ingredients are moistened. Stir in nuts.

Turn into prepared pan; smooth top. Sprinkle Cranberry Streusel evenly over batter. Arrange whole cranberries, stem end down, around outer edge of batter, 1 inch from pan. Bake 65 to 75 minutes or until a wooden pick inserted in the center comes out clean. Let stand in pan 15 minutes. Run a thin knife around inside edge of pan. Release spring and remove side of pan. Use 2 large spatulas to carefully transfer coffeecake from pan bottom to serving plate. Or leave coffeecake on pan bottom and place on serving plate.

Makes 8 to 12 servings.

Cranberry Streusel: Combine all the ingredients in a food processor fitted with the metal blade. Using quick ON/OFF pulses, process until cranberries are coarsely chopped. Refrigerate until ready to use.

Nutty Yam Bread

*T*his fragrant, spicy bread is perfect for turkey sandwiches, and leftovers make wonderful French toast. Pumpkin can be substituted for the yams, if you like.

2 (1/4-oz.) packages active dry yeast
1/3 cup packed brown sugar
2/3 cup warm water (110F, 45C)
1 cup packed canned mashed yams or pumpkin
1/4 cup vegetable oil
3 eggs
1-1/2 teaspoons ground cinnamon
1/2 teaspoon ground allspice
1/2 teaspoon ground ginger
1/4 teaspoon ground cloves
2 teaspoons freshly grated orange zest
2 teaspoons salt
5-3/4 to 6-1/4 cups bread or all-purpose flour
1 cup finely chopped toasted walnuts (Tip, page 262)

In large bowl of electric mixer, dissolve yeast and 1 teaspoon of the brown sugar in warm water. Let stand until foamy, 5 to 10 minutes. Add remaining brown sugar, yams or pumpkin, oil, eggs, cinnamon, allspice, ginger, cloves, orange zest, salt, and 1-1/2 to 2 cups of the flour. Beat at medium speed with electric mixer 2 minutes, or beat 200 vigorous strokes by hand. Stir in walnuts and enough remaining flour to make a soft dough. Change to dough hook(s) if using mixer, or turn out dough onto a lightly floured work surface.

Knead dough 10 to 12 minutes, or until smooth and elastic, adding only enough flour to prevent sticking. Clean and butter bowl. Place dough in bowl, turning to coat all surfaces. Cover with a slightly damp towel; set in a warm place free from drafts. Let rise until doubled in bulk, about 1 hour. Grease 2 (9" x 5") loaf pans; set aside.

Punch down dough; knead 30 seconds. Divide dough in half; shape into loaves. Place in prepared pans; cover with a dry towel. Let rise until doubled in bulk, about 1 hour.

Preheat oven to 375F (190C). Slash tops of loaves as desired. Bake 30 to 35 minutes, or until bread sounds hollow when tapped on the bottom. Remove from pans; cool on racks.

Makes 2 loaves.

Mini Macadamia-Eggnog Loaves

The flavor of this bread will only be as good as the eggnog you use, so use the best—you're worth it. If you like chocolate, substitute 1 cup chocolate chips for the chopped macadamia nuts. For one large loaf, use a 9" x 5" loaf pan and bake about 90 minutes.

> 3 cups all-purpose flour
> 1 cup sugar
> 1 tablespoon baking powder
> 1 teaspoon salt
> 3/4 teaspoon ground nutmeg
> 1 cup coarsely chopped toasted macadamia nuts (Tip, page 262)
> 1 egg
> 1/2 cup butter, melted
> 1-1/2 cups eggnog
> 1/2 cup plus 3 tablespoons rum
> 12 whole macadamia nuts

Grease 4 (5-1/2" x 3") mini-loaf pans; set aside. Preheat oven to 325F (165C). In a large bowl, stir together flour, 1/2 cup of the sugar, baking powder, salt, nutmeg, and chopped nuts; set aside. In a medium-size bowl, lightly beat egg. Stir in butter, eggnog, and 1/2 cup of the rum. Add to flour mixture, stirring only until dry ingredients are moistened. Turn into prepared pans; smooth tops.

Bake in preheated oven 45 to 55 minutes or until a wooden pick inserted in the center comes out clean. Let stand in pans 10 minutes. In a small bowl, combine remaining 1/2 cup sugar and the 3 tablespoons rum (sugar won't dissolve). Turn breads out onto a rack set over waxed paper. Spoon or brush sugar glaze over hot breads, allowing excess to drizzle down sides. Immediately arrange 3 whole macadamia nuts lengthwise down center of each loaf. Cool completely.

Makes 4 small loaves.

Candy Cane Bread

*C*hunks of peppermint candy dot this candy-cane–shaped bread that's just too good to hang on the tree. To crush the candy, put it into a heavy-weight plastic bag, seal, and give it a few whacks with a rolling pin or rubber mallet.

> 1 recipe Basic Sweet Yeast Dough (page 82)
> 1 cup coarsely crushed peppermint candy
> 1 egg white mixed with 2 to 6 drops red food coloring
> Coarse red decorating sugar (optional)
> Peppermint Glaze, see below
> 1/2 cup finely crushed peppermint candy

Peppermint Glaze:

> 1 cup powdered sugar
> 1 to 2 drops peppermint extract
> 1 to 2 tablespoons milk

Prepare Basic Sweet Yeast Dough through first rising. Grease 2 large baking sheets; set aside.

Punch down dough; knead 30 seconds. On a lightly floured surface, roll or pat dough out into a large rectangle. Sprinkle with 1 cup coarsely crushed candy. Fold dough over candy, then knead to distribute evenly. Work quickly to avoid melting candy. Divide dough into 4 equal pieces. Form each piece into a 22-inch rope. Tightly twist 2 ropes together; pinch ends to seal. Repeat with remaining 2 ropes. Place twists on prepared baking sheets, curving like candy canes. Cover with a dry towel; set in a warm place free from drafts. Let rise until doubled in bulk, about 1 hour.

Preheat oven to 350F (175C). Carefully brush every other section of twists with red egg-white mixture. If desired, sprinkle red decorating sugar over red sections. Bake 25 to 35 minutes, or until bread sounds hollow when tapped on top. Transfer from baking sheets to racks to cool. Spoon Peppermint Glaze over white sections of twists; immediately sprinkle with finely crushed candy.

Makes 2 loaves.

Peppermint Glaze: In a small bowl, combine powdered sugar and peppermint extract. Stir in enough of the milk to make a smooth and creamy glaze of drizzling consistency.

Cranberry Stollen

*S*tollen (STOH-luhn) originated in Dresden and is a German Christmas tradition. Dried cranberries add a distinctively American touch to this fruit-laden bread. If you prefer, dried cherries, sweet or sour, can be substituted. When stollen begins to dry out (if it lasts that long), brush it lightly all over with rum, wrap well, and let stand for a day. Many Europeans prefer stollen dry and toast slices of it in a low oven until crisp.

1-1/4 cups dried cranberries
1/2 cup golden raisins
1/2 cup currants
1/4 cup finely chopped candied orange peel
1/2 cup rum
2 (1/4-oz.) packages active dry yeast
3/4 cup packed brown sugar
1-1/4 cups milk (110F, 45C)
5-1/2 to 6 cups bread or all-purpose flour
2 eggs
1-1/2 cups unsalted butter, melted
Grated zest of 1 large lemon
1 teaspoon pure vanilla extract
1 teaspoon almond extract
1 teaspoon salt
1 cup chopped toasted almonds (Tip, page 262)
2 tablespoons granulated sugar
20 to 25 candied cherry halves (optional)
Powdered sugar

In a medium-size bowl, combine cranberries, raisins, currants, orange peel, and rum. Cover; set aside overnight or 3 to 4 hours to soak. Or, microwave at HIGH 60 seconds; let stand 10 minutes. In large bowl of electric mixer, dissolve yeast and 1 teaspoon of the brown sugar in warm milk. Let stand until foamy, 5 to 10 minutes. Add 1-1/2 cups flour. Beat at medium speed with electric mixer 3 minutes or 300 vigorous strokes by hand. Cover tightly and let sponge rise in a warm place until light and bubbly, about 20 minutes. Strain rum off fruit; set aside. Toss fruit with 3 tablespoons flour; set aside. Stir sponge down; add remaining brown sugar, eggs, 1 cup butter, lemon zest, vanilla and almond extracts, salt, reserved rum, and enough remaining flour to make a soft dough. Change to dough hook(s) if using mixer, or turn out dough onto a lightly floured work surface.

Knead dough 10 to 12 minutes, or until smooth and elastic, adding only enough flour to prevent sticking. Dough will be soft and buttery. On a generously floured surface, pat or roll out dough into a large rectangle, 1/2 inch thick. Sprinkle nuts and floured fruit over surface. Knead in nuts and fruits until evenly distributed. Clean and butter bowl. Place dough in bowl, turning to coat all surfaces. Cover with a slightly damp towel; set in a warm place free from drafts. Let rise until doubled in bulk, about 1-1/2 hours. Grease 2 large baking sheets; set aside.

Punch down dough; knead 30 seconds. Divide dough in half. Shape each half into a 12" x 8" oval, 1/2 to 3/4 inch thick. Brush 1 tablespoon melted butter over each oval. Sprinkle each oval with 1 table-spoon granulated sugar. Fold dough almost in half lengthwise, letting 1 to 1-1/2 inches of bottom dough extend beyond top edge. Place folded dough on prepared baking sheets. Press fold gently. Lightly press top edge into bottom layer to seal. Cover with buttered waxed paper. Let rise until bulk has increased by half, about 60 minutes.

Preheat oven to 350F (175C). If desired, gently tuck candied cherry halves into dough where bottom edge extends beyond top edge. Brush about 1 tablespoon butter over each loaf. Bake 35 to 45 minutes, or until a skewer inserted in center comes out clean. If tops begin to overbrown, cover lightly with foil. Transfer loaves to racks to cool. As loaves cool, brush 2 to 3 more times with melted butter. When cool, sprinkle with powdered sugar. Cut in thin slices.

Makes 2 loaves.

Gumdrop Holly Wreath

*C*hunks of brightly colored gumdrops sparkle like jewels in this holiday bread. Even Scrooge would love this fun, festive bread.

 1 (1-lb.) package small mixed gumdrops, spice or fruit-flavored
 3 cups all-purpose flour
 3-1/2 teaspoons baking powder
 1 teaspoon salt
 1/2 teaspoon ground cinnamon
 1/4 teaspoon ground nutmeg
 3/4 cup sugar
 1 egg
 1-1/2 cups milk
 2 tablespoons vegetable oil
 1 teaspoon pure vanilla extract
 3/4 cup chopped walnuts or pecans
 Vanilla Glaze, see below

Vanilla Glaze:
 1 cup powdered sugar
 1/2 teaspoon pure vanilla extract
 1 to 2 tablespoons milk

Dipping scissors in hot water to decrease sticking, cut 15 red gumdrops in half. Set aside top halves, along with 8 whole green gumdrops. Using brightest colors available, cut enough remaining gumdrops into large pea-sized pieces to equal 1 cup; set aside. Grease and flour a 9-inch-diameter, 3-inch-deep ring mold or springform pan with a center tube; set aside. Preheat oven to 350F (175C).

In a large bowl, combine flour, baking powder, salt, cinnamon, nutmeg, and sugar. Toss 1 cup snipped gumdrops with flour mixture to coat and separate; set aside. In a medium-size bowl, lightly beat egg. Stir in milk, oil, and vanilla. Add to flour mixture, stirring only until dry ingredients are moistened. Stir in nuts. Turn into prepared pan; smooth top.

Bake 50 to 60 minutes, or until a wooden pick inserted in the center comes out clean. Let stand in pan 10 minutes. Remove from pan. Cool, bottom side up, on rack. Sprinkle sugar over work surface. On work surface, use a rolling pin to flatten 8 reserved green gumdrops. Cut into 15 leaf shapes; set aside. Prepare Vanilla Glaze. Drizzle over cooled bread. Decorate top with 5 groupings of 3 reserved red gumdrop halves for the berries, and 3 gumdrop leaves.
Makes 1 loaf.

Vanilla Glaze: In a small bowl, combine powdered sugar and vanilla. Stir in enough milk to make a smooth and creamy glaze of drizzling consistency.

Panettone

Hailing from Lombardy, Italy, this rich fruit bread is traditionally served at Christmas and other special celebrations. Leftover *panettone* (pan-uh-TOH-nee) makes wonderful French toast. Serve it with Hot Buttered Rum Syrup (page 265) for pure breakfast indulgence.

3 (1/4-oz.) packages active dry yeast
1/4 cup honey
1/2 cup warm water (110F, 45C)
6 egg yolks
1/2 cup unsalted butter, melted
1-1/2 teaspoons salt
1-1/2 teaspoons pure vanilla extract
2 teaspoons freshly grated orange zest
2 teaspoons anise seeds
3-1/2 to 4 cups all-purpose flour
1/3 cup toasted pine nuts or slivered almonds (Tip, page 262)
1/3 cup finely chopped citron
1/3 cup dark raisins
1/3 cup golden raisins
1 egg white mixed with 2 teaspoons water for glaze

In large bowl of electric mixer, dissolve yeast and 1 teaspoon of the honey in warm water. Let stand until foamy, 5 to 10 minutes. Add remaining honey, egg yolks, butter, salt, vanilla, orange zest, anise seeds, and 1-1/2 to 2 cups of flour. Beat at medium speed with electric mixer 2 minutes, or beat 200 vigorous strokes by hand. Stir in pine nuts, citron, dark and golden raisins, and enough remaining flour to make a soft dough. Change to dough hook(s) if using mixer, or turn out dough onto a lightly floured work surface.

Knead dough 8 to 10 minutes, or until smooth and elastic, adding only enough flour to keep dough from sticking to surface. Dough will be soft, moist, and slightly tacky to the touch. Clean and butter bowl. Place dough in bowl, turning to coat all surfaces. Cover with a slightly damp towel; set in a warm place free from drafts. Let rise until doubled in bulk, about 2 hours. Generously grease 2 (1-quart) soufflé dishes (about 5 inches in diameter) or 2 (1-lb.) coffee cans; set aside.

Punch down dough; knead 30 seconds. Divide dough in half. Shape into 2 smooth balls; place smooth side up in prepared containers. Cover with a dry towel. Let rise until doubled in bulk, about 1 hour.

Preheat oven to 350F (175C). Brush tops of loaves with egg-white glaze. Bake 35 to 40 minutes, or until bread sounds hollow when tapped on the top. Carefully remove from baking containers; cool on racks.

Makes 2 loaves.

Griddle & Fried Breads

What could be more enticing than small breads, hot off the griddle or plucked from a sizzling hot-oil bath, all fragrant and savory? There's something almost magical about griddle and fried breads. Maybe it's being able to watch their almost-instantaneous metamorphosis from dough or batter into full-blown golden-brown glory. Whatever the answer, there's no denying these toothsome treats have long been breakfast and snack favorites throughout the world.

Take the doughnut for example. Many people resist making them because they think deep-fat frying produces greasy results. Not necessarily! All you need are a few basics for successful frying. First of all, a special deep-fat fryer isn't required—any deep, heavy pot will do. To allow for bubbling up and spattering, the pot should be filled no more than halfway with oil.

Temperature is the most important factor in frying breads. A candy or deep-fat thermometer will help you keep the oil at the necessary 370 to 375F (190C). If you don't have a thermometer, drop a bread cube into the hot oil. If it takes 60 seconds for it to brown uniformly, the temperature is 350 to 365F; 40 seconds, the temperature is 365 to 382F; 20 seconds, the temperature is 382 to 390F.

When dough is immersed in hot oil, several things happen. The heat activates the carbon dioxide in the leavening, causing the bread to puff up almost immediately. Starch in the dough stiffens, strengthening the structure, and the surface begins to brown, signaling doneness. Only fry a few pieces at a time—crowding quickly lowers the oil temperature, causing oil absorption and uneven frying.

English muffins and crumpets are griddle breads that have been a British mainstay for centuries. Both breads require a second toasting after their initial baking. One is split, the other is not; one begins as dough, the other as batter. Each one is delicious in its own inimitable manner, and both reach their ultimate glory when accompanied by gobs of sweet butter and fresh jam or marmalade.

BREADS

Scottish Griddle Scones

These griddle-baked scones are my very favorite. The rich, honey-scented biscuit dough is patted into a circle and cut into *farls*, which is Scottish for quarters. I use a nonstick electric griddle, which makes baking them a breeze. Split them while hot and spread with jam, honey, or Strawberry Devonshire Cream (page 264). Heaven!

    2 cups all-purpose flour
    2 teaspoons baking powder
    1/2 teaspoon baking soda
    1/2 teaspoon salt
    1/2 cup cold unsalted butter, cut into 8 pieces
    2 eggs
    2 tablespoons honey
    1/2 cup half-and-half

In a food processor fitted with metal blade or medium-size bowl, combine flour, baking powder, baking soda, and salt. Add butter; process in quick ON/OFF pulses just until mixture resembles coarse crumbs. Or use a pastry cutter or 2 knives to cut butter into flour mixture. In a medium-size bowl, lightly whisk eggs, honey, and half-and-half until blended. Add to flour mixture; process in ON/OFF pulses or stir only until dry ingredients are moistened.

Turn out dough onto a generously floured surface. Flour your hands. Gently press dough together only until it holds together. Cut dough in half. Pat each half into a circle about 1/2 inch thick. Lightly dust tops of circles with flour. With a floured knife, cut each circle into quarters. Preheat an ungreased griddle or large, heavy skillet over medium-high heat, or an electric griddle or skillet to 325F (165C). Gently place scones on hot griddle. When bottoms are lightly browned and scones have risen slightly, after about 13 minutes, turn and brown other side 7 to 10 minutes. Serve hot. To preserve their tender texture, pull scones apart with fingers, rather than cutting with a knife.

Makes 8 scones.

Variations

Orange Griddle Scones: Substitute 1/2 cup orange juice for half-and-half. Add 1 tablespoon freshly grated orange zest. Serve with Orange Honey Butter (page 260).

Spiced Apple Scones: To dry ingredients, add 1/2 teaspoon each ground cinnamon, nutmeg, and allspice. Substitute apple juice for half-and-half. Add 1 teaspoon vanilla and 1 small apple, chopped. Serve with Cinnamon Cream (page 263).

TIP: A food processor fitted with a metal blade makes quick work of cutting butter into biscuit dough. Process only to the point where mixture resembles coarse crumbs. Overprocessing creates tough biscuits.

Chinese Scallion Bread

Straight from San Francisco's Chinatown, these warm wedges are an anytime snack and great with soups and salads.

> **2 cups all-purpose flour**
> **1 teaspoon baking powder**
> **About 1 teaspoon salt**
> **2/3 cup water**
> **1-1/2 tablespoons sesame oil or vegetable oil**
> **9 tablespoons thinly sliced green onions, white and green portions**
> **About 1/3 cup peanut oil or vegetable oil**

In a medium-size bowl, stir together flour, baking powder, and 1/4 teaspoon salt. Add water, stirring only until dough begins to hold together. Turn out dough onto a lightly floured surface. Clean bowl; set aside. Knead dough 2 to 3 minutes, or until smooth.

Place dough in bowl; cover tightly. Let stand at room temperature 1 hour. On a lightly floured surface, knead dough 1 minute. Divide dough into 3 equal pieces. Cover with towel; let rest 10 minutes. Remove 1 piece of dough from towel covering. Roll dough into a 10-inch square. Brush top with 1-1/2 teaspoons sesame oil; sprinkle evenly with about 1/8 teaspoon salt and 3 tablespoons green onions. Roll up tightly, jelly-roll fashion. Pinch seam and ends to seal. With your palms, roll dough back and forth over work surface, stretching it to a rope 22 inches long. Wind rope around itself to form a flat pinwheel; tuck end under. Repeat with remaining 2 pieces of dough. Cover and let rest 5 minutes. With a rolling pin, gently roll out each pinwheel into a 9-inch circle. Green onions will break through dough in places.

In a large skillet over medium-high heat, heat 2 tablespoons peanut or vegetable oil until hot. Place 1 dough circle in skillet. Cook about 2 minutes on each side, or until lightly browned. Use a spatula to press down dough when it bubbles up so bread will brown evenly. Blot on paper towels. Cover with an inverted plate to keep warm. Repeat with 2 remaining rounds, adding oil as necessary. Cut breads into 6 wedges each; serve warm.

Makes 18 servings.

English Muffins

*D*ivide this dough and make half English muffins, half English muffin bread (see variation below). There are special English muffin splitters available in gourmet kitchenware shops. Or, you can simply use a fork to pierce a muffin around the side in the middle. Gently pull the halves apart at the tine marks. Fork-splitting is important to produce that typically rough, craterlike surface so wonderful for catching and holding butter as it melts. Using a knife to halve English muffins just won't produce the desired result.

2 (1/4-oz.) packages active dry yeast
1/4 cup honey
1 cup warm water (110F, 45C)
1 cup milk
1/4 cup vegetable oil
1-1/2 teaspoons salt
5-1/2 to 6 cups bread flour or all-purpose flour
Cornmeal

In large bowl of electric mixer, dissolve yeast and 1 teaspoon honey in warm water. Let stand until foamy, 5 to 10 minutes. Add remaining honey, milk, oil, salt, and 2 to 2-1/2 cups of the flour. Beat at medium speed with electric mixer 2 minutes, or beat 200 vigorous strokes by hand. Stir in enough remaining flour to make a soft dough. Change to dough hook(s) if using mixer, or turn out dough onto a lightly floured surface.

Knead dough 6 to 8 minutes, or until smooth and elastic, adding only enough flour to prevent sticking. Clean and butter bowl. Place dough in bowl, turning to coat all surfaces. Cover with a slightly damp towel; set in a warm place free from drafts. Let rise until slightly more than doubled in bulk, about 1 hour. Liberally sprinkle cornmeal over 2 ungreased baking sheets; set aside.

Do not punch down dough. On a lightly floured surface, roll out dough until 1/2 inch thick. Use a 3-inch cutter to cut dough into rounds; place on prepared baking sheets. Gather up remaining dough; reroll and cut into rounds. Generously sprinkle cornmeal over tops of rounds; lightly press cornmeal into surface. Cover rounds with waxed paper and set in a warm place free from drafts. Let rise until doubled in bulk, 30 to 45 minutes.

Preheat an ungreased griddle or large, heavy skillet over medium-high heat, or an electric skillet to 325F (165C). Sprinkle griddle with cornmeal. Place muffins on hot pan, 1-1/2 to 2 inches apart; bake 8 to 12 minutes on each side. Cool to room temperature on racks. Toast before serving.

Makes about 20 English muffins.

Variations

English Muffin Bread: Grease 2 (8" x 4") loaf pans; generously sprinkle with cornmeal. Preheat oven to 375F (190C). After first rising, punch down dough. Divide in half; shape into loaves. Generously sprinkle tops with cornmeal; press into surface. Place in prepared pans. Cover with a dry towel; let rise until doubled in bulk, about 45 minutes. Slash top as desired. Bake 30 to 35 minutes, or until bread sounds hollow when tapped on the bottom with your fingertips. Cool on racks.

Makes 2 loaves.

Whole-Wheat English Muffins: Substitute 2-1/2 cups whole-wheat flour for 2-1/2 cups bread flour. Add 1/2 cup toasted wheat germ. If desired, add 1 cup raisins with flour.

Cinnamon-Raisin English Muffins: Add 1 teaspoon ground cinnamon, 1/2 teaspoon ground nutmeg, 1 teaspoon pure vanilla extract, and 1 cup raisins with flour.

Sourdough English Muffins: Reduce water and flour by 3/4 cup each; add 1 cup sourdough starter.

TIP: Buy inexpensive metal salt shakers. Fill with flour and use to dust work surface with flour while kneading or rolling out dough.

Hungarian Langos

*I*n a pinch, you can use instant mashed potatoes, but the flavor won't be quite the same. Rub this puffy fried bread with cut garlic cloves and serve it with hearty soups.

1 (1/4-oz.) package active dry yeast
2 teaspoons sugar
1/4 cup warm water (110F, 45C)
1 cup milk
1 egg yolk
1/2 cup packed mashed potatoes
1/4 cup unsalted butter or margarine, melted
1 medium-size garlic clove, crushed
2 teaspoons salt
3/4 teaspoon ground ginger
4 to 4-1/2 cups bread flour or all-purpose flour
Peanut oil or vegetable oil for frying

In large bowl of electric mixer, dissolve yeast and sugar in warm water. Let stand until foamy, 5 to 10 minutes. Add milk, egg yolk, mashed potatoes, butter, crushed garlic, salt, ginger, and 1 to 1-1/2 cups of the flour. Beat at medium speed with electric mixer 2 minutes, or beat 200 vigorous strokes by hand. Stir in enough remaining flour to make a soft dough. Change to dough hook(s) if using mixer, or turn out dough onto a lightly floured surface.

Knead dough 6 to 8 minutes, or until smooth and elastic, adding only enough flour to prevent sticking. Dough should be slightly tacky, but not sticky, to the touch. Clean and butter bowl. Place dough in bowl, turning to coat all surfaces. Cover with a slightly damp towel; set in a warm place free from drafts. Let rise until doubled in bulk, 45 to 60 minutes.

Punch down dough; knead 30 seconds. Cover and let rest 10 minutes. Roll out dough into a 24" x 6" rectangle, about 1/2 inch thick. Cut into 12 (4" x 3") rectangles. If dough shrinks after cutting, roll each piece back into a 4" x 3" rectangle. With a sharp, pointed knife, make 3 parallel lengthwise slits 2 inches long and about 1/2 inch apart in center of each rectangle. Be sure to cut all the way through dough. Cover with a dry towel; let rest 20 minutes.

Pour oil 2 inches deep into a large, heavy skillet or deep-fat fryer; heat to 370F (190C). Use a spatula to carefully transfer dough rectangles from work surface to hot oil. Fry several at a time, without crowding, until golden brown on the bottom. Turn and fry second side until bread is puffed and golden brown. Use a slotted spatula or spoon to transfer fried bread from pan to paper towels to drain. Keep fried breads in warm oven while frying remaining dough. Serve warm.

Makes 12 servings.

Variation

Sweet Langos: Increase sugar to 1/4 cup, decrease salt to 1/2 teaspoon and omit garlic. Serve for breakfast dusted with powdered sugar and accompanied by jam or honey.

Tomato-Basil Crostini

*C*rostini (krohs-TEE-nee) are hearty Italian canapés. These are sautéed bread slices topped with cheese, basil, and tomato. They're just as wonderful with a salad for lunch as they are with aperitifs.

1/4 cup olive oil
1 garlic clove, minced
1/4 cup finely chopped fresh basil
1 tablespoon minced fresh lemon zest
8 (3/8-inch-thick) slices leftover French or other firm bread
8 to 10 thin slices mozzarella or provolone cheese
2 firm, ripe tomatoes, seeded, thinly sliced
Salt and freshly ground pepper
8 sprigs fresh basil for garnish

Preheat oven to 375F (190C). In a small bowl, combine olive oil and garlic; let stand 15 minutes. In a small bowl, combine chopped basil and lemon zest; set aside. Cut bread slices in half diagonally. Lightly brush both sides with oil mixture. Heat a large skillet over medium-high heat. Sauté bread slices on both sides until golden brown. Blot on paper towels. Arrange sautéed bread slices, 1 inch apart, on an ungreased baking sheet. Top each slice with a single layer of sliced cheese. Sprinkle with basil-lemon mixture, then top with sliced tomato. Salt and pepper to taste. Bake until cheese melts, about 3 minutes. Garnish with basil sprig. Serve warm.

Makes 8 servings.

Blueberry-Orange Yeast Cakes

These elegant, light pancakes are made with yeast, but only need an hour to rise. Assemble all the ingredients the night before, then mix when you get up and let rise while you're dressing.

> 1 (1/4-oz.) package active dry yeast
> 1 cup warm orange juice (110F, 45C)
> 1 cup milk
> 5 eggs, separated, room temperature
> Grated zest of 1 large orange
> 2/3 cup unsalted butter or margarine, melted
> 3 tablespoons sugar
> 1 teaspoon salt
> 1 teaspoon pure vanilla extract
> 3-1/2 cups all-purpose flour
> 2 teaspoons baking powder
> 1/4 teaspoon cream of tartar
> 1 to 1-1/2 cups fresh or frozen, unthawed blueberries

In large bowl, dissolve yeast in warm orange juice. Let stand until foamy, 5 to 10 minutes. Add milk, egg yolks, orange zest, butter, sugar, salt, vanilla, flour, and baking powder. Beat just until flour is moistened and batter is almost smooth. Cover with a slightly damp towel; set in a warm place free from drafts. Let rise until almost doubled in bulk, about 1 hour. Lightly grease a large heavy griddle or skillet. Heat over medium-high heat (425F, 220C on an electric griddle) until a drop of cold water dances around on surface. Stir batter down. In small bowl of electric mixer, beat egg whites with cream of tartar until stiff but not dry. Fold egg whites and blueberries into batter. Using a 1/4-cup measure, pour batter onto preheated griddle. Cook until bottoms are golden brown and bubbles break through surface. Turn and cook other side until golden brown. Dust with powdered sugar; serve with Honey-Berry Butter (page 260).

Makes about 35 to 40 pancakes.

Raised Doughnuts

Surprisingly easy, these light treats may be frozen when fresh, then quickly reheated on busy mornings.

Basic Sweet Yeast Dough (page 82)
Peanut or vegetable oil for frying
Sugar
Glaze of your choice (optional) (page 247)

Prepare Basic Sweet Yeast Dough through first rising. Punch down dough; roll out until 1/2 inch thick. Cut with a floured 2-1/2- to 3-inch doughnut cutter, or a 3-inch biscuit cutter and a 1-inch canapé cutter or bottle lid for center. Place doughnuts and doughnut holes on a lightly floured baking sheet. Cover with a dry towel; set in a warm place free from drafts. Let rise until almost doubled in bulk, 30 to 45 minutes. Or, cover doughnuts tightly with plastic wrap; let rise in refrigerator until the next morning.

Pour oil at least 3 inches deep into a 4-quart saucepan or deep-fat fryer; heat to 370F (190C). Fry doughnuts and doughnut holes a few at a time without crowding until golden brown on both sides. Use a slotted spoon to transfer doughnuts from oil to paper towels to drain. Coat with granulated sugar while warm, or cool on racks and dip in glaze of your choice. Unglazed doughnuts may be frozen.

Makes 12 to 14 doughnuts and doughnut holes.

Variations

Baked Raised Doughnuts: After first rising, place cut-out doughnuts 2 inches apart on lightly greased baking sheets. Brush with melted butter; let rise as directed. Preheat oven to 425F (220C). Bake 8 to 10 minutes, or until puffy and golden brown. Lightly brush warm doughnuts with melted butter; coat with sugar.

Spicy Raisin Doughnuts: To Basic Sweet Yeast Dough recipe, add 1 teaspoon grated lemon zest, 1 teaspoon ground cinnamon, 1/2 teaspoon ground nutmeg, and 3/4 cup raisins. Coat with cinnamon sugar made by combining 1 cup sugar with 1 teaspoon ground cinnamon.

Jelly Doughnuts: Roll dough out to 1/4-inch thickness. With a floured biscuit cutter, cut into 3-inch rounds. Place 2 teaspoons jelly or jam, or 1 teaspoon each jam and softened cream cheese, in center of half the rounds. Lightly brush edges with egg white. Top with an unfilled dough round; tightly pinch edges to seal. Let rise and fry as directed.

Cake Doughnuts

*C*hilling the dough keeps these rich, tender morsels from absorbing too much oil during frying. Cake doughnuts don't keep well and should be served the day they're made. If you're freezing part of the doughnuts, glaze after defrosting.

> 3 cups all-purpose flour
> 1 tablespoon baking powder
> 1/2 teaspoon salt
> 2/3 cup sugar
> 1/2 teaspoon ground nutmeg
> 1 teaspoon grated lemon zest
> 2 eggs
> 1/3 cup unsalted butter or margarine, melted
> 2 teaspoons pure vanilla extract
> 1/2 cup milk
> Glaze of your choice (optional), opposite

In a large bowl, stir together flour, baking powder, salt, sugar, nutmeg, and lemon zest; set aside. In a medium bowl, lightly beat eggs. Stir in butter, vanilla, and milk. Stir into flour mixture just until dry ingredients are moistened. Cover tightly; refrigerate 1 hour. On a well-floured surface, roll out dough until 1/2 inch thick. Cut with a floured 2-1/2- to 3-inch doughnut cutter, or a 3-inch biscuit cutter and a 1-inch canapé cutter or bottle lid for center. Arrange cut-out dough on a lightly floured baking sheet. Cover with plastic wrap; refrigerate until ready to fry.

Pour oil 2 to 3 inches deep into a deep, heavy skillet, 4-quart saucepan, or deep-fat fryer; heat to 370F (190C). Remove a few doughnuts and doughnut holes at a time from refrigerator. Fry, without crowding, until golden brown on both sides. Use a slotted spoon to transfer doughnuts from oil to paper towels to drain. Coat with granulated or powdered sugar while warm, or cool on racks then dip in glaze of your choice. Unglazed doughnuts may be frozen.

Makes about 18 doughnuts and 18 doughnut holes.

Variations

Chocolate Doughnuts: Substitute 1/3 cup unsweetened cocoa for 1/3 cup of the flour. Increase sugar to 1 cup. Glaze with Chocolate Glaze (opposite).

Gingerbread Doughnuts: Substitute 2/3 cup packed brown sugar for 2/3 cup granulated sugar, and 1 tablespoon molasses for 2 teaspoons vanilla. Add 2 teaspoons ground ginger and, if desired, 1 tablespoon minced crystallized ginger. Glaze with Spicy Glaze (see below), substituting 1 teaspoon ground ginger for 1/2 teaspoon each ground cinnamon and ground nutmeg; or use Maple Glaze (see below).

Spiced Doughnuts: Add 1-1/2 teaspoons ground cinnamon, 1/2 teaspoon ground allspice, and 1/4 teaspoon ground cloves to flour mixture. Use Spicy Glaze (see below).

TIPS: To sugar-coat doughnuts, place sugar in a plastic or paper bag. Add doughnuts, 1 or 2 at a time, and gently shake. If using a plastic bag, let doughnuts cool 5 minutes before coating with sugar. Heat from doughnuts could melt a hole in the plastic bag. To reheat frozen doughnuts, place them on a baking sheet, lightly cover with foil and heat 10 to 15 minutes in a preheated 350F (175C) oven.

Doughnut Glazes

Sugar Glaze: In a small saucepan, combine 2 cups sugar and 1-1/2 cups water. Bring to a boil over medium-high heat. Boil 4 minutes without stirring. Cool 15 minutes; stir in 1 teaspoon pure vanilla extract.

Orange Glaze: In a small bowl, combine 1 cup powdered sugar, 1/4 teaspoon ground nutmeg, and 1 teaspoon grated orange zest. Stir in 1 to 2 tablespoons orange juice to make a smooth and creamy glaze.

Maple Glaze: In a small bowl, stir together 1 cup powdered sugar, 1/2 teaspoon maple flavoring, and 3 to 4 tablespoons maple syrup, making a smooth and creamy glaze.

Chocolate Glaze: In the top of a double boiler, melt 4 ounces semisweet chocolate and 1/3 cup butter over simmering water. Remove from heat. Stir in 1-1/2 cups powdered sugar, 2 teaspoons vanilla, and 3 to 4 tablespoons hot water, milk, or cream, making a smooth and creamy glaze.

Spicy Glaze: In a small bowl, combine 1 cup powdered sugar and 1/2 teaspoon each ground cinnamon and ground nutmeg. Stir in 1 to 2 tablespoons milk to make a smooth and creamy glaze.

Crumpets

*O*ne side of these moist, chewy, English tea classics is riddled with dozens of tiny holes—perfect little craters for butter or honey. Crumpet or English muffin rings are available in specialty gourmet shops and the kitchenware section of many department stores. If you can't find them, use clean 6-1/8-ounce tuna cans with tops and bottoms removed. Unlike English muffins, crumpets aren't split before they're toasted.

> 1 (1/4-oz.) package active dry yeast
> 1 teaspoon sugar
> 3/4 cup warm water (110F, 45C)
> 1/2 cup milk
> 2 tablespoons unsalted butter or margarine, melted
> 1 teaspoon salt
> 1-1/4 cups all-purpose flour
> 1/2 teaspoon baking soda
> 1 tablespoon hot water

In large bowl of electric mixer, dissolve yeast and sugar in warm water. Let stand until foamy, 5 to 10 minutes. Add milk, butter, salt, and flour. Beat at medium speed with electric mixer 4 minutes or 400 vigorous strokes by hand. Cover with a slightly damp towel; set in a warm place free from drafts. Let rise until bubbly and doubled in bulk, about 1-1/2 hours. In a small bowl, combine soda with 1 tablespoon hot water. Stir into batter; beat until blended. Cover with a slightly damp towel. Let rise again until doubled in bulk, about 1 hour. Lightly grease a griddle or skillet and crumpet or muffin rings. Arrange the rings 1/2 inch apart on griddle.

Preheat griddle over medium heat until a drop of water sizzles on the surface. Spoon batter into rings, 1/2 inch deep. Cook over medium heat about 7 minutes, or until surface appears dry and has formed a thin skin. Remove rings. Turn crumpets and lightly brown other side; about 3 minutes. Repeat with remaining batter. Serve warm, or cool on racks. Toast whole crumpets just before serving.

Makes 10 to 12 crumpets.

Variation

Spicy Crumpets: Add 2 tablespoons sugar and 1/4 teaspoon each cinnamon and nutmeg to the dry ingredients.

Feather Lights

These feather-light pancakes are my husband's favorite. Lemon zest and vanilla make them truly special. Using a 1/4-cup dry measure to pour the batter onto the griddle will make pancakes about 3-1/2 inches in diameter. Too much grease on the griddle can make pancakes cook unevenly. The best technique is to rub a little vegetable oil over the surface with a paper towel.

1 cup all-purpose flour
1 teaspoon baking powder
1/4 teaspoon salt
1/3 cup powdered sugar
2 egg yolks
1 cup half-and-half
1 teaspoon pure vanilla extract
1-1/2 teaspoons grated lemon zest
2 egg whites, stiffly beaten

Lightly grease a large heavy griddle or skillet. Heat over medium-high heat (425F, 220C on an electric griddle) until a drop of cold water dances around on surface. In a large bowl, stir together flour, baking powder, salt, and powdered sugar; set aside. In a medium bowl, lightly beat egg yolks. Stir in half-and-half, vanilla, and lemon zest. Add to flour mixture, stirring only until dry ingredients are moistened. Gently fold in beaten egg whites.

Cook on preheated griddle until bottoms are golden brown and bubbles break through all over the surface. Turn and cook second side until golden brown. Sprinkle with powdered sugar or serve with honey, syrup, or your favorite jam.

Makes 12 to 16 pancakes.

Variations

Cornmeal Pancakes: Substitute 1/4 cup yellow cornmeal for 1/4 cup of the flour.

Whole-Wheat Pancakes: Substitute 1/2 cup whole-wheat flour for 1/2 cup all-purpose flour; add 2 tablespoons wheat germ.

Spicy Orange Pancakes: Substitute 1 cup orange juice for 1 cup half-and-half, and 2 teaspoons grated orange zest for 1-1/2 teaspoons grated lemon zest. Add 1/4 teaspoon each ground nutmeg and ground cinnamon.

Eggnog Pancakes: Omit lemon zest. Substitute 1 cup eggnog for 1 cup half-and-half. Add 1/2 teaspoon ground nutmeg and 1/4 teaspoon ground cinnamon.

Banana Pancakes: Once bubbles begin to break the surface, place 4 to 5 thin banana slices on each pancake.

Sunflower-Seed Pancakes: Reduce sugar to 1 tablespoon. Add 1/3 cup raw sunflower kernels.

Buckwheat-Maple Pancakes: Omit sugar; add 2 tablespoons maple syrup and 1/2 teaspoon maple flavoring. Substitute 1/4 cup buckwheat flour for 1/4 cup all-purpose flour.

Sourdough Pancakes: Reduce sugar to 1 tablespoon. Substitute 1 cup sourdough starter for 3/4 cup of the flour and 3/4 cup of the half-and-half.

Bourbon-Pecan Pancakes: Substitute 1/4 cup bourbon for 1/4 cup of the half-and-half. Add 1/2 cup finely chopped toasted pecans.

Crispy Cornmeal Waffles

*I*f you're buying a new waffle iron, invest in one with nonstick grids—it'll make cleaning much easier. For a regular, 4-square waffle iron, use about 1 cup of batter. Less batter will produce a thinner, crisper waffle. Never open a waffle iron during the first minute of baking or the waffle may break apart. Waffles are done when the lid rises slightly, the steaming stops, and the sides are golden brown. If the lid resists when you try to lift it, the waffle's not done.

1 cup all-purpose flour
1/2 cup yellow cornmeal
2 teaspoons baking powder
1/2 teaspoon baking soda
1/4 teaspoon salt
2 tablespoons sugar
3 eggs, separated
1-1/3 cups buttermilk
1/2 cup vegetable oil
1/2 teaspoon pure vanilla extract

Follow manufacturer's directions for preheating and greasing waffle iron. In a large bowl, stir together flour, cornmeal, baking powder, baking soda, salt, and sugar; set aside. In small bowl of electric mixer, beat egg white until stiff, but not dry; set aside. In a medium bowl, lightly beat egg yolks. Stir in buttermilk, oil, and vanilla. Add to flour mixture, stirring only until dry ingredients are moistened. Gently fold in beaten egg whites. Bake according to manufacturer's directions for your waffle iron.
Makes 4 to 8 waffles.

Variations

Gingerbread Waffles: Substitute 1/2 cup all-purpose flour for cornmeal. Add 3/4 teaspoon ground ginger, 1/4 teaspoon each ground cinnamon and ground allspice, and 2 tablespoons molasses. If desired, stir in 2 teaspoons minced crystallized ginger.

Whole-Wheat Waffles: Substitute 1/2 cup whole-wheat flour for 1/2 cup cornmeal. Add 1/4 cup wheat germ.

Corn-Bran Waffles: Add 1/2 cup oat or wheat bran and 1 tablespoon molasses.

Spiced Nut Waffles: Add 1/2 cup finely chopped walnuts or pecans, 1/2 teaspoon ground cinnamon, and 1/4 teaspoon each ground nutmeg and ground allspice.

Sourdough Waffles: Substitute 1 cup sourdough starter (page 34) for 3/4 cup of the flour and 3/4 cup buttermilk.

Fried Bread Dough

*T*his is one of my childhood favorites. Serve savory fried breads for dinner, sweet ones with plenty of honey and jam for breakfast. Reheat leftovers in a 375F (190C) oven 5 to 10 minutes.

Basic White Bread (page 32)
Toasted Polenta Bread (page 54)
Mighty Wheat Bread (page 73)
Basic Sweet Yeast Dough (page 82)
Maple Butter Bread (page 90)
Peanut or vegetable oil for frying
1/4 cup sugar mixed with 1 teaspoon ground cinnamon (optional)

Prepare any of the above bread doughs (or your favorite yeast dough) through the first rising. Pinch off egg-size pieces of dough. Flatten between the palms of your hands until 1/2 inch thick. Or roll dough out until 1/2 inch thick; use a floured cutter to cut into any shape desired. Cover and let stand 20 minutes. Pour about 2 inches of oil into a large deep skillet, 3- to 4-quart saucepan, or deep-fat fryer; heat to 370F (190C). Fry dough pieces, a few at a time, until crisp and dark golden brown on both sides. Use a slotted spoon to remove from oil; blot on paper towels. If desired, roll in sugar or cinnamon-sugar.

Makes 30 to 40 fried bread pieces.

Spreads & Toppings

Spreads have accompanied breads for centuries. The words *bread* and *butter* have been linked in prose, poems, and children's songs. Some of the more common phrases and rhymes include "earning one's bread and butter," "I know on which side my bread is buttered," and "The King asked the Queen, and the Queen asked the dairy maid: Could we have some butter for the royal slice of bread?"

No one really knows who made the first butter. Some say that it originated in Northern Europe; others say Egypt; and most admit there is simply no way of ever knowing. Undisputed, however, is the fact that whoever discovered how to create this creamy, moon-colored spread should have won the Oscar for the best performance of the century!

One of butter's main attractions is that it blends easily with so many ingredients to create spreads, syrups, and toppings. When making butter-based spreads use room-temperature butter, and beat it with an electric mixer or food processor until soft and creamy before combining with other ingredients. To prevent a butter-based spread from separating, add liquids very gradually while constantly beating the mixture. Be imaginative in creating butter-based spreads with additions like ground nuts, chopped herbs, mustard, seeds, garlic, chopped olives, or spices.

Cream cheese is another wonderful base for all manner of spreads. While I don't recommend nonfat cream cheese because it breaks down when mixed with many ingredients, the low-fat version works quite nicely. Because it has the bonus of already being soft and spreadable, low-fat cream cheese often doesn't require beating before adding flavorings.

Homemade syrups are fun and easy to make. Generally, all you do is combine the ingredients in a saucepan and cook for a few minutes. Because they do not have the added thickeners, homemade syrups are thinner than those made commercially. They will, however, thicken as they cool. If syrup forms crystals after being stored, reheat gently until the crystals dissolve. Store syrups containing butter in the refrigerator; others can be stored at room temperature for a few days. Syrups may be frozen, and defrosted when ready to serve. And don't just think of syrups for waffles, pancakes, and French toast; some syrups are equally marvelous on ice cream, puddings, and cakes.

Roasted Garlic

W hen garlic is roasted, its texture becomes buttery-soft, its flavor slightly sweet and nutty. Roasted garlic has many uses, the most popular of which is to squeeze the soft garlic out of the skins and spread it like butter over thick slices of French bread that have been drizzled with olive oil. Squeeze from the pointed end, so the garlic pops out of the root end. Roasted garlic is also wonderful used as an ingredient in breads, soups, sauces, salad dressings, and mashed potatoes.

3 heads of garlic
3 teaspoons olive oil

Preheat oven to 400F (205C). From the tip (pointed) end of each head of garlic, gently rub off the outer layers of papery skin. Separate the cloves, but leave their skins intact. Place individual cloves in a baking dish or pan; drizzle with oil. Cover with foil; bake 25 to 30 minutes, or until cloves are soft when pierced with a metal skewer or the tip of a pointed knife. Remove from oven and cool to room temperature. Refrigerate leftover cloves in a sealed, airtight jar up to 10 days. To use as a spread for bread, bring roasted garlic to room temperature.

Makes 3 heads roasted garlic.

Roasted Garlic Butter

T his makes delicious garlic bread, or pat a spoonful on a baked potato, grilled steak, or cooked vegetables.

2 to 4 cloves Roasted Garlic, above
1/2 cup butter, softened

In a small bowl, mash Roasted Garlic. Add butter; blend to combine.

Makes about 1/2 cup.

Cheddar Butter

*B*aked potatoes love this spread—and so do breads like Jalapeño Nacho Bread (page 116), Potatoes-au-Gratin Bread (page 42), Toasted Polenta Bread (page 54), and Triple-Corn Batter Bread (page 119).

> 1/2 cup butter, softened
> 3/4 cup shredded Cheddar cheese (3 oz.), room temperature
> 1/8 teaspoon Tabasco sauce
> Salt to taste

In blender or food processor fitted with the metal blade, combine all ingredients. Process until smooth, scraping container often. Cover and refrigerate. Let stand at room temperature 20 to 30 minutes before serving.

Makes about 3/4 cup.

Variation

Jalapeño-Cheddar Butter: Add 2 to 3 teaspoons diced jalapeño chiles.

Blue Cheese Butter

*A*s good atop baked potatoes, grilled steak, or cooked green beans as it is simply spread on bread or toast.

> 1/2 cup unsalted butter, softened
> 4 ounces blue cheese
> 1 large shallot, minced

In a blender or a food processor fitted with a metal blade , combine all ingredients. Process until almost smooth, scraping container as necessary. Spoon into small crock or serving dish. Cover and refrigerate. Let stand at room temperature 20 to 30 minutes before serving.

Makes about 3/4 cup.

Mustard-Pepper Butter

*U*se your favorite mustard in this savory spread. Dijon, of course, is a favorite, but I've also used a sweet-and-hot style with great results. This butter is great with rye breads and wonderful on steaks and corn-on-the-cob.

> 2/3 cup unsalted butter, softened
> 2 to 3 tablespoons mustard
> 1 teaspoon freshly ground pepper to taste
> Salt to taste

In small bowl of electric mixer or food processor with metal blade, process all ingredients until smooth. Cover and refrigerate. Let stand at room temperature 20 to 30 minutes before serving.

Makes about 3/4 cup.

Chocolate Butter

*A*dd chocolate flavor to your favorite bread with this easy spread.

> 1/2 cup butter, softened
> 2 ounces semisweet chocolate, melted and cooled
> 1/4 cup powdered sugar
> 1 teaspoon pure vanilla extract

In a medium bowl, combine butter, chocolate, and sugar until blended. Stir in vanilla. Cover and refrigerate. Let stand at room temperature 20 minutes before serving.

Makes about 3/4 cup.

Homemade Butter

*T*he food processor makes homemade butter quick and easy. I prefer unsalted butter for its sweet-cream flavor and the flavor control it gives a cook. Choose old-fashioned or heavy whipping cream, which produces a better butter than ultra-pasteurized cream.

2 cups very cold whipping cream
1/4 teaspoon salt (optional)

Chill food processor bowl and metal blade in freezer 15 minutes. Pour cream into work bowl; add salt, if desired. Process 2 minutes; scrape down sides of bowl. Continue to process until solids separate from liquid, 3 to 5 minutes. Pour off liquid; cover and refrigerate to use within 3 days for pastries, soups, or sauces. Remove butter from work bowl. Squeeze with your hands to extract excess liquid, or place butter in a fine strainer and press with rubber spatula. Spoon or pipe butter into a pretty glass bowl; cover and refrigerate. Let stand at room temperature 30 minutes before serving.

Makes about 6 ounces butter and 1 cup liquid.

Variation

Blender Butter: Pour 1 cup whipping cream into a chilled blender. Process at high speed 15 seconds, or until cream coats blades. Add 1/2 cup ice water. Blend at high speed 2 to 3 minutes, or until butter separates from liquid. Drain off liquid; squeeze to extract excess moisture. If desired, cover and refrigerate liquid up to 3 days. Use for baking, soups, or sauces.

Honey Butter

⬥⬥⬥

*T*his versatile spread can be varied many ways—try those below or use your imagination to create your own.

> **1/2 cup unsalted butter or margarine, softened**
> **1/3 cup honey**
> **1/4 teaspoon pure vanilla extract**
> **Pinch of salt**

In small bowl of electric mixer or food processor fitted with a metal blade, process all ingredients together until creamy. Cover and refrigerate. Let stand at room temperature 20 minutes before serving.

Makes about 3/4 cup.

Variations

Cinnamon Honey Butter: Add 1/2 to 3/4 teaspoon ground cinnamon.

Honey-Berry Butter: Blot 1/2 cup minced fresh blueberries or strawberries on paper towels. Fold into honey butter.

Orange Honey Butter: Increase butter to 2/3 cup. Add 2 tablespoons orange juice and 2 teaspoons finely grated orange zest.

Amaretto Butter

⬥⬥⬥

*H*eady with Amaretto and sweetened with honey, this butter is great on everything from pancakes to dinner rolls.

> **1-1/4 cups unsalted butter or margarine, softened**
> **3 tablespoons honey**
> **1/4 teaspoon grated orange zest**
> **1/4 teaspoon almond extract (optional)**
> **1/4 cup Amaretto liqueur**

In small bowl of electric mixer, beat butter, honey, orange zest, and almond extract, if desired, until blended. Beating constantly, slowly add liqueur until thoroughly blended. Cover and refrigerate. Let stand at room temperature 20 to 30 minutes before serving.

Makes about 1-1/2 cups.

Variations

Nutty Amaretto Butter: Stir in 1/4 cup toasted, finely chopped almonds or other nuts.

Spiked Butter: Substitute 1/4 cup other liqueur (such as orange- or hazelnut-flavored), rum, or brandy for Amaretto. Omit almond extract.

Molasses Butter

*T*his spread is subtly sweet and lightly laced with molasses. It's perfect for whole-grain breads.

> **1 cup unsalted butter or margarine, softened**
> **2 tablespoons packed brown sugar**
> **2 tablespoons molasses**
> **1 teaspoon pure vanilla extract**
> **Pinch of salt**

In small bowl of electric mixer, cream butter and brown sugar until fluffy. Beating constantly, slowly drizzle in molasses and vanilla. Beat until thoroughly blended. Cover and refrigerate. Let stand at room temperature 20 to 30 minutes before serving.

Makes about 1-1/4 cups.

Variation

Maple Butter: Substitute 3 tablespoons maple syrup (preferably natural) for 2 tablespoons molasses. If desired, stir in 2 tablespoons minced, toasted pecans.

Sesame Butter

*T*he nutty flavor of toasted sesame seeds will make this spread a favorite. Reduce calories by substituting low-fat cream cheese for half the butter.

> **1/2 cup toasted sesame seeds, finely ground, see below**
> **2/3 cup unsalted butter or margarine, softened**
> **Salt and freshly ground pepper to taste**

In a medium-size bowl, combine sesame seeds and butter; mix until well blended. Salt and pepper to taste. Cover and refrigerate. Let stand at room temperature 20 to 30 minutes before serving.

Makes about 1 cup.

Variation

Sunflower-Seed Butter: Substitute 2/3 cup toasted sunflower seeds, finely ground, for sesame seeds.

TIP: Toast seeds, nuts, and grains in a skillet over medium heat, stirring often, until golden brown. Oven-toast at 350F (175C), stirring occasionally, 15 minutes or until golden brown.

Creamy Chèvre Spread

*C*hèvre (SHEHV), French for "goat," is a pure white goat-milk cheese with a tangy flavor. Two of the more commonly available chèvres are Montrachet and Bucheron. This spread is great with rye and other full-flavored breads.

> **4 ounces chèvre cheese, room temperature**
> **1 (8-oz.) package cream cheese, softened**
> **1/3 cup unsalted butter or margarine, softened**

In small bowl of electric mixer, beat all ingredients until light and fluffy. Cover and refrigerate. Let stand at room temperature 20 to 30 minutes before serving.

Makes about 2 cups.

Cinnamon Cream

For a double flavor whammy, serve this creamy spread with any bread flavored with cinnamon. It's also great on pancakes, waffles, and French toast.

> 1 (3-oz.) package cream cheese, softened
> 1/3 cup butter, softened
> 1 to 2 tablespoons powdered sugar
> 1/2 teaspoon ground cinnamon
> 1/2 teaspoon pure vanilla extract
> 1 to 3 tablespoons milk

In small bowl of electric mixer or food processor with metal blade, process cream cheese, butter, powdered sugar, cinnamon, and vanilla until smooth. Add enough milk to create a smooth, light spread. Cover and refrigerate. Let stand at room temperature 20 to 30 minutes before serving.

Makes about 3/4 cup.

Orange Cream

Substituting low-fat cream cheese will keep the calories to a minimum.

> 2 (3-oz.) packages cream cheese, softened
> 1 to 2 tablespoons powdered sugar
> 2 teaspoons grated orange zest
> 1 to 3 tablespoons orange juice

In small bowl of electric mixer or food processor with metal blade, process cream cheese, powdered sugar, and orange zest until smooth. Add enough orange juice to create a smooth, light spread. Cover and refrigerate. Let stand at room temperature 20 to 30 minutes before serving.

Makes about 1 cup.

Variations

Lemon Cream: Add 1 to 2 tablespoons powdered sugar. Substitute lemon zest for orange zest and lemon juice for orange juice.

Prune Cream: Add 1/2 cup minced prunes.

Ginger-Orange Cream: Add 2 to 3 teaspoons minced crystallized ginger.

Maple Cream

Spread this creamy mélange on wheat bread, sprinkle a little cinnamon on top, and slip under the broiler until bubbly and brown. Maple magic! Reduce calories by using low-fat cream cheese.

1 (3-oz.) package cream cheese, room temperature
1/2 cup unsalted butter or margarine, softened
Pinch of salt
1/2 teaspoon pure vanilla extract
1/4 cup pure maple syrup

In small bowl of electric mixer, beat cream cheese, butter, salt, and vanilla until smooth and fluffy. Beating constantly, slowly drizzle in maple syrup, whipping until thoroughly blended. Cover and refrigerate. Let stand at room temperature 20 to 30 minutes before serving.

Makes about 1 cup.

Strawberry Devonshire Cream

Be sure your whipping cream, beaters, and bowl are very cold before beginning. Strawberry Devonshire Cream is wonderful on piping hot pancakes, waffles, or scones.

1/2 cup whipping cream
2 tablespoons packed brown sugar
1/2 cup sour cream, stirred
1 cup diced fresh strawberries

In small bowl of electric mixer, combine whipping cream and brown sugar; let stand 2 minutes. Whip cream until firm peaks form. Gently fold in sour cream and strawberries. Cover and refrigerate.

Makes about 2-1/2 cups.

Whipped Ginger Cream

Heavenly on Twice Gingerbread (page 207), Sherried Tea Biscuits (page 165), and Feather Lights (page 250) . . . you name it!

 1/2 cup whipping cream
 1 (8-oz.) package cream cheese, softened
 1/3 cup packed brown sugar
 1 teaspoon ground ginger
 2 to 4 tablespoons minced crystallized ginger

In small bowl of electric mixer, beat cream until firm peaks form. Transfer whipped cream to a small bowl; set aside. In same small bowl of electric mixer, combine cream cheese, brown sugar, ground ginger, and crystallized ginger. Beat until sugar dissolves and mixture is smooth. Fold whipped cream into cheese mixture. Cover and refrigerate. If mixture is too firm when ready to serve, let stand at room temperature 15 minutes before using.

Makes about 2-1/2 cups.

Hot Buttered Rum Syrup

Wonderful on blustery winter mornings over waffles, pancakes, or French toast. Just as great drizzled over ice cream for dessert.

 1 cup packed brown sugar
 1/2 cup light or dark rum
 1 large cinnamon stick, broken in half
 1/3 cup cold butter, cut into 4 pieces

Combine sugar, 1/3 cup of the rum, and the cinnamon stick in a small saucepan; bring to a boil over medium-high heat. Continue to boil, without stirring, 2 minutes. Remove from heat. Add butter; stir briskly until melted. Add remaining 3 tablespoons rum, stirring until well blended.

Makes about 1-1/4 cups.

Créme Fraîche

*I*ts tangy, nutty flavor and velvety-rich texture makes *créme fraîche* (krehm FRESH) a wonderful bread spread. It's also delicious on fresh fruit, cakes, cobblers, and puddings. Though créme fraîche can be made with ultra-pasteurized cream, the results are far superior with natural heavy whipping cream.

1 cup whipping cream, room temperature
2 tablespoons buttermilk

In a glass jar with a screw top, combine ingredients. Secure lid; shake 15 seconds. Set aside at room temperature 24 hours, or until very thick. Stir once or twice during that time. Cream will thicken faster if the room is warm. Spoon créme fraîche into a sieve lined with a double layer of cheesecloth. Set over a bowl with the bottom of the sieve 2 inches above the bowl's bottom. Cover and refrigerate overnight. May be refrigerated for up to 2 weeks.

Makes 1 cup.

Variations

Sweetened Créme Fraîche: Add 2 tablespoons powdered sugar to cream before shaking. If desired, stir 1 teaspoon pure vanilla extract into thickened créme fraîche just before refrigerating.

Chocolate Créme Fraîche: In the bottom of a glass jar, combine 2 tablespoons each unsweetened cocoa powder and granulated sugar. Add 2 tablespoons buttermilk; stir until smooth. Stir in cream. Proceed as directed.

Gingered Créme Fraîche: Stir 1-1/2 to 2 tablespoons minced crystallized ginger into thickened créme fraîche just before refrigerating.

Spiced Créme Fraîche: Add 1/4 teaspoon each ground cinnamon and nutmeg to cream mixture before shaking.

Herbed Créme Fraîche: Add 1 to 1-1/2 tablespoons minced fresh herbs to thickened créme fraîche just before refrigerating.

Spiced Honey-Butter Syrup

*T*his easy-to-make syrup is lightly spiced and buttery good. Try mixing a little with peanut butter for truly special sandwiches.

1 cup honey
1/3 cup unsalted butter
1/2 teaspoon ground cinnamon
1/4 teaspoon ground ginger
1 teaspoon pure vanilla extract

In a small saucepan, combine honey, butter, cinnamon, and ginger. Cook over medium heat, stirring occasionally, until butter melts and syrup is warmed through. Remove from heat; stir in vanilla.

Makes about 1-1/4 cups.

TIP: Homemade syrups thicken as they cool. If a syrup forms sugar crystals, reheat gently, stirring until crystals dissolve and syrup is smooth. Warm syrup before serving to intensify its flavor. Syrups containing butter must be refrigerated; warm before serving.

Spicy Fresh Applesauce

*W*hether this spicy spread is smooth or chunky is up to you. You can vary the flavor by changing the spices. On occasion, I like to add 2 teaspoons minced fresh gingerroot or crystallized ginger.

4 crisp, tart apples, unpeeled
1/4 cup orange juice
1/4 cup packed brown sugar
1 teaspoon grated orange zest
1/2 teaspoon ground cinnamon
1/4 teaspoon ground nutmeg

Remove cores from apples; cut into chunks. Soak in cold, salted water 5 minutes to prevent discoloration. Drain on paper towels. Combine all ingredients in a food processor fitted with the metal blade or a blender. Use ON/OFF pulses to process until apples reach the texture you desire.

Makes about 3 cups.

Onion-Orange Marmalade

*W*hen removing the skin from the oranges, be sure to take only the thin outer zest, which is the colored portion. The white pithy part of the peel will give this spread a bitter undertaste.

3 medium-size red onions, thinly sliced
3 tablespoons olive oil
Finely grated zest from 1 medium-size orange
1/2 cup orange juice
1 tablespoon balsamic vinegar
1 tablespoon brown sugar
1/8 teaspoon ground allspice
1/8 teaspoon freshly grated nutmeg
1/8 teaspoon ground cloves
Salt and pepper to taste

In a large heavy skillet over medium heat, sauté onions in oil until onions are soft and deep golden brown, about 20 minutes. Stir in orange zest, orange juice, vinegar, sugar, allspice, nutmeg, cloves, salt, and pepper. Reduce heat to low. Simmer, uncovered, until almost all liquid evaporates and the marmalade is thick, 20 to 30 minutes. Cool to room temperature; cover and refrigerate. Let stand at room temperature 30 minutes before serving.

Makes about 2 cups.

Metric Conversion Chart

COMPARISON TO METRIC MEASURE

When You Know	Symbol	Multiply By	To Find	Symbol
teaspoons	tsp	5.0	milliliters	ml
tablespoons	tbsp	15.0	milliliters	ml
fluid ounces	fl. oz.	30.0	milliliters	ml
cups	c	0.24	liters	l
pints	pt.	0.47	liters	l
quarts	qt.	0.95	liters	l
ounces	oz.	28.0	grams	g
pounds	lb.	0.45	kilograms	kg
Fahrenheit	F	5/9 (after subtracting 32)	Celsius	C

Liquid Measure to Liters

1/4 cup	=	0.06 liters
1/2 cup	=	0.12 liters
3/4 cup	=	0.18 liters
1 cup	=	0.24 liters
1-1/4 cups	=	0.3 liters
1-1/2 cups	=	0.36 liters
2 cups	=	0.48 liters
2-1/2 cups	=	0.6 liters
3 cups	=	0.72 liters
3-1/2 cups	=	0.84 liters
4 cups	=	0.96 liters
4-1/2 cups	=	1.08 liters
5 cups	=	1.2 liters
5-1/2 cups	=	1.32 liters

Liquid Measure to Milliliters

1/4 teaspoon	=	1.25 milliliters
1/2 teaspoon	=	2.5 milliliters
3/4 teaspoon	=	3.75 milliliters
1 teaspoon	=	5.0 milliliters
1-1/4 teaspoons	=	6.25 milliliters
1-1/2 teaspoons	=	7.5 milliliters
1-3/4 teaspoons	=	8.75 milliliters
2 teaspoons	=	10.0 milliliters
1 tablespoon	=	15.0 milliliters
2 tablespoons	=	30.0 milliliters

Fahrenheit to Celsius

F	C
200–205	95
220–225	105
245–250	120
275	135
300–305	150
325–330	165
345–350	175
370–375	190
400–405	205
425–430	220
445–450	230
470–475	245
500	260

INDEX

SHARON TYLER HERBST is a nationally known culinary expert and media personality. She appears on ABC's *Good Morning America* as their "kitchen-tip" expert, and is the award-winning author of *The Food Lover's Tiptionary, Food Lover's Companion, The Joy of Cookies,* and *Simply Sensational Desserts.*

Her 1992 book *Cooking Smart* was both a Julia Child Cookbook Award nominee and the winner of the International Association of Culinary Professionals (IACP) Cook's Choice Award. She is a past president of the IACP and served on its board of directors for eight years. She lives in the San Francisco Bay area.